1985

Emerson, Whitman, and the American Muse

Emerson, Whitman,
and the American Muse

Jerome Loving

The University of North Carolina Press

Chapel Hill and London

Manufactured in the United States of America

Library of Congress Cataloging in Publication Data

Loving, Jerome, 1941–
Emerson, Whitman, and the American Muse

Bibliography: p.
Includes index.
1. Emerson, Ralph Waldo, 1803–1882.
2. Whitman, Walt, 1819–1892. 3. Authors,
American—19th century—Biography. I. Title.
PS1633.L6   810' .9'003   82-1868
ISBN 0-8078-1523-3   AACR2

Chapter 2 was previously published in another form in
Emerson Centenary Essays, edited by Joel Myerson (Carbondale:
Southern Illinois University Press, 1982), © 1982 by the Board of Trustees
of Southern Illinois University; reprinted by permission of
Southern Illinois University Press. Permission to quote from Emerson's
unpublished sermons was given by the Houghton Library,
Harvard University, and by the Ralph Waldo Emerson
Memorial Association.

To Cathy

*The whole question of the relation of
Whitman's theory and practice of art to
Emerson's is fascinating, since, starting
so often from similar if not identical
positions, they end up with very different
results.*

F. O. MATTHIESSEN
American Renaissance

Contents

x   Contents

Acknowledgments

My interest in Emerson and Whitman began with two documents: Emerson's famous letter of greeting to Whitman in 1855 and his *Parnassus*, published in 1874. What a contrast, I thought, between Emerson's ardent letter of praise and his failure to include even one of Whitman's poems in his anthology of favorite poets. I have since learned that Whitman's exclusion had little significance—that Poe and other important American writers were also omitted and that the anthology was largely the work of Edith Emerson, the poet's younger daughter, who was merely preparing for print poems the Emerson family had over the years compiled and read to each other under the "standards of the evening lamp" (certainly not the ideal setting for *Leaves of Grass* in the nineteenth century).

Yet the intersection of these two figures continued to tease me as it has critics for over a century. And as I sifted through the mass of criticism on the relationship, I found it often full of hasty, ill-conceived, oversimplified generalizations; too many cases entailed the trotting out of parallels and echoes to show that Emerson was "master" of Whitman. But the relationship is far more complicated than most critics have allowed. Indeed, a connection so central to American literature deserves its own separate study, I decided; and that decision has led me to write this book. In doing so I have enjoyed the advice and encouragement of a number of fellow critics in American literature. Two, however, have been most prominent in their support: Norman S. Grabo and Roy Harvey Pearce. Each read my work as it unfolded and encouraged me at crucial turns in the composition of this book. I also owe a large debt to the late Arlin Turner, and my only regret in this regard is that I cannot show him the completed work. With his passing I lost both a mentor and a friend.

xii   Acknowledgments

Two more who helped me in similar ways are Gay Wilson
Allen and Justin Kaplan. Each allowed me to read the manuscript
of his forthcoming book, now respectively entitled *Waldo Emerson:
A Biography* and *Walt Whitman: A Life*. They also read the penultimate draft of this book. Still another to thank is Paul Christensen,
a poet whose observations on poetry past and present were
always compelling and often applicable to my work on Emerson
and Whitman. Others include John C. Broderick of the Library of
Congress; Ellen Dunlap of the Humanities Research Center at the
University of Texas; Charles E. Feinberg, the Whitman collector;
Marte Shaw, formerly of the Houghton Library at Harvard Uni-
versity; Stanley L. Archer; Marcia Carr; James M. Cox; Patti Lynn
Hudgens; Henry C. Johnson; Tibbie E. Lynch; Philip McFarland;
Joel Myerson; Kenneth M. Price; the late Joseph Jay Rubin; Joseph
Slater; and Eleanor M. Tilton.

For financial aid in the research and writing of this book, I
thank Walter Harding and the National Endowment for the Humanities; David H. Stewart, head of the English Department,
Texas A&M University; and Keith L. Bryant, Jr., dean of the
College of Liberal Arts, Texas A&M University.

This book is dedicated to my wife, who as always was my
warmest critic.

Part One

1. Intersection

I look in vain for the poet whom I describe.
Emerson, "The Poet"

"He is no man to mind trifles, & no book man, or writer, but as easily domesticated in ten minutes as a cat. Take him straight into the house, send for Mr Daggett, if he is in town, but no learned or fine people, only thoughtful ones, or none; & sit down & let the gentle creature talk" (*L*, 4:392). So wrote Ralph Waldo Emerson in 1853 of Amos Bronson Alcott, initially one of the most promising of the so-called Transcendentalists who formed the Concord circle. For a brief period Emerson may have even considered him as a model for the orphic poet in *Nature*. But Alcott's promise had faded for Emerson almost as quickly as it had emerged, when he read a draft of "Psyche" and suspected that his friend and neighbor was wholly lacking in the ability to reproduce his thought in any form of art whatever. He continued over the years to hope that Alcott's "apex" would become defined, but ultimately decided that the orphic philosopher was only "an intellectual *torso*, without hands or feet," who would never find the right form for his "Conversations."[1] However, unlike many of the promising youths Emerson had discovered, Alcott would remain in Concord to become what Perry Miller has mockingly called the "venerable 'Dean' of the Concord School of Philosophy."[2] This last stab at reform, America's first summer school, was the culmination of a long series of failures for Alcott, from school teaching in Boston to the utopian Fruitlands experiment in Harvard, Massachusetts.

Alcott's disappointment as an artist was not uncommon among Emerson's "geniuses." And as Emerson labored on *English Traits* in 1855, he may have doubted his prophecy in the American Scholar Address of 1837, what Oliver Wendell Holmes called "our intellectual Declaration of Independence." The Whole Man of American letters had yet to emerge. Emerson's first discovery, Jones Very, was thought to be "hopelessly mad" by 1839 (*L*, 2:191). Henry David Thoreau, once regarded by Emerson as a candidate for his country's literary laurels, had proved in *Walden* (1854) that he could celebrate the full metaphysical significance of nature, but only in irregular flashes of genius (*L*, 4:460).[3] Another hopeful, Margaret Fuller, once editor of the *Dial*, had perished in a shipwreck off Fire Island in 1850. Although many of her papers were salvaged from the sinking vessel, Emerson was never quite sure they deserved to be published, even in a memoir. Ellery

Channing, handicapped perhaps by an unhappy marriage to Margaret's sister and what Yvor Winters would have called an overdose of Emersonianism, had also not fulfilled the promise Emerson had held for him as a poet in 1840. He would outlive all the other Transcendentalists and become Concord's relic of the era. Christopher Pearse Cranch, best remembered for his caricature of Emerson as a "transparent eye-ball," had never gone beyond his deft imitations of Emerson's own verse. Finally, the man who perhaps promised more for Emerson than any other had succumbed to the Swedenborgian notion that genius is pernicious. Charles King Newcomb had delighted Emerson with "The Two Dolons," published in the *Dial* for July 1842. Only the first "Dolon" ever appeared, however, and despite Emerson's repeated supplications over the next few years, Newcomb would publish nothing. After his death in Paris in 1894, it was discovered that he had indeed been writing all the time, filling his journals with poetry that Emerson probably would have considered obscene.[4]

By 1855 Emerson dismissed his friend Newcomb, calling him "a strange perverse son of the light fighting against light" (*L*, 4:516). The letter of 9 July in which he ended the relationship was on the surface a response to what has been described as Newcomb's "Swedenborgian, rhapsodical letter," but the catalyst that probably completed Emerson's disenchantment with Newcomb was the work of another poet he had received around 4 July—what he would presently call the "wonderful gift of *Leaves of Grass*." In his letter of 21 July to Walt Whitman, he suspected a "long foreground" for such a book. For he thought for certain this time that the American Adam he had prophesied in "The Poet" (1844) had arrived. He no longer had to confess, as he had in that essay, "I look in vain for the poet whom I describe."

That foreground was already forming in 1842 when Emerson delivered the lecture that became a draft of "The Poet." Driven south from New England in search of more lecture fees, Emerson was speaking in New York City for the second winter in a row. The series of lectures he gave there was called "The Times," but it echoed the same general theme of previous courses with similar titles. Like "Human Culture," "Human Life," and "The Present

Age," this one sounded the ideas that cohere in his *Essays* of 1841 —"The infinitude of the private man." In "The Times" series, however, he focused for the first time on the American artist. "Nature and the Powers of the Poet" described clearly the poet only suggested in *Nature*—the individual, he now may have concluded, who was not to be found in New England.

It seemed clear enough that the *Dial* had not published this poet by 1842. That year he told his friend Thomas Carlyle, who had recently complained of the "perilous altitudes" to which its contributors soared, "We write as we can, and we know very little about it. If the direction of these speculations is to be deplored, it is yet a fact for literary history, that all the bright boys & girls in New England, quite ignorant of each other, take the world so, & come & make confession to fathers and mothers." They confessed their dislike for "trade" and "morning calls & evening parties," now the stock of life in a nation born out of religious reform. "They are all religious," Emerson continued, "but hate the churches: they reject all the ways of living of other men, but have nothing to offer in their stead. Perhaps, one of these days, a great Yankee shall come, who will easily do the unknown deed" (*CEC*, pp. 328, 332).

Emerson's New York City lecture on the Poet marked the beginning of his search outside New England, a search into areas where, as Carlyle termed it in his grumbling over the *Dial*, the emerging American artist still struggled with "the fact of this present universe." There literary expression called for more than Newcomb's dreamy and abstract narrative of the child Dolon, who becomes an Old Testament sacrifice in the sylvan environs of New England. There Ellery Channing's idyllic meandering lacked the identity and power of the New World. There the young artist emigrated from the country to the city and was initiated in both the beauty and the brutality of a growing metropolis. There the artist would have to comprehend the Actual (or apparent) before transcending to the Real.

The city Emerson encountered in 1842 pulsated with political activity and controversy. At the time of his visit, the two-penny presses of New York were debating the question of using public funds for Roman Catholic schools. It was also a city beginning to absorb the reform movements that had filtered down from New England. A year earlier Horace Greeley had founded the New York *Tribune* and opened its columns to many assorted dreamers. Abolitionists, Fourierists, universalists, proponents of the National Bank, those in favor of high tariffs, and other advocates of "contradictory systems" were heard from in the *Tribune* at one time or another. Grahamites warned of the dangers of sexual intercourse to intellectual growth, and spiritualists (or "table-rappers") captured the attention of thousands of Americans. Emerson found his New York colleagues naively utilitarian. "They are bent on popular action," he wrote his wife about Greeley and Albert Brisbane, the American spokesman for Fourierism who would shortly lecture him on the "high mysteries of 'Attractive Industry.' " "I am in all my theory, ethics, & politics," he protested, "a poet and of no more use in their New York than a rainbow or a firefly. Meantime they fasten me in their thought to 'Transcendentalism,' whereof you know I am wholly guiltless, and which is spoken of as a known & fixed element like salt or meal." In a letter to Margaret Fuller, he called them "dim New Yorkers" (*L*, 3:18, 21, 29n).

Greeley and Brisbane (assistant editor of the *Tribune*) were preaching the system of Charles Fourier (1772–1837). The French socialist had advocated a cooperative organization of society in which all members would equally share the profits of its combined labor. The ideal community would be divided into phalansteries containing exactly 1,680 men, women, and children, including at least one craftsman in every trade. Since, as Fourier had taught, most of the ills of society stemmed from the suppression of emotions, there would be free expression of love (an idea that became a movement of its own in the 1870s under the aegis of Ezra Heywood's New England Free Love League), free choice of vocation, communal nurseries for the workers' offspring, and so on. Like most socialistic theories, Fourierism assumed that the timeless problem of human diversity could be solved "scientifically." In 1843 Brisbane left the *Tribune* and took Fourier's "science" to the Transcendental community of Brook Farm in the West Roxbury district, near Boston. In doing so, he effectively set the date for its demise in 1847.

Even in its pre-Fourieristic days when Brook Farm had accommodated Nathaniel Hawthorne for a time, Emerson had refused to join the enterprise. He told George Ripley, founder of the cooperative, that he thought it "circuitous . . . to put on your community the task of my emancipation which I ought to take on myself" (*L*, 2:369). Reform for Emerson would always begin and end with the individual. Yet the experiment interested many in New York when Emerson made his visit. The city had expanded rapidly since 1800. What had once offered the rural village atmosphere of 60,000 inhabitants became the nation's largest metropolis in 1820 with a population of 124,000, surpassing Philadelphia. By 1842 it counted more than 350,000 residents. And with the population expansion had come the impersonality and anonymity of city life, labor problems, currency speculation, and increasing disparities in wealth. It is little wonder, then, that the sage of Concord found New Yorkers anything but self-reliant. For the likes of Greeley and Brisbane, the panacea for mankind lay in centralization, not individuality; practicality, not poetry.

Nevertheless, Emerson found the full house he lectured to during the first two weeks in March encouraging after the disappointing turnout for his lectures in Providence in late February. At one time or another during the New York series, the audience probably included some of the city's better-known figures. Besides Greeley and Brisbane, there were Henry James, Sr., whose son, the philosopher William James, was born that year, and William Cullen Bryant, already recognized as America's leading poet and editor of the *Evening Post*. Doubtless, there were also editors in attendance from the *Sun*, the *Mirror*, the *Aurora*, the *Union*, and the *Knickerbocker*. No longer content to fill their pages with advertisements and satirical accounts of police court proceedings, editors now sought out news in the race to outsell their competitors on "newspaper row," near Fulton and Nassau streets. Emerson, whether he liked the appellation or not, was New England's leading "Transcendentalist."

The *Aurora*, a new two-penny newspaper that year, said of Emerson's lecture on the Poet, delivered on 5 March at the Society Library, "There were a few beautiful maids—but more ugly women, mostly blue stockings; several interesting young men

with Byron collars, doctors, and parsons; Grahamites and abolitionists; sage editors, a few of whom were taking notes; and all
the other species of literati." The reporter making these observations was Walter Whitman, at twenty-two the editor of the
Aurora. Somewhat conservative in his political views, he was not
above using the tools of scurrilous journalism to poke fun at the
liberal Greeley. He said the editor was "in ecstasies whenever
any thing particularly good was said," adding that Greeley's
enthusiasm bubbled over about every five minutes during the
course of Emerson's remarks. Greeley "would flounce about like
a fish out of water, as a tickled girl—look around, to see those
behind him and at his side; all of which very plainly told to those
both far and near, that he knew a thing or two more about these
matters than other men" (*WWA*, p. 105).

Although Whitman was careful to measure and record the re-
actions of the auditors that evening, he did not miss the salient
points of Emerson's lecture. Already a published poet with eight
or so rather conventional pieces going back to 1838, he heard
Emerson say that the world's next great poet would be found at
home. He "is Yankee born. He is in the forest walks, in paths car-
peted with leaves of the chestnut, oak, and pine. . . . He visits
without fear the factory, the railroad, and the wharf." "When he
lifts his great voice," Emerson proclaimed, "men gather to him
and forget all that is past, and then his words are to the hearers,
pictures of all history; and immediately the tools of their bench,
and the riches of their useful arts, and the laws they live under,
seem to them weapons of romance" (*EL*, 3:362). What probably
struck Whitman as he listened was the thought of the impact the
next literary genius would have on his countrymen. This poet
would become almost a messiah whose nation (as he later wrote
in the preface to the 1855 *Leaves of Grass*) would absorb "him as
affectionately as he has absorbed it." In the *Aurora* of 7 March,
Whitman described Emerson's lecture on the Poet as "one of the
richest and most beautiful compositions, both for its matter and
style, we have ever heard anywhere, at any time" (*WWA*, p. 105).

Thirteen years would pass before the editorial "we" metamor-
phosed into the self-reliant "I" of "Song of Myself," but Emerson's words had finally found and stirred one who would become

the poet he sought. Like the young journalist Theodore Dreiser fifty years later, Whitman would serve his literary apprenticeship absorbing the sights and sounds of the city of New York, "a mighty world in itself." When he chose, he could be the "hack writer" many have called him, but like Dreiser in sketches such as "Curious Shifts of the Poor" (a vignette that anticipates the pathos of Hurstwood's fall in *Sister Carrie*), Whitman had an eye that was both imaginative and penetrating. "Here are people of all classes and stages of rank," he wrote in the *Aurora* of 8 March, "from all countries on the globe—engaged in all varieties of avocations—of every grade, every hue of ignorance and learning, morality and vice, wealth and want, fashion and coarseness, breeding and brutality, elevation and degradation, impudence and modesty" (*WWA*, p. 17). In 1855 in the book that Emerson had sought and helped to inspire, he would sing of "every hue and caste." The famous foreground had already begun, but the genius that it produced would require a long period of gestation. Over the next decade Whitman would continue to evaluate his city and people through the eyes of the journalist, though there would be repeated attempts at poetry and short fiction. These would be less useful to him in his poetic development than his newpaper observations that recorded everything from boarding house life to abandoned children. He would work for a number of newspapers, including the *Evening Tatler*, the Brooklyn *Evening Star*, the Long Island *Star*, the Brooklyn *Daily Eagle*, the New Orleans *Crescent*, and finally the Brooklyn *Freeman*. Then Whitman would end his journalistic peregrination and, as he may have told John Townsend Trowbridge in 1860, "simmer" toward the creation of *Leaves of Grass*.[5]

Probably the aspect of the Emerson-Whitman connection most often noted in studies of the two writers is the difference in their backgrounds or culture. It is often used to account for the contrast between Emerson's noble letter to Whitman of 21 July 1855 and Whitman's unauthorized publication of it along with his open letter in which he addressed Emerson as "Master." This event in American literary history has been the cornerstone of the argument that Emerson could not have seriously endorsed Whitman's 1856 and 1860 editions. Indeed, few believed that Emerson was serious in his endorsement of 1855, or even that he was the author of the letter. One distressed clerical geologist "pronounced it at once ungenuine, a malicious jest . . . [and] promised to obtain [Emerson's] word in support of my volunteered faith."[6] Thus began the debate over the Emerson-Whitman connection. On the one hand, James Russell Lowell (shortly after publication of the 1855 *Leaves*) and later Edward Emerson argued for Emerson's superiority to and nonrecognition of Whitman's genius; on the other hand, John Burroughs, William Douglas O'Connor, and later the "Whitmaniacs" insisted on Emerson's unqualified and unceasing approval of *Leaves of Grass*.[7] In our own century John B. Moore has argued that Emerson was the "master of Whitman," and Clarence Gohdes, avoiding the shrillness of Moore's assertion, has nevertheless censured Whitman for his "mawkish" response to Emerson's letter of greeting.[8] The argument implying that Emerson and Whitman were entirely different as American artists reached its nadir in 1957 in an essay that describes the connection as a meeting of "the Body Electric" and "the genteel tradition."[9]

In temperament and talent, however, Emerson and Whitman were much alike, and the similarity accounts for their complementary roles in the literature of the American Renaissance. Both overcame the stifling influences of their cultures to accept the challenge of producing a literature that was uniquely American because it reflected the spontaneity of "becoming" in the New World. It relied absolutely on the successful quest for that quality, or Character, that was at once representative of the American Character and uniquely one's own. Emerson called it the emergence of the "Slumbering Giant," the symbol of man's potential awareness of his central position in the universe. This Emersonian self-reliance became "original energy" in Whitman's *Leaves of Grass*. Their literary connection has been blurred, however, by shortsighted theories that have tended to stereotype Emerson as the "gentleman" and Whitman as the "rough" of American literature. Doubtless, it was Whitman himself who fostered the theory that left him as an "outsider" in our literary history of the nineteenth century. Like the critics who followed him, he some-times lost sight of the Emerson of *Nature* and other essays and lectures written between 1836 and 1841 and focused instead on the Emerson of "Experience" and "Fate," where culture was needed as a buffer between man and nature.

Years after Emerson died, leaving the world to its own conclu-sions regarding his lifelong view of *Leaves of Grass*, Whitman compared Emerson's culture to the condition of an overtrained athlete. Recalling a conversation with Emerson, he told his friend Horace Traubel: "He said he felt that culture had done all it could for him—then it had done something for him which had better been left undone" (*WWC*, 3:354). By this time, of course, Whit-man's attitude was tainted slightly by the fact that Emerson had never publicly confirmed his statement that *Leaves of Grass* was "the most extraordinary piece of wit & wisdom that America has yet contributed." But Whitman still discerned a quality in Emer-son that suggests he understood his genius as well as the New Englander's patience with a literary establishment that ignored or condemned *Leaves of Grass*. "I seem to have various feelings about Emerson," he told Traubel, "but I am always loyal at last. Emer-son gratified me as a young man by what he did—he sometimes tantalized me as an old man by what he failed to do. You see, I both blaspheme and worship" (*WWC*, 2:69). Such polarities of attitude in Whitman stemmed from a view of Emerson that Ste-phen Whicher later defined as the Emerson of Freedom and the Emerson of Fate.[10] The distinction is a useful one, but it is also as misleading today as it was for Whitman. For it keeps us from a clear understanding of the Emerson of Freedom, the man whose contrarieties led to his best work *and* to his recognition of Whit-man's genius.

Of all the comments pro and con by Whitman about Emerson, one idea emerges with a lucidity that is undeniable. The poet perceived two distinctly different selves in the enigmatic New Englander. The Emerson who shied away from the controversy created by the publication of his letter was the overtrained ath-lete. This was the man who became the Unitarian minister, the faithful husband, the conscientious father, and the good neigh-bor. Although he held that reform had to begin with the individual, it was also this cautious side of Emerson that made him slower than many other New England intellectuals to protest the existence of black slavery in his own country. This was the Emerson who regretted the necessity of writing to President Van Buren about America's shabby treatment of the Cherokee Indians in Georgia.[11] As an American man of letters, this Emerson held membership in the "club"—Hedge's Club, the Town and Country Club, the Saturday Club, whatever circles commonly associated with the New England Brahmins (and it should be remembered that the charter members of Hedge's Club initially considered limiting membership to ordained Unitarian ministers). As Whitman saw clearly, this was the Emerson "clipped and pruned [of] that free luxuriance" of genius that satisfied the soul (PW, 2:759). As such, he was little more perceptive as a critic than those New England writers now generally relegated to the second rank in our histories: James Russell Lowell, who promised to keep *Leaves of Grass* out of the Harvard College Library; Henry Wadsworth Longfellow, who complained that Whitman lacked the education to complement his talent; or John Greenleaf Whittier, who allegedly pitched his complimentary copy of Whitman's first edition into the fire.[12]

The other Emerson Whitman perceived required more freedom, at times "wildness." This man loved too deeply and never became completely reconciled to his losses—the early deaths of his first wife Ellen Tucker, his first son Waldo, and his favorite brother Charles. With their surrogates he was affectionate and loving, but also cautious. The caution shows in his letters, for he was never again able to give of himself with the same abandon. To his second wife in 1848, after four months' absence in England, he wrote: "Ah you still ask me for that unwritten letter always due, it seems, always unwritten, from year to year, by me to you, dear Lidian" (L, 4:33). In other letters to her during his frequent lecture tours in America, he often cautioned Lidian to watch over the children who had survived young Waldo. Despite the fact that he was probably an exemplary parent to the others, the first child's death by scarlet fever in 1842 removed the strongest part of the magnetism that had always drawn him anxiously back home again from the lecture circuit. As he wrote in "Threnody,"

Waldo took "the largest part of me" (W, 9:153). Emerson's reaction to this loss bears no resemblance to his sense of compensation in "Experience" and "Threnody." The series of letters he
issued from Concord in the days following his son's death are almost bulletins of hysteria: "My boy, my boy is gone," he wrote to
Aunt Mary Emerson. "I can say nothing to you. . . . He adorned
the world for me like a morning star, and every particular of my
daily life. I slept in his neighborhood & woke to remember him"
(L, 3:7). With Charles the loss was also profound, though not so
jarring as to compel him to open his brother's coffin as he had
Ellen's (JMN, 4:7). Yet all three—Ellen, Waldo, and Charles—
drew out the other Emerson, the one few others could touch, the
self even his friend and confidante Margaret Fuller failed to know
to her complete satisfaction. They lived in Emerson's "neighborhood," the daring, self-reliant side that accounts for his genius.

Apparently, it accounts for his singularity as the prophet and
trumpeter of an age in American letters in which the character of
a nation was for the first time accurately mirrored in its literature.
Discussing the natural and artificial in Emerson, Whitman told
Traubel: "There's no difference between Homer and Virgil—oh
no!—and yet there's every difference. . . . it is the whole gap between the fellow who sings because he is moved to, and the fellow who sets out deliberately to sing, and so sings!" He thought
Emerson had "a good deal of Virgil in him," but he was not about
to discount his Homeric side as an artist and critic, "because
in him there's a whole world, independent of cultivation, that
bubbles up, evolutes, is cast forth, naturally, superbly" (WWC,
5:322). This was the Emerson that Whitman always came back to,
was always loyal to. It was the Homeric Emerson who said in the
1842 lecture that poetry "finds its origin in that *need of expression*
which is a primary impulse of nature. Every thought in man requires to be uttered, and his whole life is an endeavor to embody
in facts the states of the mind. . . . The man is only half himself;
the other half is his Expression" (EL, 3:348–49). And it was the
natural Emerson who wrote (and whom Whitman doubtless read)
in "The Poet": "If a man is inflamed and carried away by his
thought, to that degree that he forgets the authors and the public
and heeds only this one dream which holds him like an insanity,

let me read his paper, and you may have all the arguments and histories and criticism" (*W*, 3:32).

If one theme sounds clearly over the others in Emerson's early lectures and essays, it is that the form of all genuine poetry is prescribed by one compound force: "the particular genius of the poet" and "the want of the times" (*EL*, 2:61). The challenge was to find the genius who had discovered the drama of America mirrored in himself, and not in the nation's English ancestry. Not an easy task, it appeared. For as he said in "Art," a lecture first delivered in Boston the same year *Nature* appeared, "In this country, at this time, other interests than religion and patriotism are predominant, and the arts, the daughters of enthusiasm, do not flourish" (*EL*, 2:54). He sought a literature that idealized action, the action of the New World. It had to combine, he continued in another lecture, the material and the ideal to apprise "us of how large a portion of ourselves lies within the limits of the unconscious" (*EL*, 2:56). Emerson's perception of this principle had as much to do with the evolution of his best works as it did his immediate recognition and approval of Whitman's blend of patriotism and religion ("wit & wisdom") in *Leaves of Grass*. What he found to delight and electrify him in Whitman's book was a translation and an expansion of the compound that had characterized his own art and its assaults on the American literary establishment still enamored of "the courtly muses of Europe."

Both Emerson and Whitman possessed this force and discovered its expression at periods in our literary history that mark off the dates of what F. O. Matthiessen has taught us to call the American Renaissance, 1836–55. And each discovery was the culmination of a literary apprenticeship that lasted at least ten years. In 1826 Emerson was authorized to preach as a Unitarian minister and thus accepted a philosophical and theological tradition that gradually proved too rigid for the expanding scope of his thought. Almost at the same age as Emerson, Whitman in 1842 seriously committed himself to a career in journalism and encountered the same kind of confinement. In Chapters 2 and 3 I have attempted to limn these foregrounds, showing in each case how the man and his thought could not be contained by the institution that had nurtured his genius. Suffice it to say here that each writer transcended the limits of his institution by the force of Character. As travelers lost on the public road of life, each trusted his own instincts to find the way home.

In an often-quoted passage from an 1835 letter to Lidian, Emerson confessed: "I am born a poet, of a low class without doubt yet a poet. That is my nature & vocation." At the time he was struggling with the philosophical "crack" in *Nature* and doubtless realized he was what Hyatt Waggoner has recently called the poet-preacher.[13] For *Nature* presented a kind of writing that did not belong to either the essayist or the poet. Rather, it lay somewhere between, because it constituted the language of a literary visionary. It was certainly not the cold, sledgehammer prose of the philosopher; for Emerson's metaphors led him to ignore Kant's warning that pure Reason cannot be applied practically to the world of the senses. Only the poet could mend the crack between the sections on "Discipline" and "Idealism" and thus equate Transcendental intuition with instinct.[14] Yet the final product of *Nature* is generally unpoetic, with its sermonlike divisions and "Application" (the final section labeled "Prospects"). Although his genius fully emerges in the American Scholar Address, the Divinity School Address, and "The Poet," even these are more accurately called prose-poems, not poetry. For as he told Lidian in the same letter, his singing was "very 'husky,' & [was] for the most part in prose. Still," he added, "am I a poet in the sense of a perceiver & dear lover of the harmonies that are in the soul & in matter, & specially of the correspondences between these & those" (*L*, 1:435).

On the other hand, he was too much of a poet to remain a Unitarian minister. As minister he began to find, through his study of natural history, those correspondences between Body and Soul, and so to perceive nature as fluid rather than fixed. Later, when he wrote as poet-preacher about the orphic poet in *Nature*, he unfixed "the land and the sea, [made] them revolve around the axis of his primary thought, and [disposed] them anew" (*CW*, 1:31). He accepted his genius and acted it out. He took nature, the symbol grown stale and lifeless under Unitarian complacency, and applied it to the present. And thus he enabled Whitman to proclaim in his 1855 preface that "there will soon be no more priests. . . . A new order shall arise and they shall be the priests of man, and every man shall be his own priest."[15] In Emerson's new order, the priest, like Christ who had spoken in metaphors now misapprehended, became a poet again, one who "spoke of miracles; for he felt that man's life was a miracle" (CW, 1:81). In a sense, Emerson's vision attempted to restore the poet to the pulpit, but instead created a secular church and the need for a poet-priest. Ultimately, Whitman filled that role, for Emerson is more accurately described as a poet-preacher: he provided the literary vision and Whitman conducted the celebration.

The genesis of *Leaves of Grass* occurred shortly after Emerson's 1842 lecture on the Poet, when he introduced into Whitman's fixed world of journalism the possibilities of seeing "higher laws" in the carnival of life he recorded. But like Emerson in 1826, Whitman had yet to do more than simply ponder the meaning of nature. The bard who ultimately announced "I am the poet of the Body and I am the poet of the Soul" was but "half himself" in 1842. During March and April of that year, Whitman's editorials in the *Aurora* revealed his occupation with political questions, not philosophical or literary ones. They involved Bishop Hughes's attempt to get public funds appropriated for the support of Roman Catholic schools in New York, a measure Whitman vehemently opposed. His almost cavalier dissent went beyond the question of separation of church and state to attack the Catholic population in New York City as invading foreigners. In "Insult to American Citizenship" he wrote: "We sorrow for our native land. Having no prejudices against foreigners, because they are such, we yet feel that they are becoming altogether too domineering among us." As for "that reverend villain, Hughes," and his "jesuitical knaves," Whitman suggested that they deserved nothing more than frontier justice: "In the west, where the statute book affords no remedy for outrage, the injured community takes the case into its own hands" (*WWA*, p. 58).

"Insult to American Citizenship" is fairly representative of the kind of incendiary editorials in which the young journalist indulged himself on the political front. With regard to the later poetry, it may be said that the themes are democracy and nativism, aspects of Whitman's beliefs that became more universal in *Leaves of Grass*. In the *Aurora* editorials focusing on the population and its various backgrounds and trades, however, he anticipates his vivid descriptions of the "divine average." In a piece written shortly after Emerson's lecture on the Poet ("Life in a New York Market"), we find hints of the freewheeling descriptions in his later poetry. The essay also shows the writer to be master of his subject: "How the crowd rolls along! There comes a journeyman mason (we know him by his *limy* dress) and his wife—she bearing a little white basket on her arm." And further on: "But those butchers! what jovial dogs they are! . . . With amusing perseverance, they play off on every new passenger the same lures and the same artifice that have been tried and failed in so many previous cases. And when they have nothing to do, they amuse themselves with a jig, or a breakdown" (*WWA*, pp. 20–21). The editor already knew his average well and so the poet wrote in 1855: "The butcher-boy puts off his killing-clothes, or sharpens his knife at the stall in the market, / I loiter enjoying his repartee and his shuffle and breakdown."[16] In "New York Boarding Houses" he employed what became one of his trademarks in *Leaves of Grass*, the catalog: "Married men and single men; old women and pretty girls; milliners and masons; cobblers, colonels, and counter jumpers; tailors and teachers; lieutenants, loafers, ladies, lackbrains, and lawyers; printers and parsons—'black spirits and white, blue spirits and gray'—all 'go out to board'" (*WWA*, p. 23).

It is of course nothing new to observe that Whitman moved toward his expression, or the "other half" of himself, when he loitered and observed. Hence, it was in journalism (especially the human-interest writing), the genre that confined his talent for a time as the ministry had confined Emerson's, that he also matured as a poet—and generally not in his attempts at fiction and poetry. The one exception in the poetry is found in "Time to Come," a revision of his earliest known published poem, "Our Future Lot." Published in the *Aurora* of 9 April 1842, it presented the same prosaic theme that decay or death will claim the body. There is, however, a slight but significant departure in the revision. In "Our Future Lot" the destiny of the Soul was certain: "Thy form, re-purified, shall rise, / In robes of beauty drest." In the 1842 version the question of the "soul's abiding place" is left open: "O, powerless is this struggling brain / To rend the mighty mystery; / In dark, uncertain awe it waits / The common doom, to die" (*EPF*, pp. 27–29). The question now resists traditional Christian teachings and becomes open-ended. We find evidence here that Whitman underwent the beginning of a change. It had little to do with the immediate development of his prosody, however, for the two poems are conventional in meter and differ only in rhyme scheme, with the alternating rhyme of the first becoming *a b c d* in the revision. But the crack in the conventionality of his thought had been accomplished. Perhaps he understood, but in a way not yet clear enough, Emerson's maxim that thought precedes form. He may have been stopped cold for a time by what Emerson had said in his lecture, what Whitman himself restated in his *Aurora* report of 7 March, that "the business of the poet is expression—the giving utterance to the emotions and sentiments of the soul" (*WWA*, p. 105). At any rate, after revising one other poem, he stopped writing poetry altogether and turned to short fiction. In 1843 "My Departure" of 1839 was published as "Death of the Nature-Lover" in *Brother Jonathan*. But the theme of wishing to die in nature, "where the shrubs grow and the proud trees wave," is unchanged (*EPF*, pp. 30–32). Furthermore, the quality of the metaphors is possibly inferior to that in the original, and the first-person narrator is dropped for the third.

Whitman's fiction provides a few more clues to his poetic development in the early stages of his foreground. In the story "Reuben's Last Wish," published in the *Washingtonian* of 21 May 1842, he turned to the temperance theme (expanded later that year in his only completed novel, *Franklin Evans; or, The Inebriate*). Almost as if to eschew the profound question broached in "Time to Come," he went back to preaching conventional morality. Yet "Reuben's Last Wish" may provide some indication of a change in Whitman's self-image, for the story revives the plot of the two brothers and their relationship to the father. In "Wild Frank's Return" and "Bervance: or, Father and Son," which appeared, respectively, in the *Democratic Review* for November and December 1841, the father clearly favors the first son over the second. Whitman was the second son after Jesse, an individual who eventually led the life of a drunkard and a syphilitic. But according to his niece, in his youth he was apparently thought to have "the best mind of any of the children" until he suffered an accident.[17] Perhaps the fact that the three sons born after Whitman were named for famous Americans supports the hypothesis that Walter Whitman, Sr., was disappointed with the son to whom he had given his own name. Or at least Whitman thought so. Whatever the case, Whitman appears to have disabused himself of this notion by the spring of 1842, for in "Reuben's Last Wish" both sons receive equal treatment, or mistreatment, from the father. Like Jesse Whitman, who became a member of the merchant marine in the early 1840s, the older son in the story runs off to sea, never to be heard from again. The second son becomes an invalid after his father mistreats him in a drunken tipsy. The rest of the tale follows one of the standard temperance plots: the invalid boy, never healthy, dies—but not before he has copied out the temperance pledge and persuaded his father to sign it. The story is important, however, for what it omits. In the poems and fiction written before the 1842 Emerson lecture, personal themes are mixed with public ones, as in "Fame's Vanity" in 1839 ("Ambition" in early 1842), "Death in the School-Room (A Fact)" in 1841, and "The Child and the Profligate" in 1841.[18] In "Reuben's Last Wish," however, Whitman now steps back from his experience—banishes, in effect, his older brother to a life at sea—and his writing in the spring of 1842 becomes impersonal, if also blatantly moralistic.[19]

Whitman's didacticism is also found in his journalism, but it becomes milder as he gains a clearer perspective on the life he records. His answers become questions. In the piece "About Children," which appeared in the *Aurora* of 16 April, the subject is mentally retarded children. Although it gave Whitman an opportunity to call upon the pathetic example of his youngest brother Edward, who by the age of seven was found to be both a physical and mental invalid, he presents instead a scene that omits personal echoes of earlier pieces having to do with children, "Sun-Down Papers No. 6" and "Death in the School-Room" (where Whitman's personal dislike for feruling is reflected). Rather, he provides the reader with a scenario that conjures up not the pathos but the intriguing aspect of mental illness. During a recent visit to the home of such a child, Whitman found him weirdly attracted to a portrait of the crucifixion of Christ and the two thieves. After stating that all explanation of the icon was lost on the child, Whitman concludes: "It was very singular, and we could not help noticing it, that the mind of this dumb youth seemed to respond at once to the idea of a God" (*WWA*, pp. 51–52).

Aside from the fact that the editorial avoids much of the moralizing found in the poetry and fiction, it suggests that Whitman continued to become detached from personal experience, to be "both in and out of the game, and watching and wondering at it." In the other genres he is farther from the mark; yet the preachy nature of even these endeavors argues for a drift away from the Actual toward the Real as he had heard it described in "Nature and the Powers of the Poet." Emerson's lecture may have provided a holding pattern, as it were, for Whitman, thereby keeping him from success even as a "hack writer." In the meantime he was forced to continue as a journalist. And it was from this point that his development toward *Leaves of Grass* began in earnest. Like Emerson's journals, his reporter's notebook was his "savings bank." He recorded the pathos of "the suicide [sprawled] on the bloody floor of the bedroom," the "arrests of criminals, slights, adulterous offers made, acceptances, rejections with convex lips," and "the opium-eater [reclining] with rigid head and just-opened lips."[20] Here he began to "witness and wait."

2. Emerson—The Foreground

God offers to every mind its choice
between Truth and Repose. Take which you please;
you can never have both.
Emerson, ''The Head''

The greatest delight which the
fields and woods minister is the suggestion of
an occult relation between man
and the vegetable.
Emerson, *Nature*

On 10 October 1826 Ralph Waldo Emerson was "approbated" to preach by the Middlesex Association. On 11 September 1832 he resigned as pastor of the Second Church of Boston. And on 9 September 1836 he published his first and most famous book, *Nature*. These three events punctuate a decade of development in which Emerson ultimately rejected the theological legacy based upon generations of Arminian reform of New England Protestantism and wrote what may be considered an epilogue to the movement. For surely what he inherited from his father, the Reverend William Emerson of the First Church of Boston, was the final chapter, one that opened with the installation of the Reverend Henry Ware, Sr., as Hollis Professor of Divinity at Harvard College in 1805. With that victory, the Arminians or liberals of the church declared the theological frontier of New England conquered; the reform movement that decade after decade in the eighteenth century had witnessed the rejection of innate depravity, original sin, the divinity of Christ—in short, the Calvinistic bedrock upon which the first colonies had been founded—was now concluded. Unitarianism, as the term came into general use by 1819 with William Ellery Channing's famous Baltimore sermon, retained only two of the original puritan concepts: the validity of scripture as a manifestation of God's will and the conviction that the religious community had an obligation and a right to exercise its influence over society.

When Emerson resigned from the Second Church, he selected as his ostensible reason the applicability of the sacrament of the Lord's Supper, which he believed clothed Christ with "an authority which he never claimed and which distracts the mind of the [Unitarian] worshipper" from God to Jesus (*W*, 11:17). The challenge was not without historical precedent, for the Arminian movement had really begun with an earlier controversy over the same ceremony. Probably more than any other New England congregational minister, it was Solomon Stoddard who blurred the puritan distinction between the saints and sinners of the church by allowing all of his parishioners, regenerate and unregenerate alike, to receive the sacrament of the Lord's Supper. First-century American puritanism had thrived on adversity (papism, anglicism, the wilderness of New England), but most of all on the fear of unregenerate souls in its midst. Indeed, the uncertainty of the New World enhanced the Calvinistic principle of innate depravity, for it served as a symbol of the hidden evil in the world. But as the settlers gained a foothold in New England, turning the hostile land into a source of prosperity, their apprehensions declined with their fear of the wilderness. This corresponding decline of spiritual determination led to a decline in religious conversions by the second generation of puritans. By 1662 church leaders instituted the "Half-way Covenant," which allowed children of the "unconverted" to seek membership in the church. Stoddard merely enlarged this first crack in puritan idealism by using the ceremony as a means to salvation rather than as evidence of justification in the eyes of God and therefore hastened the inevitable disappearance of the concept of innate depravity in the New World. For if everyone could receive the sacrament, how were church leaders to retain a vivid sense of God's election among their congregation?[1]

Of course there were many attempts by church conservatives to reverse Stoddard's precedent and its liberating effect on American Calvinism, the most dramatic being made by the minister's grandson, the great theologian Jonathan Edwards. He advocated a return to more pristine Calvinistic principles, but after the Great Awakening (1740–45) and its emotional excesses, ministers who had been encouraged by Stoddard's experiment and thus opposed to the concept of exclusive membership in the church began to grow bolder in their views. As Conrad Wright notes, "The effect of the revival was not so much to spread Arminianism as to prepare the way for its rapid growth. Down to the Awakening, a sense of community in New England still existed. For all of Stoddard's differences with the Mathers, he still came to Boston every year at Harvard Commencement time. . . . But after 1745, New England was so divided that there was a sense of community among the liberals and a sense of community among the evangelists [Calvinists], but any wider sense of common purpose was wearing thin."[2]

Emerson's reluctance and ultimate refusal to administer the Lord's Supper in 1832, then, was the first step in rejecting what the previous generations of liberals had firmly stopped short of challenging: the validity of scripture as proof of God's will. Between the close of the Awakening and the election of Ware at Harvard, they had adopted the Arian view that Christ is not divine but an archangel or intermediary between God and man; however, they balked at the idea of ceasing to address Christ as God with the Lord's Supper. In doing so, they acted upon the justified fear that without the ceremony the Unitarian creed would be open to the Socinian interpretation of Christ as simply a great man, a view in fact advocated in 1838 when Emerson complained of the Unitarian preoccupation "with the noxious exaggeration about the *person* of Jesus" (*CW*, 1:82). And once Christ was removed from the ambiguous status as an intermediary, the Unitarians would have been hard-pressed to defend the New Testament as necessary for spiritual progess. Indeed, with the Arian view of Christ, Unitarianism already came perilously close to English Deism and a dependence on the empirical principles of Locke. It was doubtless because such Harvard leaders as Ware and Andrews Norton realized the possible outcome of Arminian reform that they incorporated into the college curriculum between 1805 and 1819 the writings of the Scottish Common-Sense philosophers. Thomas Reid, Dugald Stewart, and Thomas Brown offered relief from the cold empiricism of Locke by denying that man's apprehension of God could be gainsaid by logical analysis; they also maintained that man had an innate moral sense of right and wrong.[3]

Yet, as Perry Miller argues in an essay that is still useful in locating the source of Emerson's antinomianism, the New England tradition "gave with one hand what it took away with the other; it taught that God is present to their intuitions and in the beauty and terror of nature, but it disciplined them into subjecting their intuitions to the wisdom of society and their impressions of nature to the standards of decorum."[4] The Arminians had carried into the nineteenth century many of the social checks and balances that the original puritans had used to contain individual religious fervor. It is not surprising, therefore, that Emerson's epilogue to the history of his father's religion opens with the complaint that Unitarianism built "sepulchres of the fathers" and also asks for "a religion by revelation to us, and not the history of theirs." For the theological world he assailed in *Nature* was almost as spiritually fixed as that of the first-generation American puritans.

The clearest origins of the young preacher's misgivings are exemplified by the following journal passage in 1827. Reflecting dubiously on his new calling (from which poor health had temporarily relieved him), Emerson wrote from St. Augustine, Florida: "Satisfy me beyond the possibility of a doubt of the certainty of all that is told me concerning the other world and I will fulfill the conditions on which my salvation is suspended. The believer tells me he has historical & internal evidence that make the presumption so strong that it is almost a certainty that rests on the highest probabilities. Yes; but change that imperfect to perfect evidence & I too will be a Christian. Now it must be admitted that I am not certain that any of these things are true. The nature of God may be different from what He is represented" (*JMN*, 3:68–69). Although these doubts were real, they were also private ones at the beginning of his preaching career and thus were committed to his journal, where he allowed his ideas wide range and free play. Publicly, he was still pledged to the Unitarianism of the day, albeit not as firmly as he had once been. In his undergraduate essay "On Genius" (1820), he had belittled the tendency of modern scholars to overemphasize "their own unassisted exertions" and to underestimate the wisdom "of the wonderful men of old" (*JMN*, 1:207).[5] And in 1827 nature as the source of spiritual elevation was still "an unsubstantial pageant." Yet Emerson's doubts were growing, and the Unitarian way was his way only for the time being. "I will embrace it this time by way of experiment," he declared, "& if it is wrong certainly God can in some manner signify his will in the future" (*JMN*, 3:69). So he continued to accept his father's theological legacy and went on preaching.

Notwithstanding Emerson's vacillation in 1827, the hundred or so sermons he preached prior to his first wife's death in 1831 suggest that he was clearly trying to fulfill his responsibilities as a Unitarian minister. From "Pray Without Ceasing" (15 October 1826) to "Miracles" (23 January 1831), Emerson supports traditional Christian concepts, although he occasionally gives hints of his later rebellion. These concepts are duty, conscience, charity, piety, public and private prayer, the pettiness of life compared to the kingdom of God, the need for ceremony (i.e., the Lord's Supper), belief in miracles other than the ordinary works of nature, civic responsibility, God-reliance, underdevelopment of the soul, and so on. His public dedication to the institutional way of knowing God is well demonstrated in "A Feast of Remembrance" (27 September 1829). Although he would conclude his ministerial career with a denunciation of the Lord's Supper, here he sees it as "a means of quickening your moral perceptions and amending your character in its personal and social regards." In "Trust Yourself" (3 December 1830), his theme is not self-reliance but God-reliance. Indeed, it is God-reliance achieved through the religious community; for he announced that "it is the effect of religion [i.e., the institution] to produce a higher respect." Now far from the concept that "society scatters your force," he preaches that one's spiritual growth depends on the quality of his native religion: "cultivate in every soil the grapes of that soil." Finally, in "Miracles," Christ's supernatural accomplishments are regarded as sometimes necessary to startle those who are blind to the presence of God's miracle of nature itself (*YES*, pp. 58, 105, 107, 121).

Emerson's sermons suggest that he was a "Channing Unitarian" between 1826 and 1831. Like the elder William Ellery Channing, the young minister was imaginative in supporting the Arminian concepts that did away with the Calvinistic degradation of human nature, but remained more or less impervious to the subsequent currents of religious thought that blew west from the Romantic movements in England and Germany. Emerson shared Channing's dedication to the idea that Christian churches have an investment in contemporary civilization and must therefore exercise a leadership in the social order. But also like Channing, Emerson stretched the Unitarian reforms to their limits in many of his sermons. In "The Christian Minister" (15 March 1829), his first sermon as ordained junior pastor of the Second Church, he implied the importance of individual spiritual growth by declaring his own preference for preaching over public prayer (because the minister "merely utters the petitions which all feel"). He also announced that preaching equal to the demands and hopes of the times "must be manly and flexible and free beyond all the example of the times before us" (YES, pp. 25, 27).

Of course, it was the "Gospel and its universal applications" that Emerson intended to advance with such freedom in 1829. Yet Emerson's analogies between man's spiritual life and nature frequently took him into areas of theological ambiguity, in the fashion of Channing's sermon on man's "Likeness to God." Channing, for example, had declared that God "dwells within us," but concluded his sermon with the caveat against "extravagance" in appreciating this concept. "Let none infer from this language," he warned, "that I place religion in an unnatural effort, in straining after excitements which do not belong in the present state, or in any thing separate from the clear and simple duties of life."[6] Generally, Emerson was also content (although he questioned the practice in his journal) "simply to hunt out & to exhibit the analogies between moral & material nature in such a manner as to have a bearing upon practice" (JMN, 3:130). Ultimately, of course, the means of the analogies became far more enticing than their ends, leading him to conclude in 1836 that Unitarianism, in its refusal to allow the miracles of nature to supersede those recorded in scripture, was groping "among the dry bones of the past."

Perhaps the earliest and most dramatic example of Emerson's shifting focus is found in the sermon entitled "Summer" (14 June 1829). Here he is still preaching in support of "the truth of Religion," in this case following the Unitarian practice of adapting Christianity to the eighteenth-century theory of nature as the world machine. (Later, in a sermon on "Providence," he would quote Paley's theology "with pleasure.") In calling "all nature . . . a book on which one lesson is written . . . the omnipresence of God," he cites scripture as "always appealing" to nature "as the emblems of our mortal estate. It was the history of man in the beginning, and it is the history of man now" (YES, pp. 40, 44). Yet in the context of the sermon, which dwells more on the analogy with nature than on scripture as a source of the analogy, the biblical references appear obligatory and forced.

In his recent study of Emerson, Joel Porte compares "Summer" to the Divinity School Address, noting that it was last preached almost exactly a year before the Harvard address of 15 July 1838 and therefore seeing it as a kind of translation.[7] As Porte demonstrates, there is an obvious similarity between the opening metaphors: "In this grateful season" and "In this refulgent summer." But since Porte sees the language of the sermon as archaic and flaccid in the shadow of the 1838 address, it may be more accurate to view "Summer" as the earliest precursor to *Nature*. The Divinity School Address is Transcendental doctrine at its Emersonian apex in terms of prose-poetry in the lectures and essays, whereas "Summer" and *Nature* are clearly seminal in doctrine and are preoccupied, sometimes laboriously, with the analogy between man's condition and the harmony of nature.

Like the theme of *Nature*, the theme of "Summer" takes the form of a rhetorical question. After cataloging the ways in which nature ministers to man, Emerson asks: "To what end this unmeasured magnificence?" (*YES*, p. 43). Surely, it has a greater purpose than simple commodity, though "man shuts his eyes to this sovereign goodness, thinks little of the evidence that comes from nature, and looks upon the great system of the world only in parcels as its order happens to affect his petty interest" (*YES*, p. 40). In *Nature* he would remark: "A man is fed, not that he may be fed, but that he may work." As in *Nature*, the complaint about man's nearsightedness takes him from the level of commodity to that of beauty in nature. God's benevolence, Emerson says in "Summer," is more profoundly visualized "when it is considered that *the same results might have been brought about without this beauty*. . . . all this food might have been prepared as well without this glorious show." Nature gives us pleasure (the first level of beauty in *Nature*), but "there is more in nature than beauty; there is more to be seen than the outward eye perceives." Nature exists to tell us something about our spiritual destiny: "There is the language of its everlasting analogies" (*YES*, pp. 43–44). Although here Emerson hints at concepts in the next section of *Nature* on "Language," such a detailed analysis of the way nature speaks to man was not to come until he had left the ministry and studied science, biography, and literature in conjunction with his lyceum lectures between 1833 and 1836. Now he is satisfied to imply that nature is somehow the language of the soul. But in doing so, he establishes his definition of nature as the "Not-Me." "There is nothing in external nature," he contends, "but is an emblem, a hieroglyphic of something in us" (*YES*, p. 44). In *Nature*, of course, he will be more exacting and declare: "Every man's condition is a solution in hieroglyphic."

Like Channing's "Likeness to God," Emerson's "Summer" dwells dangerously close to the later Transcendental analogies. Yet, perhaps because of the Channing sermon, or the Channing influence in general, Emerson could venture freely into such areas of potential infidelity without offending Unitarian sensibilities. For in "Summer" nature is not what Emanuel Swedenborg called "the dial plate of the invisible," but merely an aid to appreciating the validity of Christian revelation. Here harmony with nature is a means, not an end. The same caution is exercised in Channing's sermon. God may indeed dwell within us, but "God's infinity places him beyond the resemblance and approach of man." In "Summer" man is not "part or particle with God," but merely in orbit around him: "Whilst thus directly we depend on this process [of nature], on the punctuality of the sun, on the timely action of saps and seed vessels, and rivers and rains, *are we as punctual to our orbit?*" (*YES*, p. 45).

Emerson's transformation from Unitarian to Transcendentalist was probably gradual and not marked by any particular event, such as Ellen Tucker's death on 8 February 1831.[8] Yet it is certain that his use of nature became an end in itself rather than a theological tool in his sermons a year after her death. In this sense, the change is *associated* with an external event just as Whitman's metamorphosis from journalist to poet is associated with his reading (or rereading) of Emerson in the late 1840s or early 1850s. For Emerson, 1831 was a watershed year, the year in which he finally decided to act upon the theological doubts that had been piling up in his journals. Ellen's death in the beginning of that year was probably the most traumatic experience of his life. Only the loss of his first son eleven years later can be compared to it for the level of intensity and grief. In 1842, however, his grief was soon assuaged and finally muffled in "Experience" and "Threnody." But in 1831 he was not so well prepared for tragedy. His letters to his brothers William and Charles suggest that his life had lost much of its value without Ellen. This young woman not yet twenty, her person representing everything truly good in life, had vanished.

Death, it seemed, became attractive as the only means of escaping his misery. Daily he visited his wife's grave, regardless of the weather. On 29 March he recorded in his journal: "I visited Ellen's tomb & opened the coffin." Whether he actually did so is a matter of conjecture, although he did, in fact, open Waldo's coffin in 1857 (*JMN*, 4:7; 14:154). The act suggests the macabre fiction of Edgar Allan Poe. Interestingly, Poe's first "biographer" opened his own wife's coffin in 1842, forty days after her funeral. Rufus Wilmot Griswold admitted that he entered the burial vault with the aid of a sexton. While alone with the coffin in a fit of melancholy, he pried off the lid and lay "beside the ruin of all that was dearest in the world" until a companion persuaded him to retire. If Emerson is recording an act instead of a dream (and he usually identifies dreams as such in his journals), he would have viewed Ellen's remains at about the same period after death as Griswold. What Griswold saw, he described as "the terrible changes made by Death and Time." He "kissed for the last time her cold black forehead [and] cut off locks of her beautiful hair, damp with the death dews, and sunk down in senseless agony."[9] Since the practice of filling the arterial system with embalming fluid did not begin until the Civil War, the sight must have been gruesome. If Emerson did indeed look upon Ellen in this state, he probably saw little more than a skeleton—the decay of the emblem that had brought him so much happiness.

The sight must have confirmed what Emerson had declared in "Consolation for the Mourner," preached twelve days after Ellen's demise. "All that part of man which we call the *character*, survives and ascends. Not a shade, not a thought of it cleaves to the cold clay we have put in the ground" (*YES*, p. 141). Decay, or change in nature, brought death, Ellen's death, but it also brought life. Death, as Whitman would say in "Song of Myself,"

is merely a transfer and a promotion. The particular may change
—indeed must change—but the universal sense of life remains.
What remained and grew, Emerson realized, was Character, its
growth symbolized by the alteration of nature. In 1835, the same
year in which he married Lydia Jackson ("Lidian" after her marriage), Emerson was still assessing the impact of Ellen's death.
He told his Aunt Mary: "The severest truth would forbid me to
say that ever I had made a sacrifice. . . . I loved Ellen, & love her
with an affection that would ask nothing but its indulgence to
make me blessed. Yet when she was taken from me, the air was
still sweet, the sun was not taken down from my firmament, &
however sore was that particular loss, I still felt that it was particular, that the Universe remained to us both" (*JMN*, 5:19–20).
By then he could accept the truth that life is change and the hope
for permanence in the particular is life's greatest illusion.

In "Grief," a sermon preached on 27 February 1831, Emerson
returned to the orthodox Christian idea that "religion makes circumstances indifferent" (MH). But that year he already must
have concluded that religion exalted the particular instead of the
universal. Thus, as if emerging from his year of mourning and
learning, he reversed himself—almost a year to the very day after
Ellen's death. In "Find Your Calling" (5 February 1832) Emerson
complained, "We hear a great deal of the empire of circumstances
over the mind, but not enough of the empire of the mind [or
Character] over circumstances, that the mind is capable of ex-
erting this power." On the contrary, he submitted to his congregation, is there "not reason to think that every man is born with a
particular character or having a peculiar determination to some
one pursuit or one sort of usefulness[?]" This pursuit may be
hidden from him for years because of unfavorable associations or
bad advice, "but he will never be at ease, he will never act with
efficiency, until he finds it" (*YES*, pp. 164–65, 167). "Find Your
Calling" represents most directly the thoughts of 1831, his determination to call forth his own character as it was mirrored in the
flux of nature. He took the same theme in "The Genuine Man"
(21 October 1832), following the acceptance of his resignation
from the office of pastor. The Genuine Man, he said, "acts always
in character because he always acts *from* his character. . . . He

therefore speaks what he thinks. He acts his thought'' (*YES*, pp. 184–85).

Whereas ''Find Your Calling'' and ''The Genuine Man'' are fundamental to Emerson's resignation, ''The Lord's Supper'' (9 September 1832) is not. For the ceremony was only a symptom of a larger malady. ''To exalt particular forms, to adhere to one form a moment after it is outgrown,'' he told his congregation two days before his resignation was tendered, ''is unreasonable, and it is alien to the spirit of Christ'' (*W*, 11:20). But actually, as he had learned during his year of mourning for Ellen, to exalt the particular in any aspect of life was alien to life itself and hence to the development of Character. Not only did Unitarianism violate the spirit of its Arminian past by continuing to worship Christ as God, but it also restricted the believer's appreciation of the growth of his character by defining it in terms of tradition instead of insight. Like the corpse of Ellen, the church, as he would declare in *Nature*, represented only ''the dry bones of the past.''

Ellen's death and her husband's reflection on it during 1831 were the catalyst and not the cause of Emerson's resignation. He had already been exposed to various Romantic writings, including Coleridge's *Aids to Reflection* and Goethe's memoirs. And he had read Sampson Reed's *Observations on the Growth of the Mind*, finding in it ''the aspect of a revelation'' (*JMN*, 3:45). His change in vocation was clearly the result of five years or more of inner struggle. Looking back in 1837 on his ordeal with the clergy and his decision to leave it, he said: ''God offers to every mind its choice between Truth and Repose. Take which you please; you can never have both. Between these as a pendulum man oscillates ever. He in whom the love of repose predominates will accept the first creed, the first philosophy, the first political party, he meets, —most likely his father's. He gets rest, commodity, and reputation. But he shuts the door of truth'' (*EL*, 2:256).[10] It was a choice between Repose and Truth. The one exalted the particular symbol (as Emerson in *Nature* would accuse Swedenborg of doing), whereas the other represented a life in touch with the flux of nature. As Emerson would declare in the Divinity School Address, the problem with Christianity was that it fastened its vision on one man who was merely the first to see that ''God incarnates himself in [every] man." The particular example was valuable only insofar as it represented the universal experience. Christ, as seen through Emerson's version of the Socinian view, was the first *representative* man because he had called forth his character to shape the circumstances of his life.

Five days after Ellen's death, Emerson asked himself, "Shall I ever again be able to connect the face of outward nature, the mists of the morn, the star of eve, the flowers, & all poetry, with the heart & life of an enchanting friend?" "No," he concluded, "There is one birth & one baptism & one first love and the affections cannot keep their youth any more than men" (*JMN*, 3:227). The lesson of her death helped him to confront the errors of Christianity. It was no longer mirrored in the flux of nature but mired in the particular of Christ's legacy. The church, as it were, had never fully emerged from its period of mourning.

These considerations led him in 1832 to emphasize the growth of Character in "Find Your Calling" and "The Genuine Man." The idea would later be developed in his most famous essays, especially "The Poet": "Doubt not, O poet, but persist. Say 'It is in me and shall out.'" However, he would need a theory of the Soul based upon the visible image in nature before he could enshrine the concept in Neoplatonic terms. For this he turned to the study of natural history. It has been suggested recently that Emerson's 1833–34 lectures on science "reveal his reading and thinking about science before he had fused his ideas thus derived with the Neoplatonic and 'transcendental' ideas of Plotinus, Swedenborg, Wordsworth, Coleridge, Carlyle, and seventeenth-century English Platonists."[11] But that interest in science and its spiritual relationship began while he was still a minister grappling with the superstitions of the past. His first "lecture" on natural history, in fact, is found in the sermon on "Astronomy" (27 May 1832), in which he suggested that the stars awakened in man religious sentiments that had been distorted by present-day Christianity. "Religion in the later ages, suffering from the caprices and errors of men, wanders often far from her object into strange paths; and the attempt is resisted as a sort of violence which strives to reunite Religion with the love of nature." Yet astronomy has always been at hand as the visible image of every truly exalted sentiment: "The song of the morning stars was really the first hymn of praise and will be the last; the face of nature, the breath of the hills, the light of the skies, are to a simple heart the real occasions of devout feeling more than the vestries and sermon hearings; and are those natural checks that are ever exciting an insensible influence to hold us back from fanaticism and keep us within sight of the true God" (*YES*, p. 171).

"Astronomy" also marks the beginning of Emerson's emancipation from anthropomorphic religion: "Even God himself, the infant religion of all nations has clothed in human form. . . . Astronomy corrects all these boastful dreams." He added this statement (though there is evidence to suggest that he did not include it when the sermon was first delivered to the Second Church): "When the student of nature, quitting the simplicity and perfectness of natural laws, came into the churches and colleges to learn the character of God they [*sic*] there found such gross and unworthy views of him as not agreed but contrasted with their own conclusions respecting the cause of Nature, and as with one voice they rejected these creeds" (*YES*, pp. 173, 175). The theme reminds us of Whitman's "When I Heard the Learn'd Astronomer," but it also clearly anticipates Emerson's use of astronomy in *Nature* and the Divinity School Address.[12] In 1832, however, he felt obliged to retreat (as he had done in "Summer" and other sermons) from his theory of nature and declare that his observations were "not denial but purification" of the authority of Christ: "Does it take away any authority from his lips? It abridges what belongs to persons, to places and to times but it does not touch moral truth" (*YES*, p. 177). Yet the time was soon approaching when he would unburden himself of Christian doctrine. For astronomy, he thought privately, "proves theism but disproves dogmatic theology. . . . It operates steadily to establish the moral laws[,] to disconcert & evaporate temporary systems." Therefore, in order to be a "good minister," he decided the next month to leave the ministry. "The profession is antiquated," he wrote in June. "In an altered age, we worship in the dead forms of our forefathers. Were not a Socratic paganism better than an effete superannuated Christianity?" (*JMN*, 4:26–27). He was almost ready now to act upon the suspicions of 1827, that the nature of God is different "from what he is represented."

The same month Emerson sent a letter to the church committee requesting a change in the communion ceremony. The request was refused, and by the middle of July he decided to resign his pastorate. The formal resignation was presented on 11 September and accepted by the Second Church on 21 October. Emerson's health had been poor during the fall of 1832, and on Christmas day he sailed for Europe in search of a stronger constitution as well as a way to work out of his spiritual quandary. Ten months later, on 9 October 1833, he returned to Boston, having regained not only his health but a renewed and more vigorous interest in natural history.

Emerson's experiences in Europe have been recounted in numerous biographies and critical studies. He met John Stuart Mill, Wordsworth, Coleridge, and Carlyle, among others. It has also been noted that his visits to the Jardin des Plantes in Paris left him with a feeling only somewhat short of revelation. On 13 July 1833 he wrote in his journal: "The fancy-coloured vests of these elegant beings [in the ornithological chambers] make me as pensive as the hues & forms of a cabinet of shells, formerly. It is a beautiful collection & makes a visiter calm & genial as a bridegroom. The limits of the possible are enlarged, & the real is stranger than the imaginary. . . . Walk down the alleys of the flower garden & you come to the enclosures of the animals where almost all that Adam named or Noah preserved are represented" (*JMN*, 4:198–200). Perhaps only with a visit to this Paris sanctuary today can one fully appreciate the serenity that Emerson must have enjoyed during his tours of the garden. Originally a botanical garden opened in 1793, it had also become the first public zoo in France by the time of Emerson's visit. Wandering through the sixteen-acre menagerie and attending lectures on science, Emerson seemed to leap forward with a new vision.[13] The experience confirmed what he had come to accept as his new religion: "Nature is a language & every new fact that we learn is a new word; but rightly seen, taken altogether it is not merely a language, but a scripture which contains the whole truth" (*JMN*, 4:95).[14]

Emerson made his debut as a lecturer on 4 November 1833, when he was asked to speak on the "Uses of Natural History" at the Masonic temple in Boston. The American lyceum movement, begun in 1826, encouraged individuals to speak on various subjects without being "experts" in the fields. Emerson's lecture was assigned to him and sponsored by the Natural History Society of Boston. Yet his theme, "To what end is nature?" was similar to that of "Summer" and "Astronomy" and would become the centerpiece of his first book.

In inquiring about "the advantages which may be expected to accrue from the greater cultivation of Natural Science," he recalled his experiences in the Jardin des Plantes and the feelings it excited in him. He saw in that collection of life's curiosities "Nature's proof impressions." In his recent assessment of the lecture, Gay Wilson Allen remarks that it clarifies Emerson's famous "transparent eye-ball" passage in *Nature*. For though the passage has been attributed to personal experience, it was more likely an imaginative illustration of the occult relation Emerson found between man and the rest of nature.[15] "We feel," he said, "that there is an occult relation between the very worm, the crawling scorpions, and man. I am moved by strange sympathies. I say I will listen to this invitation. I will be a naturalist" (*EL*, 1:10).

Like the fabled Greek giant Antaeus, whose strength in combat with Hercules was renewed every time he touched the earth, "Man is the broken giant, and in all his weakness he is invigorated by touching his mother earth, that is, by habits of conversation with nature" (*EL*, 1:11). In *Nature* Emerson would write, "The reason why the world lacks unity, and lies broken and in heaps, is, because man is disunited with himself" (*CW*, 1:43). The idea of unity or correspondence between the material and spiritual worlds had found its first public expression in "Summer" and "Astronomy," but in these sermons the Neoplatonic overtones were vague and absorbed ultimately into Christian doctrine. Although Emerson did not read the Neoplatonists directly until 1837 (and then through the controversial translations of Thomas Taylor), he had been familiar with the doctrine since his college days through Ralph Cudworth's *True Intellectual System of the Universe*.[16] Furthermore, between 1831 and 1834 his journals indicate at least a casual reading of Plotinus and Porphyry. In "Uses of Natural History," however, Emerson was free to develop the Neoplatonic theme of Character by dwelling upon the evolutionary process of nature and how it prepared the globe for the advent of man. Astronomy may have suggested the exaltation of true religious sentiment, but geology presented an even stronger case for the use of nature in awakening the "Slumbering Giant" in man. Coal, for example, was once covered by layers of granite, slate, and chalk. But like so many "coats of the onion," they were peeled away and vast beds of fuel were brought within the reach of man's puny hands. The discoveries of the geologists suggested that all the workings of nature were made to contribute to man's "pleasure and prosperity at this hour." Finally, this awareness of nature's benevolence produced a "salutary effect" upon man that was directly related to the evolution of his character; indeed, it generated "the highest *state* of character" (*EL*, 1:15–21). For he saw that the whole of nature, or its evolution in the particular, was a metaphor for the growth of the human mind or spirit.

The theme is repeated and clarified in his next lecture, "On the Relation of Man to the Globe." Speaking sometime in December, he declared that man is "no upstart in the creation, but has been prophesied in nature for a thousand thousand ages before he appeared" (*EL*, 1:29). And not only has the globe been prepared for man, but necessity has adapted man to the globe. For example, "the history of navigation affords the most striking instances, but by no means the only ones, of the accurate adjustment of the powers to the wants of man. The same balance is kept everywhere. A man is always in danger, and never" (*EL*, 1:38). Certainly, we have here anticipations of Emerson's theory of compensation, but the focus now is really on self-reliance through the realization of Character and its constant evolution. Man's adaptation to the globe encourages his love for it, the love of nature for its "accord between man and the external world." Self-reliance, then, is the perception of how truly all his senses, "and beyond the senses, the soul, are tuned to the order of things." For the first time, Emerson articulated his distinction between God-reliance and self-reliance. No longer simply in orbit around God, man the naturalist finds in nature a delight that transcends commodity and encourages faith in himself. "I am thrilled with delight by the choral harmony of the whole," Emerson concluded. "Design! It is all design. It is all beauty. It is all astonishment" (*EL*, 1:44, 49).

In his journal for 22 March 1834, Emerson determined that the subject most requiring presentation was "the principle of Self reliance, what it is, what it is not, what it requires, how it teaches us to regard our friends" (*JMN*, 4:269). In "Water," which was delivered to the Boston Mechanic's Institution at the Athenaeum Library on 17 January, he gave his most technical lecture on natural science. Un-Emersonian in its literal rendering of the facts about water and its service to man, it probably conformed more to the spirit of the lyceum movement by emphasizing the practical rather than the moral aspects of scientific inquiry to the working class. His only Neoplatonic digression was the observation that there is a parallel between the circulation of water on the globe and the circulation of blood in the body (*EL*, 1:63). But Emerson returned to his Neoplatonic theme in "The Naturalist," addressed to the Boston Natural History Society on 7 May. In his three earlier lectures, he had held back the full force of the implications of natural history for man, in much the same way that he had played down in his sermons between 1826 and 1831 the significance of nature as a means of informing (and superseding) scripture. Now he was ready for a summary of his ideas on natural history that would take for granted commodity and go directly to the heart of his concern, the "occult relation" between man and nature: "I shall treat this question not for the Natural Philosopher, but for the Man, and offer you some thoughts upon the intellectual influences of Natural Science" (*EL*, 1:70).

The intellectual influences of nature are not as clearly outlined as they would be in *Nature*, but in both the ultimate result of man's love of nature is self-reliance. First of all, this love persuades man that "composition is more important than the elegance of individual forms. . . . The most elegant shell in your cabinet [he offered in anticipation of the poem "Each and All"] does not produce such an effect on the eye as the contrast and combination of a group of ordinary shells lying together wet upon the beach." Also, "The tree is not, the botanist finds, a single structure but a vast assemblage of individuals." Second, the realization that the whole is made of individual parts discourages imitation (thus confirming what he had discovered in 1831, that it is baneful to look for permanence in the particular). The study of natural science leads man back to the "truth" that nature is permanent only in its whole; indeed, that its permanence thrives upon the transitory nature of the particular. "Imitation," he declared, "is [the] servile copying of what is capricious as if it were permanent forms of Nature" (*EL*, 1:73–75).

Much of the doctrine in "The Naturalist" had already been suggested in the first two lectures; here it comes together to suggest a more coherent outline for *Nature*. "The Naturalist" also departs from the others in its attack on society, on the refinements of civilization that keep man from a clear vision of nature. Just as he had assailed Christianity for imposing barriers between man and God in "Astronomy," he now accused the cities of putting man in danger of forgetting his relation to the planet and the system. "The clock and compass do us harm by hindering us from astronomy," he offered. "We have made civil months until the natural signs, the solstices and the equinoxes most men do not know. Find me a savage who does not know them." Society took man down the same "strange paths" as he thought Christianity had in "Astronomy." And it resulted in a loss of Character that could be recovered only through a rediscovery of nature. "I cannot but think," he said, "that a ramble in the country with the set purpose of observation to most persons whose duties confine them much to the city will be a useful lesson. . . . go out into the woods, break your hours, carry your biscuit in your pocket, and you shall see a day as an astronomical phenomenon" (*EL*, 1:76–77).

It has been said of Walt Whitman that he is one of the very few in the history of world literature who wrote the same book over and over again, expanding it but always returning to the same essential theme. Sir Francis Bacon is another who kept beginning again, writing twelve different drafts of the *Novum Organum* in as

many years. Beginning with the sermon on "Summer," Emerson
in a sense rewrote his book about nature throughout his strong
years as a prose-poet. His ideas reach their pinnacle in terms of
classification in *Nature*, then are applied with greater eloquence
and force to individuals in academe, the clergy, and literature.
They become somewhat diluted but also more humanized in the
biographical sketches of *Representative Men* (1850); yet the idea of
biography is implied throughout the successive "versions" of
Nature. Indeed, as Joel Porte remarks, it was the same with
Whitman, whose intuitive grasp of *representation* suggests that
the poet uncannily "had read not only *Representative Men* but
also been given the opportunity to leaf through Emerson's journals."[17] The similarity undoubtedly explains Emerson's "un-
canny" ability to see, when no one else could, that Whitman's
celebration of self was the work of genius. But back in the winter
of 1835, Emerson still had to articulate clearly what he had already
known, namely, that natural history by itself had little value: "It
is like a single sex. But marry it to human history, & it is poetry"
(*JMN*, 4:311). Two more lecture series would be required to complete the rehearsal for *Nature*, one on biography and another
on literature.

   Between 29 January and 5 March 1835, Emerson delivered six
lectures on "Biography" to the Society for the Diffusion of Useful
Knowledge at the Masonic temple. As the editors of the first
volume of *The Early Lectures* note, the pervasive influence of Plutarch's *Lives* and *Morals* is more apparent than it is on *Representative Men*, "when other influences such as Carlyle's had taken full
effect" (*EL*, 1:94). Yet the lectures go far beyond the influences of
his early reading in the sense that this series joined for the first
time Emerson's observations on natural science with human history as it was best represented or idealized. Unfortunately, Emerson's intention in the series at the outset can be determined only
generally from the biographical sketches that followed the introductory address because the manuscript to the opening lecture is
lost. His theme anticipates the one in "Uses of Great Men," the
essay that introduced *Representative Men*: history is really a composite of individual biographies of great men; these, when strung

together, suggest the ideal qualities of the Whole or Central Man. This is more or less confirmed by two journal entries from 1834 and 1835.

As Emerson wrote in his journal for 19 January 1834, "The reason why the Luther, the Newton, the Bonaparte . . . was made the subject of panegyric, is, that in the writer's opinion, *in some one respect* this particular man represented the idea of Man" (*JMN*, 4:256; italics mine). In other words, biographies of particular men taken together suggest the ideal of the whole man, an individual not really possible on earth. Instead, he is a paragon to be achieved eventually through change or amelioration in nature, or, as Whitman would exclaim, through a "passage to more than India." Biography, then, Emerson continued in his journal for 13 January 1835, is "history taken together [and] is as severely moral in its teaching as the straitest religious sect." By studying it, "We recognize with delight a strict likeness between their noblest passions & our own. . . . We participate in their act by our thorough understanding of it. . . . that the faintest sentiments which we have shunned to indulge from fear of singularity are . . . eternal in man" (*JMN*, 5:11–12).

Emerson chose for his representative men in 1835 Michelangelo, Martin Luther, John Milton, George Fox, and Edmund Burke. They exemplified, respectively, the worshiper of beauty, the epitome of self-reliance, the gifts of the poet, the exaltation of religious sentiment, and the philosopher as statesman. Of Michelangelo, Emerson said he was "so true to the laws of the human mind that his character and works . . . seem rather a part of Nature than arbitrary productions of the human will" (*EL*, 1:99). Yet the essay is really about beauty and the artist's perception of it. It is the great whole that the Understanding cannot embrace. Of course, Reason—or its potential—resides in all men, but most are able to use it only to *appreciate* beauty. This is called taste. But Michelangelo was an artist who possessed the ability to reconstruct the conversations with nature that lesser men can only grasp through taste. Martin Luther was also a poet in this sense: "He wrote no poems, but he walked in a charmed world. Everything to his eye assumed a symbolical aspect. . . . No man in history ever assumed a more commanding attitude or ex-

the church and cries aloud for new and more appropriate prac-
tices." Fox and his followers laid stress "upon the doctrine of
the infinitude of Man as seen in the conviction that his soul is a
temple in which the Divine Being resides" (*EL*, 1:174, 180–81).

In introducing the final lecture in the series, the editors of *The
Early Lectures* remark that the role that Edmund Burke filled as
statesman "had less personal appeal for Emerson than did those
of poet, philosopher, and religious leader" (*EL*, 1:183). Yet Emerson's interest in Burke was aligned with his enthusiasm for the
others in the series. It might be compared to our own yearning
for the statesman instead of the politician in American politics.
Burke was not merely a statesman but "the *philosophical politician*,
not a man who, quoting Latin and German, Aristotle and Hume,
acted with a total disregard to general principles,—but one who,
drawing from the same fountain with these theorists, brought
principles to bear upon the public business of England" (*EL*,
1:189). As the philosopher in action, Burke anticipates Emerson's
model for the American Scholar. But as we shall see, he also con-
tributes to the Central Man theory that lies at the heart of *Nature*.

Of course, the most *central* of men for Emerson was the Poet,
and hence the biographical sketch of Milton was appropriately
the centerpiece of the series. Milton, Emerson's favorite poet for
years, combined to a lesser extent all those qualities that the
others represented in part. He perceived the whole of beauty in
nature. He was self-reliant, writing with failing eyesight his
greatest works. And he possessed the moral sentiment to celebrate in his poetry man as "Adam in the garden again" (*W*, 8:31).
Finally, as Emerson remarked in his sketch, Milton was the
philosopher in action and "obtained great respect from his contemporaries as an accomplished scholar, and a formidable contro-
vertist. . . . His prose writings, especially the 'Defence of the
English People,' seem to have been read with avidity" (*EL*, 1:146).
Emerson also made reference to *Areopagitica* and other pamphlets
having to do with public affairs. And if we might look ahead for a
moment, Emerson may have found in Whitman the same blend
of solitude and society. Indeed, despite the scandal that resulted
from Whitman's publication of his letter of "greeting," he may
have silently applauded at least the less exuberant descriptions

of Whitman in *The Good Gray Poet* (1866), a copy of which William Douglas O'Connor sent to Emerson. O'Connor wrote of Whitman: "He is deeply cultured by some of the best books, especially the Bible, which he prefers above all other great literature; but principally by contact with things themselves, which literature can only mirror and celebrate."[18] Emerson would see Whitman as both a man of letters and a man of the world.

———————

In his recent biography of Emerson, Gay Wilson Allen writes of the lectures on English literature: "None of these lectures is of particular importance in Emerson's biography except his Introduction, in which he explained his theory of literature. . . . it was a dress rehearsal for *Nature*."[19] It is true that the series was hastily prepared and often careless in its use of factual material. For example, Emerson's assessment of Chaucer as a talented imitator sounds ridiculous today. It is also true that many of the observations in the introductory lecture were lifted almost unchanged into *Nature*. But this lecture, delivered 5 November 1835, while certainly the closest thing to *Nature*, is perhaps more important as a benchmark in the development of Emerson's theory of language. We have seen in the sermons and earlier lectures many of the ideas that went into *Nature*, but that development had stopped short of anticipating "Language," one of the most important sections in *Nature*. In "English Literature: Introductory," Emerson finally laid the foundation for this section that most directly presented his theory of poetry. And with this accomplished, he had served his apprenticeship as the prophet of the American literary renaissance. In this sense, Allen is correct in calling the introductory lecture a dress rehearsal for *Nature*; for once the "Language" section had been worked out, the sections on "Discipline," "Idealism," "Spirit," and "Prospects" followed almost automatically.

We must keep in mind that Emerson's greatness lies in his use of language, not in any philosophy he originated. Meaning for him was possible only through language, through its ability to clothe the spiritual world with words. "Of the various ways in which a man endeavors to utter the great invisible nature which gives him life, the most perfect vehicle of his meaning is Language," he said in the opening lecture to "English Literature" (*EL*, 1:219). What followed will be familiar to every student of *Nature*: "Every word which is used to express a moral or intellectual fact, if traced to its root, is found to be borrowed from some corporeal or animal fact. *Right* originally means *straight*; *wrong* means *twisted*. Spirit primarily means *wind*. Transgression, the *crossing a line*. Supercilious, the *raising of the eyebrow*." And further on: "It is not words only that are emblematic; it is things which are emblematic. Every fact in outward nature answers to some state of the mind and that state of the mind can only be described by presenting that natural fact as a picture" (*EL*, 1:220). Good writing, then, is a perpetual allegory representing man's connection with the unseen. Only the Poet, of course, is capable of this level of discourse, which teaches us the emblematic character of the flux of the material world: "He converts the solid globe, the land, the sea, the sun, the animals into symbols of thought. . . . it is his office to show this beautiful relation, to utter the oracles of the mind in appropriate images from nature. And this is Literature" (*EL*, 1:224–25).

With his lectures on "English Literature," Emerson completed the triad of primary ingredients appearing in *Nature*: natural history, biography, and poetry. Like the series on biography, "English Literature" focused on representative men but now on those singularly gifted in the highest form of expression, the "august geniuses . . . who had just views on their vocation as Teachers." They did not sing the tune of their times but obeyed the spirit within them, preferring "its whisper to the applause of their contemporaries" (*EL*, 1:231–32). Their fables were true allegories of man.

Although Emerson failed to appreciate Chaucer's gift for satire, he did say of the bard that he "never writes with timidity. He speaks like one who knows the law, and has a right to be heard" (*EL*, 1:274). Like Milton, Chaucer was a moralist and a reformer, lashing out at the clergy (though Emerson failed to cite "The Pardoner's Tale" as an example of his satire on the religious community). Emerson considered Spenser for his next lecture but chose Shakespeare instead, probably because he thought the poet's example better fitted his theory of language. "The power of the Poet," he said, "depends on the fact that the material world is a symbol or expression of the human mind and part for part. Every natural fact is a symbol of some spiritual fact." In "Shakspear" Emerson also gave the definition he would apply to his orphic poet in *Nature*: "He converts the solid globe, the land, the sea, the air, the sun, the animals into symbols of thought. . . . And this act or vision of the mind is called Imagination. It is the use which the Reason makes of the material world, for purposes of expression" (*EL*, 1:289). As in the introductory lecture—and indeed as far back as Emerson's discovery of the meaning of Character in 1831—the fluidity of nature is again paramount.

Lord Bacon's *Novum Organum* was certainly a logical continuation of this theme, for Emerson clearly appreciated Bacon's argument that experience is the source of all knowledge and induction is its method. The syllogism, or deductive reasoning, Bacon said, "is no match for the subtlety of nature." Of the other writers covered in the series (Jonson, Herrick, Herbert, and Wotton), only the observations on the author of "Upon Julia's Clothes" add any new facts about Emerson's future as a writer and judge of poetry. Though he commended the poet for his lyrics "upon the objects of common life," he also censured Herrick's sexual pieces: "Herrick by the choice often of base and even disgusting themes, has pushed this [poetic] privilege too far, rather I think out of the very wantonness of poetic power . . . to make his book sell, by feeding the grosser palates of his public" (*EL*, 1:346–47). Ironically, he would warn Whitman on Boston Common in 1860 that the "Children of Adam" sequence would keep his third edition from selling. In fact, Whitman emphasized that the whole basis for Emerson's objections to his poetry was practical, not philosophical or literary. As has been demonstrated recently, Emerson viewed Whitman's sexual candor as only a minor problem in the poetry. In a confidential letter written in 1889, shortly after the publication of *Emerson in Concord*, in which Edward Emerson stated that his father quickly lost interest in the poetry of "this young mechanic" after the 1855 *Leaves*, Frank Sanborn told Horace Traubel: "Emerson took views of his subject, whatever it might be, from more than one point; and that which he expected of Whitman in 1855 was his more constant way of looking at Whitman's genius. [Nevertheless:] He was, in fact, greatly annoyed by W's printing of his letter of commendation, and he disliked the too frequent mention of the organ of generation."[20] But the question of Emerson's position toward Whitman and his book must wait for a later chapter. We are now ready to examine briefly the book that played, indirectly, a major role in the development of Whitman's poetry.

Ever since the shock with which the Unitarians received Emerson's "transparent eye-ball" passage, critics have pointed to it as the eclectic statement in *Nature*, calling it a description of a mystical experience and also comparing it with Whitman's famous passage in section 5 of "Song of Myself." Yet I agree with Gay Wilson Allen that it is more likely an imaginative illustration of man's occult relation with nature. Allen cites the passage from the "Uses of Natural History" (quoted on p. 39 above), but that passage is echoed in *Nature*. There it is a more accurate if less imaginative description of what the Transcendentalist experiences. "The greatest delight which the fields and woods minister is the suggestion of an occult relation between man and the vegetable. I am not alone and unacknowledged. They nod to me, and I to them." The Transcendentalist is the Central Man, representative of all men in their truest moments. But a description of these is beyond the language skills of most men, and only the Poet can freeze the music of nature's song. Only the epitome of the representative man, Emerson would say again in "Prospects," can help us "become sensible of a certain occult recognition and sympathy in regard to the most unwieldy and eccentric forms of beast, fish, and insect" (*CW*, 1:10, 40).

The sensibility that the Poet brings to us is the subject of "Language" and indeed the theme of *Nature*. He makes the veil of society (a theme in "The Naturalist") somewhat diaphanous; he lifts "our discourse above the ground line of familiar facts" by dressing the spirit with images. "The poet, the orator bred in the woods [Burke, for an example of the latter], whose senses have been nourished by their fair and appeasing changes, year after year, without design and without heed—[does not] lose their lesson altogether in the roar of the cities or the broil of politics." This master of language, who sees a *fact* as "the end or last issue of the spirit," also teaches us "that nature is a discipline." He comprehends the laws of physics, for he sees that "a leaf, a drop, a crystal, a moment in time is related to the whole, and partakes of the perfection of the whole" (*CW*, 1:21–23, 27). Emerson remarks in "Discipline" that the language of the Poet helps the Understanding to approach intellectual or spiritual truths—the Poet shapes "the Hand of the mind." This perhaps is as far as most men can soar in their knowledge of nature and how its flux mirrors the growth of their character.

The Poet knows that with discipline "all parts of nature conspire," Emerson says in "Idealism." And it matters not to the Poet "whether nature enjoy a substantial existence without, or is only in the apocalypse of the mind." For like the Genuine Man of 1832, he shapes the circumstances of his life and finds meaning. In 1836 Emerson reiterates his theme of self-willed evolution of Character: whereas "the sensual man conforms thoughts to things; the poet conforms things to his thoughts. The one esteems nature as rooted and fast; the other, as fluid, and impresses his being thereon" (*CW*, 1:29, 31). Relying on Shakespeare again, he likens the Poet to the magician Prospero of *The Tempest* to illustrate the "transfiguration which all material objects" receive under the power of the Poet's language. So Prospero calls for music to soothe his companions:

> A solemn air, and the best comforter
> To an unsettled fancy, cure thy brains
> Now useless, boiled within thy skull.
> [*CW*, 1:33]

Through Reason and the gift of language, the Poet transfers "nature into the mind, and [leaves] matter like an outcast corpse." He detects "God in the coarse," Emerson continues in "Spirit." In "Prospects" appears the final aphorism: "Build, therefore, your own world" (*CW*, 1:32, 34, 37).

Of course, *Nature* is general doctrine, the so-called "bible" of Transcendentalism. It urges man to undergo a change of character, to act from Character. But underlying all is the message that we need an intermediary or archangel, and he is the Poet, just as Christ had been to the first Christians, Emerson would say two years later at the Harvard Divinity School. And by acting from his own character, the Poet perceives the fluid world and acts for us all. For he is the representative man.

Nature was a logical boundary of Emerson's foreground, for it brought together Neoplatonic concepts that had been masked in various Christian and "scientific" disguises in his sermons and early lectures. His literary apprenticeship concluded with the discovery of language as a vehicle for perceiving the truth about the emblematic significance of Character. *Nature* is even more important, however, because it served as a dividing line between Emerson the clergyman and Emerson the poet-preacher—indeed, the bardic evangel for a new vision. But this aspect will be discussed in Part Two. It is now time to examine the famous yet obscure foreground of Whitman, as well as Emerson's association in the 1850s with the poet it produced.

3. Whitman—The Foreground

And as to you corpse I think you are good manure,
but that does not offend me,
I smell the white roses sweetscented and growing,
I reach to the leafy lips. . . . I reach to the
polish'd breasts of melons.
Whitman, *Leaves of Grass*, 1855

Whitman was the first to break the mental allegiance.
He was the first to smash the old moral conception
that the soul of man is something "superior"
and "above" the flesh.
D. H. Lawrence, *Studies in Classic American Literature*

In April 1833 William Leggett, assistant editor of Bryant's New York *Evening Post*, spat upon a rival journalist to avenge a personal attack that had recently appeared in the *Courier and Enquirer*. "Colonel Webb," he shouted at James Watson Webb, "you are a coward, and I spit upon you." Webb immediately responded with a few quick blows from his cane and then fled across the street. Leggett pursued his victim, snatched the cane from him, and delivered several blows—spitting on Webb once again as gathering onlookers stood by.[1] Such a scene was not uncommon on "newspaper row" in New York City in the 1830s and 1840s. Two years earlier, the much less excitable William Cullen Bryant had avenged an attack upon his character in the *Commercial Advertiser* by thrashing editor William L. Stone with a horsewhip. After several successful lashes, a witness reported, "the whip was wrested from Bryant and carried off by Stone."[2] "Every journalist is a politician, of course," wrote Bryant in 1839 shortly after Leggett's early death, "but in how many instances does he aspire to no higher office than that of an ingenious and dexterous politician?"[3] It was partisan politics, an arena in which newspapers aligned themselves with either the "Locofoco" Democrats or the Whigs. And scurrilous editorials often lost sight of the political issues and stooped to personal attacks on rival editors. Such an atmosphere may lend some credence to the legend that Walter Whitman, as editor of the Brooklyn *Daily Eagle* in 1848, was dismissed from his job in part for kicking an influential Hunker politician down a flight of stairs in retaliation for a personal insult.[4]

To Whitman, Leggett and Bryant were men of principle during this stormy and ugly period of American journalism. Looking back in 1889 he told Traubel: "I remember William Leggett's saying, saying so wisely, that nothing, nothing in the whole range of thought, life—not a thing, sacred or profane—but what in the hands of a skilled controversialist, a cute lawyer, can be shown to have opposed sides, reasons for and against it" (*WWC*, 4:476). A radical Democrat of the Jeffersonian school, Leggett was in fact as fiery and sometimes reckless in his crusades for freedom and equality as William Douglas O'Connor a few decades later. Prior to his journalistic career, he had been a settler in Illinois and a member of the United States Navy. He had also published two volumes of verse and one of fiction, calling upon his knowledge of the sea in the latter.[5] Shortly after Leggett had published two laudatory reviews of Bryant's poetry, Bryant signed him on as assistant in the early 1830s. During his tenure (which lasted until 1836), Leggett expounded furiously on such incendiary issues as the right of the laboring classes to unionize, the evils of the National Bank, and the degradations produced by slavery. His editorials against slavery were so biting that many postal stations in the South burned copies of the *Post* intended for local subscribers. But like O'Connor, Leggett seldom knew when to draw back. During Bryant's absence in Europe between 1834 and 1836, the circulation of the *Post* dropped off significantly. Without Bryant's restraint (perhaps acquired after the 1831 fracas), the newspaper's political posture was simply too forceful for an era in which abolitionist meetings were disrupted by angry mobs and lecturers often compelled to flee for their lives.

Bryant's temperament, on the other hand, came closer to Whitman's. When the two men met in the 1840s, they shared to some extent the same views in both politics and poetry. "I had known Mr. Bryant over thirty years," Whitman wrote after the editor's death in 1878, "and he had been markedly kind to me. Off and on, along that time for years as they pass'd, we met and chatted together. . . . We were both walkers, and when I work'd in Brooklyn [for the *Eagle*] he several times came over, middle of afternoons, and we took rambles miles long, till dark, out towards Bedford or Flatbush, in company" (*PW*, 1:166). Whitman recalled that Bryant had talked of "scenes in Europe," but he may have also discussed poetry with the young journalist and budding poet. Having spent much of his youth in Stockbridge, Massachusetts (among the Berkshires), Bryant had somewhat involuntarily emigrated from the country to the city and from poetry to journalism—meeting Whitman, as it were, on his passage in the opposite direction.

By their examples, Leggett and Bryant contributed to Whitman's development as a poet by reminding him that the events he recorded might have a deeper significance. Although in a sense ex-poets who had themselves become immersed in the day-to-day drama of journalism, they nevertheless could apprehend the spiritual significance of life, a significance only obscured by journalistic observation. The presence of these two poet-turned-journalists among so many scurrilous members of the fourth estate may have led the young editor to use the profession in much the same way that Melville had allowed a whaling ship to serve him in his apprenticeship as an artist. Politics, social questions, the slavery issue—these were the matters that filled the young journalist's notebook and his mind in the 1840s. Emerson, too, had his influence, but the course of Whitman's journey was without question set by his newspaper experiences. His passage from journalism to poetry was a zigzag voyage on which his attention was riveted to numerous interests as the editor explored his environment for items to fill his daily columns.

One aspect of inquiry to the man who would ultimately believe with Emerson that ''the unseen is proved by the seen'' was the area of what was loosely defined as natural science. For the nineteenth century witnessed discoveries in astronomy, geology, physics, anatomy, and even the pseudosciences like phrenology. Even more than Emerson, however, he would use his knowledge of science with a ''free margin.'' ''You must not know too much, or be too precise or scientific about birds and trees and flowers and water-craft,'' Whitman wrote in *Specimen Days* (1882); ''a certain free margin, and even vagueness—perhaps ignorance, credulity—helps your enjoyment of these things'' (*PW*, 1:269). In 1855, however, he had been more direct in suggesting the influence of science on his work:

> Hurrah for positive science! Long live exact demonstration!
>
> .   .   .   .
> Gentlemen I receive you, and attach and clasp hands
>   with you,
> The facts are useful and real. . . . they are not my dwelling.
>   . . . I enter by them to an area of the dwelling.
>   [''Song of Myself,'' sec. 23]

Tracing Whitman's interest in the scientific knowledge of his time is more difficult than tracing Emerson's, whose journals for

the period of his awakening are available and whose responses
to science are clearly recorded in his early lectures. Whitman was
a journalist, however, and his responses were often limited to
no more than short notices and book reviews in newspapers
whose formats seldom extended beyond four pages. Furthermore, though the future poet probably listened with interest to
lectures by such figures as Ormsby MacKnight Mitchell and Deni-
son Olmstead on astronomy, he was less methodical in the way
he absorbed the material as a confirmation of spiritual laws. In
his study of the poet's interest in science (one that stresses astronomy over the other sciences), Joseph Beaver sees both Emerson and Whitman as having the same angle of vision in science
but also an important difference in outlook: "Emerson held that
man was the measure [or proof] of the universe; Whitman held
that the universe is the measure of man. To Whitman, man is the
'microcosm of all Creation's wildness.' To Emerson, the universe
is the 'externization of the soul,' but to Whitman, man is the
condensation of the universe."[6]

This is an important distinction, for it helps to explain how
Whitman could put the body and the soul on an equal footing in
the early editions of *Leaves of Grass*. He later wrote of his work
that his aim (unlike Emerson's, which used science as a means to
an end) was to combine scientific materialism and mysticism:
"My two theses—animal and spiritual—became gradually fused
in *Leaves of Grass*."[7] And as he had written in "Song of Myself,"
alluding to "exact demonstration," such facts were "not my dwelling." That they were indeed *part* of his "dwelling," however, is
shown in one of the three 1855 anonymous reviews he wrote of
Leaves of Grass. In the *American Phrenological Journal* for October,
he described himself as "sterile on the old myths, and on all the
customary themes of romantic and classical writers, but pregnant
with the deductions of the geologist, the astronomer, the great
antiquary, the chemist, the phrenologist, the spiritualist, the
mathematician, and with the ideas and practice of American politics."[8] Curiously, this passage was omitted in the reprint of the
review that was included in the 1856 edition of his book.[9] It may
have been done after a reexamination of his statements about
science in what became section 23 of "Song of Myself." Or he

may have realized more clearly just how science had affected his work. For in his open letter to Emerson (in the second edition), he does praise "the amativeness of Nature," or its love for man on the globe.[10]

The importance of the canceled passage from the review also lies in its variety, or catalog, of influence that Whitman recognized in his development. Not only do we find legitimate sciences like geology and chemistry, but also the pseudosciences of phrenology and spiritualism. (Later Whitman would grow suspicious of phrenology, which today has disappeared even from the boardwalk in Atlantic City: "Remember in scientific and similar allusions that the theories . . . are continually changing. Be careful to put in only what *must* be appropriate centuries hence.")[11] Furthermore, the list includes "American politics," an influence that had the greatest impact on Whitman's first edition.

Hence, science, although it played an important role in Whitman's foreground, was perhaps less crucial than it was for Emerson, who wrote of natural history: "It is like a single sex. But marry it to human history, & it is poetry" (*JMN*, 4:311). This is indeed what happens in section 5 of "Song of Myself" with Whitman's marriage of the body and the soul. However, in achieving the result, the process for Whitman was reversed. In other words, the first ingredient in his "marriage" was not science but human history—more precisely, American politics. This before all else was the preoccupation of the New York journalist in the 1840s: questions on labor, public education, ward chicanery, "foreigners" (a word Whitman wanted to ban from the vocabulary as editor of the *Eagle*), women's rights, temperance, and, above all, American slavery and its expansion into the new territories. In fact, it was not until 1846–48, during the debates over the Wilmot Proviso (which would have forbidden the expansion of slavery), that Whitman became more than casually interested in science. Until that time he had written on matters social and political. The only known exception is a notice of a lecture in New York City by the famed geologist Charles Lyell in 1842, and here the journalist was more interested in reconciling the differences between the doctrines of geology and those of scripture. He also noted that in addition to the controversy aroused in the religious community of the city, "Brownson's lectures 'On Civilization,' and Emerson's 'On the Times,' [also] gave a severe shock to the religious mind."[12] As Joseph Jay Rubin has demonstrated, Whitman's world was social and political, with little time in the 1840s for any extended scientific inquiries. It was also a busy one when we consider that between 1842 and 1848 he either edited or wrote for eleven different newspapers in New York and Brooklyn.[13]

Whitman's activities before 1846, when he became editor of the *Eagle*, suggest a pattern formed largely by external circumstances. In other words, he had yet to make the discovery of Character as Emerson had done in 1831–32. He became involved in politics through his various journalistic stints, wrote occasional short fiction and the temperance novel *Franklin Evans* (1842), and generally subscribed to the principles of conventional Christianity. As to the latter, it can be said that as late as 1848 he was in no clear sense a Transcendentalist, in spite of the impact of Emerson's 1842 lecture and whatever he read of Emerson's shortly afterward. In criticizing the ornate architecture of the newly constructed Grace Church, for example, he found its pomp in no way representative of "the genuine spirit of Christ." Two years later he indicated a belief in the Calvinistic notion of damnation. In describing the engine room of the Fulton Street ferry, he wrote: "It is enough to make a sinful man feel any other feeling on earth than that of pleasurable anticipation." Finally, in a review of *The Life of Christ*, he said in 1847: "In looking over such a book as this, one is impressed with the interest, even as a narrative, and apart from its sacred character, of the history of 'him who spake *as never man spake*'" (*GF*, 2:92, 211, 305; italics mine). Of course, much of his commentary in this vein constituted a pose—the journalist as moral paragon, offering advice on everything from personal hygiene (use of public baths) to the necessity of leisure time for shop girls. The same tone prevailed in his fiction. As late as 1848, in "The Shadow and the Light of a Young Man's Soul," his protagonist moves from the city to the country and substitutes "action and cheerfulness for despondency and a fretful tongue" (*EPF*, p. 330).

Yet by 1848, and even before that, as he approached his thirtieth year, Whitman began to sort out the experiences of the 1840s.

In "The Shadow and the Light," he asked with regard to his protagonist's search for happiness: "Has God's all-wise providence
ordered things wrongly, then? Is there discord in the machinery
which moves systems of worlds, and keeps them in their harmonious orbits?" In line with his fatherly pose (as a journalist but
also not unlike the role Emerson filled in the Unitarian pulpit),
the author found the source of chaos not in the universe but in
the human heart: "in that, lies the darkness and the tangle" (*EPF*,
p. 328).

It was during this time that Whitman may have begun to look
beyond scripture and conventional morality. The 1848 story, in
fact, is the first time he looked—so directly if rhetorically—in his
fiction for solutions beyond the quotidian level. The use of the
term "harmonious orbits" suggests a familiarity with astronomy,
especially with the work of Sir William Herschel, whose writings
were then being popularized in America by Mitchell. Whitman's
introduction and genuine interest in science (which can be shown
conclusively only through his poetry) began, however, with his
fascination for phrenology. Starting in 1846, he reviewed a number of books on the subject for the *Eagle*: J. G. Spurzheim's *Phrenology, or the Doctrine of the Mental Phenomena*, George Moore's
The Use of the Body in Relation to the Mind, O. S. Fowler's *Hereditary
Descent; Its Laws and Facts Applied to Human Improvement*, and
others. In an early and noteworthy article on Whitman's interest
in this pseudoscience, Edward Hungerford writes: "It is clear,
then, that Whitman knew phrenology. He read, underscored and
preserved articles on the subject, reviewed several extensive trea-
tises, copied passages into his own notes, and presumably subscribed to one of the leading journals [*The American Phrenological
Journal*]."[14]

Whitman's association with the phrenologists Fowler and Wells
is well known, of course, and need not be rehearsed here. It is
also a familiar fact that the future poet permitted Fowler to chart
the bumps on his head in July 1849 and was quite pleased with
the results. In part, Fowler's report said: "This man has a grand
physical constitution, and power to live to a good old age. He has
undoubtedly descended from the soundest and hardiest stock.
. . . Leading traits of character appear to be Friendship, Sympa-

thy, Sublimity and Self-Esteem." The reading was not altogether favorable (Whitman showing a tendency toward "Indolence" and "Voluptuousness"), but in quoting the report Hungerford calls it a "remarkable phrenology."[15] Furthermore, the general optimism of phrenology may have helped Whitman to develop his theory of Body and Soul. That is, the phrenologists (especially Moore) believed in a correspondence between physical beauty and spiritual beauty. They also believed that once one found out who he was from a phrenological reading, he would improve himself by "depressing" the faculties that were prominent and "elevating" those that needed further development.[16] Doubtless, the theory did much to enhance the self-reliance of the journalist who was now thirty years old and in excellent health but had yet to find his real calling in life.

In John Burroughs's first book on Whitman (partially written by the subject himself), it was stated that the poet never *read* Emerson's essays until 1856.[17] This seems a strange turnabout when we remember how zealously Whitman had tried to capitalize on the Emerson letter in the 1856 edition, even addressing the New Englander as "Master." But by 1867, when Burroughs's book first appeared, the poet was being denounced as a wild and obscene imitator of Emerson. The truth is, however, that Whitman read in whole or in part *Essays* (1841) and quite possibly *Essays: Second Series* (1844) shortly after they appeared.

Evidence of the journalist's familiarity with the essays, in fact, is found in the *Eagle* of 15 December 1847, where Whitman quotes Emerson. The passage suggests that Whitman was becoming aware of Emerson's theory of character:

> In one of Ralph Waldo Emerson's inimitable lectures, occurs the following striking paragraph, which every heart will acknowledge to be as truthful as it is beautiful: "When the act of reflection takes place in the mind, when we look at ourselves in the light of thought, we discover that our life is embosomed in beauty. Behind us, as we go, all things assume pleasing forms, as clouds do afar off. Not only things familiar and stale, but even the tragic and terrible, are lures of memory. The river bank, the weed at the water side, the

old house, the foolish person, however neglected at the passing, have a grace in the past. Even the corpse that has lain in the chambers has added a solemn ornament to the house.—The soul will not know either deformity or pain."
[*GF*, 2:270–71]

The quotation comes from the opening paragraph of "Spiritual Laws" in *Essays*. According to the editors of the Emerson centennial edition, the essay was never given as a lecture in its final form. An earlier version, they add, may have been used as a lecture in Concord and Boston before 1841, but never in New York City, where Whitman might have heard it (*W*, 2:402n). Moreover, Emerson was in England in the latter part of 1847 and had not lectured in Whitman's city since 1843 (*L*, 3:295–96).

Hence, we know for certain that the journalist "cracked" the 1841 *Essays*. And doubtless he did much more.[18] The passage quoted in the *Eagle* is an excellent description of what the Transcendentalist is supposed to experience, that "things familiar and stale" awaken "the lures of memory" or the "Slumbering Giant" in man when seen transcendentally. The true context for the soul emerges to dispel "all mean egotism." Coincidentally perhaps, Whitman's protagonist in the 1848 short story discovers that his life, properly viewed, is "embosomed in beauty." Even the corpse becomes beautiful if seen from the right angle of vision, for the soul "will not know either deformity or pain." The statement also reminds us of Emerson's comment to his Aunt Mary (quoted in Chapter 2) about the beauty and serenity of nature in spite of Ellen's death. Especially noteworthy in this context is the statement further on in the essay: "All loss, all pain is particular; the universe remains to the heart unhurt" (*CW*, 2:77). But if we look in the other direction, the essay anticipates one of the more striking passages in "Song of Myself": "As to you corpse I think you are good manure, but that does not offend me, / I smell the white roses sweetscented and growing, / I reach to the leafy lips. . . . I reach to the polish'd breasts of melons."

"Spiritual Laws" helped to teach Whitman the lesson that Emerson had learned back in 1831–32. For the focus of the essay is upon Character and its necessary change or growth. Echoing

Jonathan Edwards on freedom of the will (i.e., that man cannot *will* his will but only act it out), Emerson warns us not to *choose* but rather to follow the choice of our "constitution" or Character. "What business has [man] with an evil trade [i.e., one not suited to his talents]? Has he not a *calling* in his character? Each man has his own vocation. The talent is the call. . . . By doing his own work he unfolds himself. . . . He must find in that an outlet for his character" (*CW*, 2:77, 82–83). The implications of these statements are rather obvious in "Song of Myself," whose 1856 title was "Poem of Walt Whitman, An American" (simply "Walt Whitman" in 1860) and whose theme is the unfolding of Character. But the effect can be found in an earlier work, a sketch possibly written and published after the newspaper citation of one of "Emerson's inimitable lectures." In "Lingave's Temptation" Whitman described a poet who, though poverty stricken, remains true to his calling. Lingave curses "the contrast between [his] own lot, and the fortune of the rich"; yet he resists the temptation to prostitute his talents in the service of "a *money-maker*." He tells himself, "Do justice, philosopher, to your own powers. While the world runs after its shadows and its bubbles . . . we will fold ourselves in our circle of understanding, and look with an eye of apathy on those things it considers so mighty and enviable" (*EPF*, pp. 331–34).

For Whitman, "Spiritual Laws" provided the insights that Emerson had first articulated in the sermons "Find Your Calling" and "The Genuine Man." "What a man does, that he has," Emerson wrote in the essay. "In himself is his might. Let him regard no good as solid, but that which is in his nature, and which must grow out of him as long as he exists" (*CW*, 2:84). The poet Lingave makes this discovery, that the world of money is not the proper fortune for the Poet. "O Lingave! be more of a man! Have you not the treasures of health and untainted propensities, which many of those you envy never enjoy? Are you not their superior in mental power, in liberal views of mankind, and in comprehensive intellect?" (*EPF*, p. 331). There is no reference to the evils of money in "Spiritual Laws," but the following passage occurs in "Manners" (*Essays: Second Series*), an essay that expresses the same theme: "A plentiful fortune is reckoned necessary, in the

popular judgment, to the completion of this man of the world.
. . . Money is not essential, but this wide affinity is, which transcends the habits of clique and caste and makes itself felt by men
of all classes" (*W*, 3:125). The "wide affinity" is a character in
harmony with God. As the narrator of Whitman's story tells
Lingave: "Wrap yourself in your own virtue" (*EPF*, p. 334).

Looking back in old age on his pre-1855 prose and poetry,
Whitman remarked that the "tales came from the surface of the
mind, and had no connection with what lay below. . . . At last
the time came when the concealed growth had come to light."[19]
It is true that much of what he wrote then was maudlin and un-
original. Whitman was still much the journalist-preacher. Yet the
influence of Emerson's essays brought forth from time to time
"what lay below." During his editorship of the *Eagle*, for example,
he wrote on the need for a national literature free from the
influences of England. His arguments are more palatable than his
earlier chauvinism (exemplified by the Bishop Hughes controversy). What comes through are the universal sentiments he may
have absorbed from "Spiritual Laws" and essays such as "The
Poet" and "Self-Reliance."

Whitman probably read the two volumes of Emerson's essays
long before his 1847 allusion to "Spiritual Laws." As in the case
of the 1842 lecture on "The Poet," however, he was slow to absorb
and to apply Emerson's ideas on Character. Their effect is not
clearly evident until 1846. In the *Eagle* of 11 July that year he
complained of the anglomania that kept Americans from a full
appreciation of their home literature. "We have not enough confidence in our judgments," he told his Brooklyn readers. "We
forget that God has given the American mind powers of analysis
and acuteness superior to those possessed by any other nation on
earth." He went on to praise England's greatest writers (Shakespeare and Milton, for example) but at the same time to ridicule
the "Toryism" of writers like Cowper, Johnson, and Southey—
scorners of the "common people." In contrast to the general
inferiority American critics felt when American literature was
compared to English, he preceded Melville in his famous defense
of Hawthorne in 1850: "Shall Hawthorne get a paltry *seventy five
dollars* for a two volume work [*Mosses from an Old Manse*]?" The

remedy, he concluded, was in *"ourselves. . . . Let those who read,* —(and in this country who does not read?)—no more conde- scend to patronize an inferior foreign writer, when they have so many respectable writers at home" (*GF*, 2:242–45).

Less than a year later (*Eagle*, 10 February 1847), he took up the theme again. He lamented that America continued to worship at the shrine of British literature and criticism. *"Are* we not," he asked, " 'a mere suburb of London'?" Yes, he thought, "as long as we wait for English critics to stamp our books and our authors, before *we* presume to say they are very good or very bad—as long as the floods of British manufactured books are poured over the land, and give their color to all departments of taste and opinion—as long as an American society, meeting at the social board, starts with wonder to hear any of its national names, or any national sentiments, mentioned in the same hour with for- eign authors or foreign greatness." Whitman was careful not to allow praise "of *writing that is merely American because it is not written abroad.*" Rather, he sought a literature electrified by the national *character*. Again he thanked such worthies as Shake- speare, Spenser, Milton, Bunyan, and Defoe. But the day of such English treasures, he argued, had passed: "How the world has 'spread itself' since their day! And have *we* in this country noth- ing to add to the store of their manifold genius?" (*GF*, 2:237–41). In another editorial (*Eagle*, 4 September 1846) he extended his criticism to American drama: "When will American writers, even the best of them, learn to be true to the soul and thoughts God has given them? When will they pass the slough of the imitation of the conventionalities of other people?" (*GF*, 2:320–21).

The "best of them" included even Emerson, whose *Poems* (1847) Whitman would shortly read and complain (although pri- vately) of the New Englander's failure to follow his own advice in "The Poet," that "it is not metres, but a metre-making argument that makes a poem" (*W*, 2:9). In reading a review of the *Poems* in *The Democratic Review* for May 1847, he agreed with the anony- mous reviewer that Emerson cared more for the meaning than the melody in his poetry, "that he attempts no experiments in versification, and makes no effort for variety." The reviewer in- tended his remarks as favorable criticism, however, saying rather obsequiously that "the monotony ceases when the ear and mind are called in." To this Whitman responded in the margin of the article (which he subsequently clipped and preserved in his papers): "The perfect poet must be unimpeachable in *manner* as well as matter."[20] Here the future poet of *Leaves of Grass*—which he would consider "a language experiment" (*DN*, 3:729)—was perhaps beginning to move beyond slavish imitation himself. For Emerson (who was virtually the inventor of American self-reliance) not to adopt a manner or meter as experimental as that of his prose-poems he found unacceptable. Indeed, whatever Emerson might say in his poetry, it would echo the thoughts of all men since Plato. The thought was "original," therefore, only when it took on the dress of the American character.

   In challenging the American character to emerge, Whitman was in effect challenging his own to show itself. He was beginning to realize that "God exists. [That] there is a soul at the centre of nature, and over the will of every man, so that none of us can wrong the universe" (*CW*, 2:81). A product of the New World, he was beginning to spread *himself*. The seeds of the first *Leaves of Grass* were indeed germinating. The journalist-dandy-preacher in Whitman was beginning to dissolve, giving way to another self that would ultimately celebrate the character of a nation. "We are always reasoning from the seen to the unseen," Whitman had read in "Spiritual Laws." Doubtless, the essay had an important impact: "He that writes to himself, writes to an eternal public. . . . The laws of disease, physicians say, are as beautiful as the laws of health. . . . Human character evermore publishes itself" (*CW*, 2:85, 89–90).

Many explanations have been offered for Whitman's transformation from journalist to poet between 1848 and 1855 (none completely satisfying). In one of the most compelling studies of Whitman, Richard Chase finds that three hypotheses occur most frequently. The first is that Whitman may have become sexually liberated by an octoroon woman he apparently met during his stay in New Orleans, when he edited the *Crescent* between 5 March and 26 May 1848. The second explanation is that sometime after his return from New Orleans in the spring of 1848 he confronted the "fact" that part of his character was homosexual. But as Chase reminds us, "the [external] evidence that Whitman had heterosexual relations is almost as substantial as the evidence that he was homosexual—and neither is *very* substantial."[21] I tend to doubt that Whitman was an active homosexual for any substantial length of time, if at all. Certainly, during the Civil War when he befriended hundreds of young soldiers, many of whom became emotionally dependent on him for a time, some evidence of homosexual overtures and rebuffs (and not simply fatherly affection) would have come down to the present among the voluminous mass of extant documents dealing with those years. Hence, the term *homoerotic* (suppressed homosexuality) may still be more accurate than *homosexual*, although this is not to discount the impact that the discovery of such a sexual preference would have had on the poet's development. As one recent argument for Whitman's homosexuality concedes, it is possible that the poet never "engaged in genital sex with another man [but was nevertheless] fully and consciously aware of himself as a homosexual." (To quibble over the term, of course, is to argue the definition of homosexuality. Many gay critics insist that the tendency itself qualifies one as a homosexual in that homosexuality is not simply a sexual preference but an identity. But it was doubtless an identity Whitman resisted, at least outside of the poetry, since he tried to conceal his feelings by using number codes in some letters and destroying others. Hence my preference for *homoeroticism* with regard to Whitman.)[22] A third explanation is that Whitman had a mystical experience that led him to what his first biographer, Richard Maurice Bucke, called "cosmic consciousness." But this theory is useless unless we interpret it to mean that Whitman suddenly became conscious of the power of his identity to confirm spiritual facts.

It seems clear that through a merging of his sexual preference with an understanding of the Neoplatonic concept of amelioration, Whitman simply discovered his character. And he discovered that as "abnormal" as it was—indeed, because of its "abnormality"—it held the key to comprehending the Universal Character, or the One Mind from which all life emanated. Furthermore, having heard Emerson's lecture on the Poet and read the essays, he was ultimately provided with a theory and a language to articulate his identity, in a sense, to clothe his character with words and to fuse it with the American character in *Leaves of Grass*. Along the way, *Representative Men* (1850) may have helped to drive home Emerson's lesson, but the volume came out too late to influence Whitman significantly. For Emerson implies throughout his earlier work that the basis of representation is self-reliance. "Absolve you to yourself," he advises in "Self-Reliance," "and you shall have the suffrage of the world" (*CW*, 2:30).

But Whitman's belief in representation came from his own background as well. Like Emerson in his development, Whitman compiled his own list of representative men (although "representative Americans" is more precise). As might be expected from his preoccupation with politics, the calling he regarded as the highest was not that of the Poet (the case in Emerson's 1835 lectures on "Biography") but that of the statesman. Later, of course, Whitman would view Lincoln as the paragon of that sphere of activity. His affinity for Lincoln was based upon the same quality that attracted him to certain statesmen in the 1840s: their "grass-roots" American origins. Faced with the growing (and often frightening) fact of his own "peculiar" identity, he sought to reinforce his self-confidence by celebrating famous men of similar backgrounds and stock.

Whitman's gallery of such individuals also included the "divine average" he featured in his journalism and extolled in his poetry, but in the 1840s it was dominated by political heroes, those who made it possible for the "Americano" to act out his democratic character in the New World. One of Whitman's most admired representatives was Andrew Jackson. In the *Eagle* of 8 January 1848, he declared that Jackson was "a *Man of the People*, worth more than hundreds of political leaders—worth, indeed, more than all the selfish ones that ever lived." (Whitman harshly criticized Daniel Webster, for example. Long before Webster's compromise over slavery, the journalist denounced him as "overrated more than any other public man ever prominent in America. . . . A cynical, bad, corrupt man—distrustful of the people" [*GF*, 2:180–83].)

Another was Silas Wright, congressman and senator from New York, and a Jacksonian democrat. In an obituary in the *Eagle* of 28 August 1847, Whitman wrote: "Our hopes, in common with those of nearly all the members of the Democratic party of this State, and indeed the other States, were so identified with this man . . . that we indeed feel pressed to the very earth by such an unexpected blow!" Adding that Wright could have become president, Whitman wrote that the statesman "thought it best to serve his country as she needed him, and then retreat from the tinsel and the crowd, to the simplicity of his farm—to his fields, his plough—to nature and his books" (*GF*, 2:185–88). It appears that the general qualities looked for in his ideal personalities, then, were an agrarian background, courage of belief, and a commitment to the "good cause" of liberty. Even the proslavery John Calhoun was included in the list as "*morally* heroic." Calhoun may have been the bitterest foe of the Wilmot Proviso, but "a higher souled patriot never trod on American soil" (*GF*, 2:191–92). Others who received Whitman's approval in the *Eagle* were General Zachary Taylor, who was compared to George Washington (certainly one of Whitman's heroes); George Bancroft, secretary of the navy during the Mexican War; and Colonel Jefferson Davis ("a braver man never wielded a sword"). Finally, though Whitman never devoted an essay to him, there was Thomas Jefferson. In fact, Whitman felt that the Wilmot Proviso should have been renamed the "Jefferson Proviso" in recognition of the statesman's efforts to exclude slavery from the Constitution.[23] For Whitman, Jefferson and the others personified Emerson's concept of the Whole Man. For they were individuals who defended the right of all men to be "average," to be free to develop in the direction of their character. With the exception of Calhoun, they supported the concept of democracy, which (as Whitman envisioned it) invited man to become himself (*whatever* was himself) and to allow others to do the same. In *Leaves of Grass*, therefore, he had no fear that such freedom would lead to evil; like Emerson, he trusted man's instinct or Character.

After Whitman's departure from the *Eagle* in 1848, the facts about his life before 1855 become increasingly hazy. The most comprehensive study of the "foreground" is probably *The Historic*

Whitman (1973). Yet it is essentially an outsider's view. We are left with few "inside" facts about the poet—Whitman, sometimes journalist, sometimes housebuilder. We have only "faint clews and indirections." Hence, like many before me, I am driven back to the 1855 *Leaves* in search of clues to Whitman's florescence as a poet in the 1850s. In this regard I find the preface especially revealing, not exclusively as a summation of the spirit of the twelve poems and their possible sources in his book, but as a sort of spiritual autobiography of the five years or so prior to its publication.

In a letter to the editor of *The National Era* (dated 25 October 1850), Whitman lamented the irreconcilable differences between the Hunker (or "American") Whigs and the Wilmot Proviso Whigs over the question of the expansion of slavery. He saw a bloodless battle going on, but feared it would ultimately extend to the people themselves and lead to real bloodshed. (In fact, the Civil War could have begun in 1850, had not the South become pacified by the Fugitive Slave Act.) The letter suggests that Whitman was losing faith in the political process, in its present leaders' ability to keep the cause of liberty alive in America. *"But let me leave politics,"* he wrote (italics mine). "Whatever is said or written, on either side, or all sides, the cause of Hunkerism and Slavery must eventually go down. It may be years yet; but it *must go"* (Whitman's italics).[24] In the context of the letter, Whitman was merely shifting to another topic (the cantatrice Jenny Lind), but it was also about this time (the year of the Fugitive Slave Act and that of the publication of his poem "Resurgemus," which applauded the 1848 French Revolution) that he turned within. He began to turn away from the national leaders and put his faith in his own kind, the common people who were now truly representative of New World principles. We find, for example, no national leaders celebrated in the preface. Although "America does not repel the past" (the Washingtons and the Jeffersons), it does perceive that era of statesmanship as a "corpse . . . slowly borne from the eating and sleeping rooms of the house." For Whitman during the period of composition of his first book of poetry, the time for pure Jacksonian democracy had arrived: "Other states indicate themselves in their deputies. . . . but the genius of the United States is not best or most in its executives or legislatures, nor in its ambassadors or authors or colleges or churches or parlors, nor even in its newspapers or inventors . . . but always most in the common people."[25]

Of course, this passage refers to the European past and its undemocratic nations as well, but really in the context of how that example now threatened to infect the political climate of nineteenth-century America. Whitman feared for the cause of liberty under the current leadership in Washington, especially after 1852 when Hawthorne's Bowdoin classmate, the proslavery Franklin Pierce, occupied the White House. Further along in the preface, in a passage that might be subtitled "When Liberty Goes," he sees one of the first stages of its demise when "the memories of the old martyrs are faded utterly away . . . when the large names of patriots are laughed at in the public halls from the lips of the orators." In other words, the people were now being led by false political gods, whose Hunkerism, or political patronage, took priority over the welfare of the people. Their character was no longer mirrored in their legislators: "When those in all parts of these states who could easier realize the *true American character* but do not yet—when the swarms of cringers, suckers, doughfaces, *lice of politics* [italics mine], planners of sly involutions for their own preferment to city offices or state legislatures or the judiciary or congress or the presidency, obtain a response of love and natural deference from the people whether they get [deserve?] offices or not," then liberty goes. "When it is better to be a bound booby and a rogue in office at a high salary than the poorest free mechanic or farmer with his hat unmoved from his head . . . then only shall the instinct of liberty be discharged from that part of the earth."[26] The mechanic or the farmer is now preferred over the president or the chief justice. And it is the poet's calling to refocus the nation's attention on this individual, to celebrate his American Character in "the age transfigured."

Whitman's preface was written in haste,[27] but its sentiments accurately reflected the democratic ideals contained in the first *Leaves of Grass*—certainly "Song of Myself," but also such pieces as "A Song for Occupations," "Faces," "Resurgemus" ("Europe"), and "A Boston Ballad." Of course, the first is superior to the rest, but their significance to the poet's discovery of the national character and his own is rather obvious. The book as a whole is Whitman's answer to the politicians. During his apprenticeship as a poet, he had been, above all else, a political observer. And as such, he found the election year of 1852 to be a bleak one. Evidence of his dissatisfaction, in fact, comes in a letter he wrote on 14 August to John Parker Hale, a senator from New Hampshire and the Free-Soil party choice for the presidency. When it was indicated in the press during the summer that Hale might not accept the nomination at the Pittsburgh convention, Whitman, writing as "a stranger, a young man, and a true Democrat," urged Hale not to decline. "Out of the Pittsburgh movement and 'platform,'" he told the senator, "it may be that a real live Democratic party is destined to come forth, which, from small beginnings, ridicule, and odium, (just like Jeffersonian democracy fifty years ago,) will gradually win the hearts of the people, and crowd those who stand before it into the sea. Then we should see an American Democracy with thews and sinews worthy of this sublime age" (C, 1:39).

The "sublime age" became the "age transfigured" in the preface, the era of the common man in America. The preface introduced poems that celebrated what Emerson had sought in the future American epic: "Our log-rolling, our stumps [speakers' platforms] and their politics, our fisheries, our Negroes and Indians, our boasts and repudiations" (W, 3:37). It stands to reason, therefore, that the animus for the 1855 *Leaves* was formed sometime between 1850 and 1852, as Whitman became almost as disenchanted with American politics as Emerson during the same period.[28] His loss of enthusiasm for politicians as representatives of the people also accounts in part for his transformation from political journalist to poet. For, as he implied to Senator Hale, he felt he was better acquainted with the real America than the politicians: "How little you at Washington—you Senatorial and Executive dignitaries—know of us, after all. How little you realize that the souls of the people ever leap and swell to any thing like a great liberal thought or principle, uttered by any well-known personage—how deeply they love the man that promulges such principles with candor and power" (C, 1:40).[29] The "great liberal thought," of course, was pushed "into the sea" by the overwhelming victory of Franklin Pierce. The sublime age now needed a spokesman with powers surpassing the politician. Doubtless, Whitman started writing his manifesto shortly after what he viewed as a setback for the "good cause" in 1852. "Of all nations the United States with veins full of poetical stuff most need poets and will doubtless have the greatest and use them the greatest," he declared in his preface. "Their Presidents shall not be their common referee so much as their poets shall."[30]

As Nathaniel Hawthorne went off to England in 1853 as U.S. consul in Liverpool, which was his reward for having written Franklin Pierce's campaign biography ("Hawthorne's New Romance," according to the New York *Times*),[31] Walter Whitman began to make his passage from journalism to poetry. As noted earlier, Whitman differed from Emerson in his view of the universe; he saw it as the measure of the individual's identity. For Whitman, man had evolved from "the huge first Nothing" ("Song of Myself"). It is not surprising that both Emerson and Whitman expressed and relied upon the theory of evolution before Darwin's publication of *The Origin of Species* in 1859. Such concepts as nebular hypothesis and geological evolution were already known through the writings of Herschel and Lyell, for example. It might be said that Darwin merely "proved" that the preparation for man on the globe had been immense. The pre-Darwinian theories solidified Whitman's belief in the "divine average." In 1855, however, this divinity may have been confined to the New World average, considering Whitman's focus on representative Americans in the 1850s. Even the American slave's body at auction, he wrote in "I Sing the Body Electric," was part of the whole that had evolved in the New World:

> Gentlemen look on this curious creature,
> Whatever the bids of the bidders they cannot be high
>   enough for him,
> For him the globe lay preparing quintillions of years

without one animal or plant,
For him the revolving cycles truly and steadily rolled.[32]

Representation lay with the average—now personified by Walt
Whitman, who believed he could express what the American
politico could not. The Poet, Emerson had written, speaks for
those "who cannot report the conversation they have had with
nature" (*W*, 3:5). He might have said *their* nature, or Character. In
"Song of Myself" Whitman made the message clearer:

> It is you talking just as much as myself. . . . I act as the
> tongue of you,
> It was tied in your mouth. . . . in mine it begins to be
> loosened.

What follows is (for Whitman) a short catalog of the kind of
people he hoped to represent in 1855: the roughs and little children, the young mechanic, the woodsman, the farmboy, the
sailor, the hunter, the wagon driver, the young mother. It is significant that the poet concludes his survey with the hope that
"they and all would resume what I have told them."[33]

"I remember," Whitman wrote. "I resume the overstaid fraction."[34] Trooping forth "replenished with supreme power, one
of the average unending procession," the poet strikes up "for a
New World" (as he wrote in the 1856 edition). The "overstaid
fraction" is Whitman's version of Emerson's part-man theory in
the American Scholar Address, the average American whose
character was yet to be drawn out and extolled. Other interesting
parallels between Whitman's book and the Emerson address are
worth mentioning. Emerson had written: "Events, actions arise,
that must be sung, that will sing themselves." Though Whitman
fails to "sing" himself in the first line of the 1855 edition, the
word is implied throughout the first poem and the other eleven.
Furthermore, Emerson had noted in the same lecture: "You must
take the whole society to find the whole man" (*CW*, 1:52–53).
Without doubt, the poet in the first *Leaves* becomes all men, turn
by turn, in his imaginative catalogs of America. There is no proof
that Whitman read the printed version of this Harvard College
address, but the possibility is not beyond belief. What is remark-

able, however, is this parallel between an 1834 journal entry of Emerson and Whitman's vision of God in section 48 of the 1855 version of "Song of Myself":

> EMERSON: God sends us messengers always. I am surrounded by messengers of God, who send me credentials day by day.
>
> WHITMAN: I hear and behold God in every object, yet I understand God not in the least, / . . . I see something of God each hour of the twenty-four, and each moment then, / In the faces of men and women I see God, and in my own face in the glass; / I find letters from God dropped in the street, and every one is signed by God's name.

Another noteworthy parallel in "Song of Myself" is of Emerson's journal reponse to the passage of the Fugitive Slave Law: "I will not obey it, by God." Whitman writes: "By God! I will accept nothing which all cannot have their counterpart on the same terms."[35]

By the 1850s both Emerson and Whitman believed in the potential equality (or divinity) of man; hence their anger over slavery. Yet it was Whitman who democratized the Transcendental message in this regard. He boldly stated what had lost some of its emotion for Emerson in the translation from journal to essay. Whitman later realized Emerson's shortcoming. "His idea of God (as in the oversoul)," he wrote, "is beautiful & tender & orthodox, but is not the modern Scientific idea, now rapidly advancing, far more sublime & resplendent, and reflect'g a dazzl'g light upon Democracy, *its twin*" (italics mine).[36] For Emerson all action on earth was penultimate at best; hence his inability to embrace the ideals and to confront the problems of democracy directly. His separation of the Body and the Soul is clearly established in *Nature* and repeated either tacitly or directly in his subsequent essays and poems. But it is most clearly expressed in an 1837 lecture on "The Individual," that "science is ever teaching us to separate between the body and the principle of life, and not with the vulgar, to identify this trunk with myself" (*EL*, 2:183). For Whitman in 1855, however, the flesh was not vulgar but the "body electric," the twin of the Soul. A generation later D. H. Lawrence expressed the difference: "Whitman was the first to break the mental [puritan] allegiance. He was the first to smash the moral conception that the soul of man is something 'superior' and 'above' the flesh. Even Emerson still maintained this tiresome 'superiority' of the soul."[37]

Malcolm Cowley is probably correct in his argument that the first edition was Whitman's "one completely realized work" and that after 1855 the poet began to celebrate himself "in the guise of a simple separate person—greater than other persons" instead of celebrating the "deeper self" or Character.[38] But the question of the Transcendental authenticity in Whitman's subsequent editions must wait for another chapter. Suffice it to say that in 1855 Whitman was wholly Transcendental because he was celebrating his deeper self, and through it the American character. Later, in poems like "Proud Music of the Storm" and "Passage to India," where he was trying harder to please Emerson, he fell out of *character* and into a false pose by extending his message to the world.[39] But the greatness of the 1855 book lies in its celebration of the New World come of age. "The Americans of all nations [states]," he wrote in the preface, "at any time on earth have probably the fullest poetical nature. . . . Here at last is something in the doings of man that corresponds with the broadcast doings of the day and night."[40]

Here at last was a national character that expressed its true evolution through its surly but genuine manners. "I think I could turn and live with the animals," Whitman wrote to the dismay and disgust of many readers enamored of the "gentleman" in literature. "They are so placid and self-contained / . . . / They bring me tokens of myself." Again a catalog of America follows, the longest one in "Song of Myself" (section 33), in which the poet is "afoot" with his vision of the New World. He is confident of its "rendezvous" with God. Certainly, the final sentence in the preface argues for the theme of nationality in the poem: "The proof of a poet is that his country absorbs him as affectionately as he has absorbed it." Yet further evidence of the poet's motive is found in the anonymous reviews of *Leaves of Grass* (really extensions and restatements of the preface) that he published in 1855.

"We shall cease shamming and be what we really are," he said in "Walt Whitman and His Poems." "We shall start an athletic and defiant literature." Further on, he asks the question Emerson had asked in "The Poet": "Where in American literature is the first show of America? . . . Where is the spirit of the strong rich life of the American mechanic, farmer, sailor, hunter, and miner?" In another review he described himself as the "rude child of the people!—No imitation—No foreigner—but a growth and idiom of America." Other poets might celebrate great events, individuals, war, love; but this "poet celebrates natural [American] propensities in himself; and that is the way he celebrates all." Although in a third review he praised the literature of England as he had in the 1840s, he nonetheless declared: "No nation ever did or ever will receive with national affection any poets except those born of its national blood."[41]

As already stated, the composition of the first *Leaves* probably began soon after the election of Franklin Pierce. During that administration, the Kansas-Nebraska Act (1854) was passed. In effect, it nullified the Missouri Compromise of 1820, which had forbidden the extension of slavery in the remaining and unsettled portions of the Louisiana Purchase, or north of latitude $36° 30'$. This act allowed the two territories (also created by the legislation) to leave the question of slavery up to popular sovereignty, thus precipitating in 1856 the "Bleeding Kansas" episode in American history. The act incensed abolitionists everywhere, including the wild and messianic John Brown, who brutally executed five men and boys only vaguely associated with the proslavery party in Kansas.[42]

Whitman's disenchantment with American politics under the leadership of Pierce, therefore, was closely associated with his idealization of the American workingman in *Leaves of Grass*. And though we find no really solid and outright condemnation of national leaders, in the preface they are more or less sacrificed in the poet's praise of the "divine average." The acknowledgment of evil anywhere in America, of course, would have made Whitman's book quite different and untranscendental, to say the least.

Even though there is an undercurrent of criticism of the ruling class in the preface, the result was a blend of the high and low under the aegis of democracy. With almost revolutionary zeal, the political elite were not condemned but forgotten in his over-whelming enthusiasm for the average. His anger was simply ab-sorbed in the process. Evidence of this catharsis is found in one of the most remarkable essays the poet ever wrote: "The Eighteenth Presidency! Voice of Walt Whitman to each Young Man in the Nation, North, South, East, and West."

Whitman's stinging criticism of both presidential candidates seeking to become Pierce's successor—Millard Fillmore and James Buchanan—suggests that the final version of the pam-phlet, which was never published in the poet's lifetime, was intended for circulation during the 1856 campaign. Yet the essay began to germinate around 1854. Whitman probably began to draft it shortly after the passage of the Kansas-Nebraska Act, for he wrote: "The governor & part of the legislature of the State of Kansas are chased, seized, chained, by the creatures of the Presi-dent, and are to-day in chains." This of course could be a ref-erence to the 1856 violence, but the poet may also have been speaking metaphorically. Another possibility is that the allusion is literal and factual, but also an updating of an earlier mention of the turmoil in Kansas. Further and more convincing evidence of an earlier draft, however, comes from Clifton J. Furness's *Walt Whitman's Workshop*, which includes a version of the pam-phlet. Furness writes: "A preliminary germ of this pamphlet: 'The [blank]th Presidency. Voice of Walt Whitman to the mechanics and farmers of These States, and to each American young man, north, south, east and west' (*N[otes]* & *F[ragments]*, 176). Then follows the introductory paragraph, in which he speaks of 'more than five millions' of workingmen. This seems to indicate that the plan was originally conceived a good while before the campaign of 1856, since in the completed version the number had increased to 'some six millions.' The pamphlet was probably the fruit of a long slow growth, like many another of Whitman's creations."[43]

Whitman's thesis in the final draft calls for the average working-man to come forth and usurp the political offices of the "swarms of dough-faces,[44] office vermin, kept-editors, clerks, attaches of the ten thousand officers and their parties, aware of nothing further than the drip and spoil of politics—ignorant of principles, the true glory of a man." Gay Wilson Allen complains that Whitman at the time "did not have even a rudimentary understanding of practical politics."[45] But this judgment seems a bit severe when we remember that Whitman as a journalist had been both a long-time observer of and participant in city and state politics. The important feature of the pamphlet, however, is its exaggeration, the same kind of idealization of the American average we find in *Leaves of Grass*. Furthermore, even though the essay got into proof sheets, we have no evidence that Whitman ever tried to publish it. He could have published it himself (as he had the 1855 *Leaves*), but he probably realized that the spirit of his polemic had already been absorbed into the poetry.

In *Democratic Vistas* (1871) Whitman would say that the "people are ungrammatical, untidy, and their sins gaunt and ill-bred" (*PW*, 2:376). Then he was concerned about America's postwar bent for materialism ("a vast and more and more thoroughly-appointed body and then left with little or no soul"), but in the 1850s he believed that the national leaders were materialistic and the nation sorely needed leadership from "the real America." As though in anticipation of Lincoln, he wrote: "I would be much pleased to see some heroic, shrewd, fully-informed, healthy-bodied, middle-aged, beard-faced American blacksmith or boatman come down from the West across the Alleghenies, and walk into the Presidency, dressed in a clean suit of working attire, and with the tan all over his face, breast, and arms; I could certainly vote for that sort of man, *possessing the due requirements*, before any other candidate" (italics mine).[46] The statement certainly challenges the notion of Whitman's political naiveté; he sought a *representative* man, one qualified in the Jeffersonian sense—a man of virtue and talent.

Whitman must have believed in the political reality of such a man; otherwise, it is doubtful he could have written *Leaves of Grass*. But an important part of its element, as noted, was his anger or pessimism over the expansion of slavery into Kansas. In fact, he viewed it as a threat, not so much to the black man, as to the white American. "In fifteen of the States," he wrote, "the three hundred and fifty thousand masters keep down the true people, the millions of white citizens, mechanics, farmers, boatmen, manufacturers, and the like, excluding them from politics and from office, and punishing by the lash, by tar and feathers, binding fast to rafts on the rivers or trees in the woods, and sometimes by death, all attempts to discuss the evils of slavery in its relations to the whites." Whitman sounds like an abolitionist (as he does in section 10 of "Song of Myself," where the protagonist cares for a runaway slave), but he was really concerned about the white man. For this divine average was degraded by having to perform in the North what was the work of a slave in the South. Moreover, the abolitionists were often fanatics and willing to risk anything, even disunion, to rid the country of slavery. But in "The Eighteenth Presidency!" Whitman supported slavery (confined to the South) as long as it was upheld by the Constitution. It was wrong, but it had to be allowed until abolished by consent of the states. "Must run-away slaves be delivered back?" he asked. "They must."[47]

Gay Wilson Allen comments on this passage, "To Whitman the Constitution was sacred and every section must be observed 'in spirit and in letter.'"[48] What was truly sacred to the poet was the judgment and foresight of men like George Washington, Thomas Jefferson, and John Adams, leaders whose example had been more or less forgotten in the nineteenth century. As noted in Chapter 1, three of Whitman's brothers were named for such patriots as these. He had been raised to cherish the unselfish deeds of such statesmen. During the composition of the first *Leaves*, Whitman put his faith completely in the American people, believing (foolishly perhaps) that, given the chance, they too would act unselfishly and strike slavery from the Constitution. It was the poet's job in 1855, he thought, to rally them to action, "to cheer up [white] slaves and horrify despots."[49]

Malcolm Cowley finds the 1855 preface full of "a rather bumptious American nationalism."[50] Yet Whitman's nationalism pervades the poems that follow as well. It may be that both the preface and the poems are too hopeful, too idealistic, but such sublime confidence is appropriate for verse and not for prose. The fact remains that the primary influence on the poet's foreground was his strong sense of nationalism, a political idealism that became sublimated in his poetry through a combination of his background and the writings of Emerson. The reason for Whitman's concealment of the latter is rather obvious, but why did he obscure the other? Why did he permit O'Connor, Burroughs, Bucke, and others to embellish the legend of the American Homer, who had roamed the streets of America before emerging with his vision? His friends contrived to foster the myth, but it was Whitman himself who created it—in his first *Leaves* and in the three anonymous book reviews.

Doubtless, Whitman was not a little embarrassed that the foreground Emerson had praised contained much that he wanted forgotten. In his letter to Whitman, Emerson had written: "I am very happy in reading [*Leaves of Grass*], as great power makes us happy. It meets the demand I am always making of what seemed the sterile & stingy nature, as if too much handiwork, or too much lymph in the temperament, were making our western wits fat & mean." There had indeed been too much "lymph" in the background of the poet, and Whitman was not at all sure how he had found his calling. But he did know that his foreground had been constellated by the life of Walter Whitman, Jr., the dandy, the scurrilous journalist, the moralist, the temperance man, the student of phrenology, often the frustrated member of a family that, in the words of Richard Chase, "tended in the poet's generation to suffer neurosis, idiocy, poverty, sickness, and hard luck."[51] In 1855 and forever after, the poet wanted Walter Whitman, Jr., buried with his father, who had died less than a week after the phrenological house of Fowler and Wells began to issue the first *Leaves of Grass*.

4. Emerson and Whitman in the 1850s

Poems! we have no poem, the Iliad is a poor
ballad grinding—whenever the Poet shall appear!
Emerson's Journal, 1854

Walt Whitman stands to-day in the midst
of the American people, a promise, a preface,
an overture. . . . Will he justify the
great prophecy of Emerson?
Whitman's Notebook, 1855–56

"I am really very willing to see no new face for a year to come,—
unless only it were a face that made all things new," Emerson told
Lidian from England in June of 1848 (*L*, 4:93). Having spent the
last eight months lecturing there and now preparing to return
home in July, he had seen many new faces and several old ones,
including that of his friend Thomas Carlyle. But this reunion after
fifteen years had resulted in a strain on their friendship. Their
quarrel was mainly over politics, in which the Englishman found
his friend "rather *moonshiny, un*practical in his speculations, and
it must be confessed a little wearisome from time to time!" (*CEC*,
p. 42). For Emerson's part, he found Carlyle "no idealist in opinions, but a protectionist in political economy, aristocrat in politics,
epicure in diet, goes for murder, money, punishment by death,
slavery, & all the pretty abominations, tempering them with epi-
grams" (*JMN*, 10:551). As he would write in *English Traits* (1856),
he had gone to England for "a change and a tonic," but had
returned with the conviction that the English mind was becoming
too provincial in politics, science, and poetry. The British power,
he thought, had already culminated, was "in solstice, or already
declining" (*W*, 5:26, 37).

Emerson was even more disenchanted, however, with America
after 1850, the year in which the Fugitive Slave Act became law.
In 1851 he vowed all he had "in opposition to the execution of the
law" (*JMN*, 11:344). He felt particularly ashamed because this
latest compromise on the status of slavery had been the work of
Massachusetts senator Daniel Webster. "The word *liberty* in the
mouth of Mr Webster," he wrote in his journal, "sounds like the
word *love* in the mouth of a courtezan" (*JMN*, 11:346). Like Whitman in his reaction to the election of Pierce in 1852, he also saw in
the current leadership a reversal of the high standards set by the
founding fathers: "The head of Washington hangs in my dining-
room . . . & I cannot keep my eyes off of it. It has a certain Apa-
lachian strength, as if it were truly the first-fruits of America, &
expressed the country. . . . We imagine him hearing the letter of
General Cass, the letter of Gen. Scott, the letter of Mr Pierce, the
effronteries of Mr Webster recited. This man listens like a god to
these low conspirators." The actions of such politicians "soft"

on slavery drove him to conclude "that the Union is no longer desireable" (*JMN*, 13:63; 11:349).

As the national tension over slavery grew in the middle 1850s, Emerson even lamented the outcome of the Revolutionary War; for if America had remained a colony, the slaves, he thought, would have been freed with their counterparts in the British West Indies. His political anger increased with the passage of the Kansas-Nebraska Act. "There is nobody in Washington who can explain this Nebraska business to the people," he wrote during the three months of bitter debate over the merits of the legislation, "nobody of weight. . . . It is only done by Douglass & his accomplices by calculation on the brutal ignorance of the people, upon the wretched masses of Pennsylvania, Indiana, Illinois, Kentucky, & so on, people who can't read or know anything beyond what the village democrat tells them" (*JMN*, 13:283). Even though Emerson may have regretted not including "the unexpressed greatness of the common farmer & labourer" in *Representative Men*, he did not, like Whitman, look to the West for America's political savior (*JMN*, 11:192). Nor did he necessarily think, of course, that sane leadership might be found in the average, because they were the ones so easily duped by the likes of Pierce and Stephen Douglas. "Shall we judge the country by the majority or by the minority?" he asked in his journal for 1854. "Certainly, by the minority. The mass are animal, in a state of pupilage, & nearer the chimpanzee" (*JMN*, 13:302).

In fairness to Emerson, however, it should be observed that he shared Whitman's admiration for the average. He simply distrusted its judgment as a mass. On an individual basis, Emerson applauded the average man's self-reliance and tenacity, a faith that extended even to his Irish caretakers. As noted in Chapter 3, Whitman also required learning from those who rose from the cellar to the senate house. Like Hugh Henry Brackenridge of the Jeffersonian era, neither would have approved of an "unnatural hoist."

Slavery was not Emerson's only concern in the 1850s. He still awaited the appearance of the native American Poet. Thoreau's publication of *Walden* in 1854 apparently lacked the literary force he sought, for there is no mention of the one-man Brook Farm experiment in his journals. In a 28 August letter to his old friend George Bradford, he could only call the book "cheerful, sparkling, readable, with all kinds of merits, & rising sometimes to very great heights." He then added, "We account Henry the undoubted King of all American lions." But the comment may have been only half serious or sardonic, for he described the "King" as "walking up & down Concord, firm-looking, but in a tremble of great expectation" (L, 4:460).

Alcott and Channing as well showed only the *promise* they had exhibited for the last twenty years. Each, as he noted on his return from England, possessed the painter's eye but neither could "draw a tree so that his wife could know it was a tree" (*JMN*, 11:130). He was even more disappointed (and annoyed) at the failure of Charles King Newcomb, Emerson's "genius" during the *Dial* years. In 1850 he noted in his journal: "Charles Newcomb came, & yesterday departed, but I do not ask him again to come. . . . the unique, inspired, wasted genius!" (*JMN*, 11:316). The fate of the once promising men and women Emerson had praised in his 1842 letter to Carlyle was now grimly determined. He could console himself only with the theory that each age ends with the man of genius who absorbs the genius of his nation. After Dante what followed in Italy was "rubbish" in comparison. "So that we ought rather to be thankful that our hero or poet does not hasten to be born in America, but still allows us others to have a little, & warm ourselves at the fire of the sun, for, when he comes, we others must pack our petty trunks & begone" (*JMN*, 13:120).

In July 1855 Emerson undoubtedly believed such a poet had arrived when he received from the phrenological house of Fowler and Wells his copy of the anonymous *Leaves of Grass*. Possibly on Independence Day, ten years after Henry Thoreau had tested his own independence in the woods overlooking Walden Pond, copies went on sale for two dollars apiece at Swayne's Newspaper and Book Store on Fulton Street in Brooklyn. Shortly afterward the book was also offered for sale at Fowler and Wells at 308 Broadway in New York and at the Old Corner Bookstore on Washington Street in Boston.[1] Approximately eight hundred copies were printed by the Rome brothers of Brooklyn (*C*, 6:30), and the thin quarto was advertised in the New York *Tribune* between 17 July and 6 August.

By the time the book reached Concord, Emerson was finishing his draft of *English Traits*. He may in fact have been writing the chapter on "Literature," taking a theme that may not have been further strengthened by Whitman's book but one that shows he was prepared to find in *Leaves of Grass* what he had sought in contemporary poetry. In discussing British poetry, for example, he complained: "The English have lost sight of the fact that poetry exists to speak the spiritual law, and that no wealth of description or of fancy is yet essentially new and out of the limits of prose, until this condition is reached." The exception, he felt, was Wordsworth. Quoting Walter Savage Landor, he said Wordsworth "wrote a poem without the aid of war" (*W*, 5:256–57). This was indeed Whitman's intention, as Emerson doubtless realized in reading the preface: "The greatest poet has less a marked style and is more the channel of thoughts and things without increase or diminution, and is the free channel of himself. He swears to his art, I will not be meddlesome, I will not have in my writing any elegance or effect or originality to hang in the way between me and the rest like curtains."[2] In the summer of 1855, Emerson was persuaded that English literature was in decline, but only in England. The next generation, "the elasticity and hope of mankind[,] must henceforth remain on the Allegheny ranges, or nowhere" (*W*, 5:314).

Emerson sought evidence of the Whole Man in the *American* generation—the expounding of matter from thought, as he called it. Yet the brains of the contemporary poets were poorly formed: "One man sees a sparkle or shimmer of the truth, & reports it, & his saying becomes a legend or golden proverb for all ages; and other men report as much; but no man wholly & well. Poems! we have no poem. The Iliad is a poor ballad grinding—whenever the Poet shall appear!" Moreover, he thought the great poem could only be written organically: the Poet "must plunge into the universe, & live in its forms,—sink to rise. None any work can frame unless himself become the same" (*JMN*, 13:285). Emerson certainly was the first, then, to catch the drift of what became section 5 of "Song of Myself": "I mind how we [Body and Soul] lay in June . . . / You settled your head athwart my hips and gently turned over upon me, / And parted the shirt from my bosom-bone, and plunged your tongue to my barestript heart, / And reached till you felt my beard, and reached till you held my feet."

Emerson's letter of 21 July was therefore no "letter of thanks" (as he later called it).[3] For he told Whitman that *Leaves of Grass* met "the demand [he was] always making of what seemed the sterile & stingy nature" of poetry. Emerson could give Whitman "joy of [his] free & brave thought" because it contained the two essential elements, originality and experimentation. Later that summer he would use almost the same phrasing in a letter to Delia Bacon upon the completion of her controversial *Philosophy of the Plays of Shakespeare Unfolded* (1857), which argued for Sir Francis Bacon as the true author of the plays. "I give you joy on the good news you send me," he wrote, after having read only the initial chapter of the tract.[4] In an 1857 letter to Caroline Sturgis Tappan, he again voiced his enthusiasm for these two writers, dismissing the results of the works of Newcomb and Channing as "zero": "Our wild Whitman, with real inspiration but choked by Titanic abdomen, & Delia Bacon, with genius, but mad, & clinging like a tortoise to English soil, are the sole producers that America has yielded in ten years" (*L*, 5:86–87).

Of course, Emerson had to temper his joy in 1857 with the concern that neither Bacon nor Whitman always knew when the muse had departed. In Bacon's case, it was clear by then that her obsession to prove Shakespeare a fraud had become an insanity. She died in 1859, after two years of sometimes violent delusions. In Whitman's case, however, Emerson's doubts, at least until 1860, had more to do with the poet's unauthorized publication of his letter of 21 July 1855, a circumstance that proved to be merely incidental in the light of his appreciation of Whitman's first three editions.

The printing of this letter in the New York *Tribune* of 10 October 1855, as well as its later use by Whitman in a broadside (pasted into copies of the 1855 edition) and in the appendix to the 1856 *Leaves*, wedded from that day forward Emerson's name with Whitman's poetry. And for allowing Charles A. Dana, then acting editor of the *Tribune*, to print the letter, Whitman has been repeatedly scolded by critics ever since. Generally, the act has been viewed as a slick promotion scheme, done by a man with little sense of propriety. It is difficult even today to excuse Whitman for his actions, but a closer look at the circumstances may mitigate the offense. Whitman wanted the world to know what Ralph Waldo Emerson thought of his poetry; but he also used the letter in self-defense, as a counterbalance to what he considered a partially negative review (the very first review of his book) in the *Tribune* of 23 July 1855. Charles Dana described the anonymous poet as an "odd genius," whose "language is too frequently reckless and indecent." There were aspects of the review that Whitman doubtless welcomed, especially Dana's assertion of originality for the poet and his liberal quoting of passages from the poetry. But Dana himself probably did not consider the review to be wholly favorable either. For when he printed Emerson's letter, he introduced the epistle with the following statement: "We some time since had the occasion to call the attention of our readers to this original and striking collection of poems, by Mr. Whitman of Brooklyn. In doing so we could not avoid noticing certain faults which seemed to us to be prominent in the work. The following opinion, from a distinguished source, views the matter from a more positive and less critical stand-point."

Naturally, the question arises of why Whitman, if indeed he was acting in self-defense, waited until October to offer the letter to the *Tribune*. Legend has it that the poet was profoundly affected by Emerson's unqualified praise and actually carried the letter around in his pocket all summer, until Dana finally persuaded him to allow its publication.[5] I suspect, however, that the poet did not receive the letter until late September or early October, at which time he insisted that Dana print it as a balance to his review of 23 July. The evidence for this conjecture is admittedly not altogether solid, but for one thing Whitman may have spent the latter half of the summer of 1855 visiting his sister, Mary Elizabeth Van Nostrand, at the east end of Long Island, "around Shelter Island and Peconic Bay."[6] Furthermore, Emerson sent the letter not to Whitman's Brooklyn address but to New York City in care of Fowler and Wells.

The theory finds surer support in a letter by Moncure Daniel Conway, Emerson's first emissary to Whitman (followed by Alcott and Thoreau in 1856). A recent graduate of the Harvard Divinity School, Conway had heard Emerson highly recommend the first *Leaves*: "Americans abroad may now come home: unto us a man is born."[7] He promptly bought a copy in Boston and read it on a ship to New York the same day, in search of Whitman "with the feeling of an astronomer told of an unexpected comet visible in the western sky."[8] Conway's letter to Emerson of 17 September (at "the earliest moment I could command since my return") is well known to Whitman scholars. He described the poet, whom he found in the Romes's printing office, as a "man you would not have marked in a thousand; blue striped shirt, opening from a red throat; and sitting on a chair without a back. . . . His eye can kindle strangely; and his words are ruddy with health. He is clearly his book." More significant, though, is that Whitman did not indicate that he had received Emerson's letter of 21 July. "I told him that I had spent the evening before with you, and that what you had said of him, and the perusal of his book had resulted in my call," Conway wrote. "He seemed *very eager to hear from you* and about you, and *what you thought of his book*" (italics mine).[9]

According to an article in the *Tribune* of 22 June 1884, Emerson first learned about the newspaper publication of his letter from an acquaintance by the name of Frank Bellew. Bellew reported that Emerson was shocked by the publication and told him: "Had I intended it for publication, I should have enlarged the *but* very much."[10] Of course, there is no *but* or qualification of any kind in the letter, no indication that Emerson found anything in *Leaves of Grass* offensive. It is perhaps useful at this point, even though the letter has been printed (and misprinted) many times, to quote the text once again, this time with Emerson's original paragraphing, which Whitman altered when he allowed its publication.

Dear Sir,
    I am not blind to the worth of the wonderful gift of "Leaves of Grass." I find it the most extraordinary piece of

wit & wisdom that America has yet contributed. I am very happy in reading it, as great power makes us happy. It meets the demand I am always making of what seemed the sterile & stingy nature, as if too much handiwork or too much lymph in the temperament were making our western wits fat & mean. I give you joy of your free brave thought. I have great joy in it. I find incomparable things said incomparably well, as they must be. I find the courage of *treatment*, which so delights us, & which large perception only can inspire. I greet you at the beginning of a great career, which yet must have had a long foreground somewhere for such a start. I rubbed my eyes a little to see if this sunbeam were no illusion; but the solid sense of the book is a sober certainty. It has the best merits, namely, of fortifying & encouraging.

   I did not know until I, last night, saw the book advertised in a newspaper, that I could trust the name as real & available for a post-office. I wish to see my benefactor, & have felt much like striking my tasks, & visiting New York to pay you my respects.

                                                              R. W. Emerson.

Mr Walter Whitman.[11]

   Ralph L. Rusk speculates that Emerson probably received his copy of Whitman's book by 4 July, certainly a reasonable estimate, because Fowler and Wells were experienced booksellers and would have sent out review copies prior to the date of publication.[12] This means that Emerson allowed himself more than two weeks with the volume before writing his letter to Whitman. And his remarks were neither frivolous nor hasty; he stamped the book a success in all respects, emphasizing the poet's "courage of *treatment*." "My quarrel with poets," he had written in 1853, "is that they do not believe in their own poetry" (*JMN*, 13:236). The geography and the nation were sublime, he thought, but the poets were not. Here at last was someone who had celebrated these "incomparable things . . . incomparably well."

   Emerson's copy of the 1855 *Leaves* is now lost. Sometime in the fall of that year he loaned it to Frank Sanborn, who apparently never returned it.[13] Hence we have no hints as to what in particular delighted Emerson in the book. Yet it is probable that his enthusiasm was not short-lived. He endeavored to interest a number of his friends in the book that fall. Writing to James Elliot Cabot on 26 September, he asked: "Have you seen the strange Whitman's poems? Many weeks ago I thought to send them to you, but they seemed presently to become more known & you have probably found them. He seems a Mirabeau of a man, with such insight & equal expression, but hurt by hard life & too animal experience. But perhaps you have not read the American Poem?" (L, 4:531). On 1 October he asked his old friend and former Harvard classmate, William Henry Furness, "Have you read that wonderful book—with all its formlessness & faults . . . 'Leaves of Grass'?"[14] Cabot replied on 5 November saying, "Certainly there is *somebody there* [in *Leaves of Grass*], tho' whether he be a poet or not I have not sufficient judgment to say."[15] If Furness's response was more favorable, there is no record of it. Doubtless, Emerson soon gave up trying to increase Whitman's small circle of readers. He may have begun to realize that Whitman's "hard life" and "too animal experience" would undercut anything he could say in the poet's behalf. Silent approval must have seemed the only course of action.

Nevertheless, we can be fairly sure that Emerson, despite his friends' indifference to *Leaves of Grass*, kept his promise to strike his tasks and visit his "benefactor"; for his pocket diary of 11 December reads "Brooklyn" (*JMN*, 13:510). Of their first meeting Whitman told Traubel in 1888: "I shall never forget the first visit he paid me—the call, the first call: it was in Brooklyn: no, I can never forget it. I can hear his gentle knock still—the soft knock—so . . . and the slow sweet voice, as my mother stood there by the door: and the words, 'I came to see Mr. Whitman': and the response, 'He is here'—the simple unaffected greeting on both sides—'How are you, Mr. Whitman.' 'How are you, Waldo'—the hour's talk or so—the taste of lovableness he left behind when he was gone" (*WWC*, 2:130). Whitman knew, of course, that his friend Traubel was taking notes for what would become the *With Walt Whitman in Camden* volumes, and hence he probably romanticized the description a bit. It is difficult to believe, for example, that Whitman would have greeted the renowned essayist by his first name. And how could he have known that Emerson was known as "Waldo" instead of "Ralph" to his friends? Furthermore, this account differs from the one Whitman gave Traubel later that year:

> Did I ever tell you the story of a visit he paid me *once* [my italics] on the way to lecture at Newark: Emerson called—I was in Brooklyn at the time: it was early afternoon: he was free from then on to the lecture hour: he said to me at once: "I have a lecture to deliver at Newark this evening: I therefore have three hours to spend with you." I invited him to take a bite or two, but he answered: "No—it is but a little after dinner: I am stopping at the Astor House: you don't want anything now? Nor do I." I was entirely satisfied. He asked me how should we go: we lived three miles from the ferry: I answered him that I would rather walk. He was agreeable to that: so we went along in that way talking: the long stroll being very happy, memorable. We went to New York—to the Astor House. [*WWC*, 2:504]

In his treatment of their first meeting in his biography of Emerson, Rusk ignored or overlooked both of Whitman's statements and relied instead upon the pocket diary entry and an 1877 anecdote by Edward Carpenter, one of Whitman's English disciples. "It may have been December 11, 1855," Rusk wrote, "that Emerson first had Whitman to dinner at a New York hotel. He seems to have been only mildly surprised when his poet shouted for a tin mug for his beer. Later, Whitman took him to 'a noisy fire-engine society.'"[16] Carpenter had no reason to lie, but I tend to doubt the validity of Emerson's statement. First, Emerson's memory was failing by 1877. Second, such behavior would have been out of character for Whitman, who, as a former journalist and part-time politician, was not unfamiliar with the more elegant New York hotels. Third, Emerson could not have been taken to "a noisy fire-engine society" that evening because he had a lecture to give in Newark (according to Whitman). It is important, too, to remember that Emerson's rather negative picture of Whitman on that evening (and we have no substantial evidence that they ever dined together again in New York, despite Whitman's probable exaggeration of "twenty or so" meetings) followed the Anglo-American debate of 1876 over America's treatment of the author of *Leaves of Grass*. In the exchange of angry editorials that crossed the Atlantic that year, Robert Buchanan, one of the poet's fiercest English advocates for a time, compared Emerson to Whitman as "that other eagle of American literature, aquiline in breed but born and degenerated in captivity," the captivity of respectability that had "so weakened the heart of Emerson that he falters from his first faith [in Whitman and] no longer recognises the wild eagle his kinsman, because that kinsman's flight is afar off, and his wings, though old and feeble, are still free!"[17]

It appears that Rusk fueled the fires of the old controversy, that he distorted the facts of the Emerson-Whitman relationship by making Emerson out to be the gentleman in the company of a semibarbarian. Liberal-minded, patient certainly, the gentle Emerson (who had managed to overlook or forget the publication of his letter in the *Tribune*) is presented as slightly annoyed at and not a little embarrassed by Whitman's behavior at the Astor House. Rusk even went so far as to edit out of Carpenter's statement the unlikely account of Emerson's objecting to the absence of meter in *Leaves of Grass*. Emerson, in fact, soon tired of Whitman's endless catalogs, but it is improbable that the man who had called for "metre-making" arguments in 1844 would find the lack of conventional meter in *Leaves of Grass* a liability.

It may appear that I have given more attention to the first meeting of Emerson and Whitman than the matter warrants. However, an examination of the "facts" shows how the controversy over the Emerson letter has beclouded the details of their relationship after 1855. Testimony comes from either the Emerson disciples or the Whitman disciples, and the problem is further compounded by those individuals who held allegiance to both. Moncure Conway, for example, was one of the first to support Whitman's cause in England, but he was also an Emerson devotee (describing his first meeting with him as "the most memorable day" of his life).[18] In an 1866 article on Whitman he contradicted his earlier and more reliable statement by saying that he first met Whitman "on a

Sunday in midsummer." This time he reported that he had found the poet on a Brooklyn beach, "stretched upon his back, and gazing straight up at the terrible sun."[19] John Townsend Trowbridge was another who may have confused his allegiance with the facts. A popular writer of boys' books and a once hopeful candidate for the Concord circle, it was he who reported Whitman's alleged confession in 1860: "I was simmering, simmering, simmering; Emerson brought me to a boil." Curiously, he chose to keep this dramatic statement a secret until 1902, ten years after Whitman's death.[20]

More than anyone, however, it was Whitman himself who obscured the facts almost as well as he did his foreground. It appears that he existed in a state of sustained euphoria between 1855 and 1857. Indeed, in the latter year he even contemplated "The Great Construction of the New Bible . . . three hundred and sixty-five [poems]," and thought it "ought to be ready in 1859."[21] Even clearer evidence of his euphoria can be found in the 1856 edition of *Leaves of Grass*. Here he not only reprinted the Emerson letter again, but also had inscribed in gold letters on the spine of the volumes: "I Greet You at the / Beginning of A / Great Career / R W Emerson." He thus made Emerson ipso facto the blurb writer for a book of poems he had never examined. "At no other time," one witness reported after having seen Emerson first examine the book, "had I seen a cloud of dissatisfaction darken [Emerson's] serene countenance."[22] It is probably safe to assume that there were no more meetings after this incident—none, at least, until their confrontation on Boston Common in 1860.

In his biography of Whitman, Emory Holloway assumed that Whitman sent Emerson a "personal reply" to his letter of 21 July. Unfortunately, he offered no evidence to support the conjecture.[23] A private message to Emerson would have been awkward and superfluous if we accept the theory that Whitman did not pick up his letter from Fowler and Wells until after the Conway visit in September 1855. For its publication in the *Tribune* followed almost immediately. Whitman's first reply to Emerson, then, was his open letter in the 1856 edition. Like Emerson's eloquent letter of greeting, it was both well rehearsed and euphoric. Gay Wilson Allen calls it "boastful and garrulous,"[24] but in the light of Whitman's state of mind—a period in which he now utterly believed he was standing at "the beginning of a great career" after almost fifteen years of literary experiments and obscurity—the letter provides a useful insight into the continued growth of one of America's greatest poets. The recent publication of one of his 1856 notebooks, for example, suggests not only the ecstasy but the anxiety that so propelled the new poet onto the American literary scene. Sometime in the fall of 1856, shortly after he had recorded Alcott's first visit to Brooklyn on 4 October, Whitman wrote: "Walt Whitman stands to-day in the midst of the American people, a promise, a preface, an overture. . . . Will he fulfill the half-indistinct promise?—Many do not understand him, but there are others, a few, who do understand him. Will he justify the great prophecy of Emerson? Or will he too, like thousands of others, flaunt out one bright commencement, the result of gathered powers, only to sink back exhausted—to give himself up to the seduction of [Whitman left blank]" (*DN*, 3:779).

The editors of the *Comprehensive Reader's Edition* of *Leaves of Grass* express their astonishment that the open letter has not been regarded as a preface to the 1856 edition. The point is a good one, because in the letter Whitman announced his program for American poetry of the future. He wanted a poetry (and thought he had further introduced it in 1856 with twenty poems added to the original twelve of 1855) that resumed the "overstaid fraction" of the American identity, a poetry to encourage Americans to "resume Personality, too long left out of mind." Like the 1855 preface, the letter (really an essay without the opening and closing paragraphs addressing Emerson as "Master") also regretted the forgotten legacy of Washington and Jefferson. Because of the current political situation (with "such a rascal and thief [as Pierce] in the Presidency"), American literature has been "distasteful to our instincts, foreign to our soil. . . . Its costumes and jewelry prove how little it knows of Nature." The letter at times reads very much like a literary version of Whitman's unpublished political tract, "The Eighteenth Presidency!" "How much," he asked, "is there anyhow, to the young men of These States, in a parcel of helpless dandies, who can neither fight, work, shoot, ride, run, command?" Finally and most important, he advocated the "unabashed development of sex,"[25] backing up the suggestion with poems whose final titles are "Unfolded Out of the Folds," "A Woman Waits for Me," and "Spontaneous Me."

But Whitman doubtless intended the letter also as an answer and a tribute to Emerson, to whom he obviously felt a great obligation in 1856. Like the tribute Ezra Pound paid Whitman in "A Pact," Whitman's letter celebrated Emerson as the man who had broken the "new wood" of American literature. "Those shores you found," he freely admitted. "I say you have led The States there—have led Me there. I say that none has ever done, or ever can do, a greater deed for The States, than your deed." He then concluded: "We demand to take your name into keeping. . . . We understand what you have indicated, and find the same indicated in ourselves, and that we will stick to it and enlarge upon it through These States."[26] As annoyed as Emerson might have been with the liberties Whitman had taken with his letter (once again), he could not but silently approve of the literary manifesto it had inspired. To respond publicly, of course, would have been out of the question because the poet's statement, like Melville's exuberant praise of Hawthorne six years earlier, had recognized Emerson as one of the geniuses of the American Renaissance. As John P. Quincy recalled, Emerson was troubled by having his sentence isolated from the text of his letter and "so emblazoned." But after expressing his annoyance, he loaned Quincy the book, "saying that the inside was worthy [of] attention even though it came from one capable of so misusing the cover."[27]

In 1859 Emerson confided to his journal: "I have been writing & speaking what were once called novelties, for twenty five or thirty years, & have not now one disciple. Why? Not that what I said was not true; not that it has not found intelligent receivers but because it did not go from any wish in me to bring men to me, but to themselves. . . . What could I do, if they came to me? they would interrupt & encumber me. This is my boast that I have no school & no follower. I should account it a measure of the impurity of insight, if it did not create independence" (*JMN*, 14:258). We can be fairly sure that Emerson suspected that he had brought

Whitman to himself, especially after the 1856 edition had reached Concord. However, he wanted no disciple as such, no one taking his name into keeping and clamoring about the master's deeds instead of celebrating his own character. Hence Emerson's silent approval of Whitman's second book.

Whitman said almost the same thing about disciples in an essay in the *Boston Literary World*, in an 1880 issue devoted to the celebration of Emerson's birthday. "The best part of Emersonianism is, it breeds the giant that destroys itself. Who wants to be any man's mere follower? lurks behind every page. No teacher ever taught, that has so provided for his pupil's setting up independently—no truer evolutionist" (*PW*, 2:517–18). The statement has been taken generally as Whitman's continued ploy of denying the Emerson influence, but I think it demonstrates that he understood the Emerson doctrine, the lesson of self-reliance, perfectly. Otherwise, he could not have issued the poems of 1855 and 1856. The "Master" letter therefore stemmed more from his euphoria and the fact that he felt obligated to Emerson for his letter of 21 July 1855. But the Emerson letter also gave Whitman the courage to go beyond Emersonianism, beyond what Whitman called in his open letter the "neuter gender" of literature. And this intent in the 1856 edition manifested itself in the sexual poems.

Despite the uproar caused by the publication of the second *Leaves of Grass*, this edition has been relatively overlooked by critics of the poet's life and work.[28] Yet some of Whitman's finest poems took their first form in the small 16 mo volume of 384 pages. It was also the first time Whitman attempted to give titles to his works. Most of them, however, were verbose and awkward. "Song of the Answerer," for example, first appeared as "Poem of The Singers, and of The Words of Poems." "Respondez!" began in 1856 with the title "Proposition of Nakedness." He did hardly better with the 1855 (untitled) poem, "A Song for Occupations"; this reappeared in 1856 as "Poem of The Daily Work of The Workmen and Workwomen of These States." With most of the titles, "Poem of" became "Song of" by the time of the 1881 Osgood edition.

It should also be noted that Whitman included in his two appendixes, called "Leaves-Droppings," along with the Emerson letter, two reviews that were highly critical of the 1855 volume. Of course, these were among many complimentary opinions. Under the heading "Opinions, 1855–6," he reprinted extracts from eight reviews. The fifth, "From the American Phrenological Journal: An English and American Poet," was a reprinting of one of the three anonymous reviews that the poet had published in 1855. He also used the one he had written for the Brooklyn *Daily Times*, "Leaves of Grass: A Volume of Poems Just Published." A third, from the *Christian Spiritualist* and not by Whitman, reinforced the Emerson letter by placing the poet on the same "upper mind-sphere of the age" as Emerson. "We can not take leave of this remarkable volume," the review concluded, "without advising our friends, who are not too delicately nerved, to study the work as a sign of the times." A review from the English *Critic*, however, saw the matter differently. Supercilious and anti-American, the editors wrote: "We had ceased, we imagined, to be surprised at anything that America could produce. We had become stoically indifferent to her Woolly Horses, her Mermaids, her Sea Serpents, her Barnums, and her Fanny Ferns; but the last monstrous importation from Brooklyn, New York, has scattered our indifference to the winds." The review also ridiculed the steel engraving of the poet (the same that had been used in the 1855 *Leaves*), noting that his "damaged" hat, along with the rest of his ("hard democrat") costume, presented a man who "scorns the delicate arts of civilization." They thought Whitman "as unacquainted with art, as a hog is with mathematics." Finally, the review scolded Emerson for confusing generosity with justice in his appraisal of the 1855 volume.

One can think of no other author who included negative reviews among the "puffs" now relegated to dust-jacket copy. In another critique, from the Boston *Intelligencer*, the editors declared that Whitman "should be kicked from all decent society as below the level of the brute. There is neither wit nor method in his disjointed babbling, and it seems to us he must be some escaped lunatic, raving in pitiable delirium." Whitman knew what he was about, however. He wanted to attract attention to his book (a volume whose first edition had sold fewer than ten copies [*WWC*, 3:116]) and so attempted to generate an aura of controversy around it. (He did so again in 1876 with his anonymous essay in the *West Jersey Press*.)[29] As Gay Wilson Allen writes in his discussion of the 1856 edition, "Much sex imagery is to be found in the first edition . . . but beginning with the second edition it [was] now to be a program, a 'cause,' a campaign against both asceticism and puritanism."[30]

Emboldened by the Emerson letter, Whitman reintroduced his theory of sex, a theme that had begun with "Song of Myself" and "I Sing the Body Electric" in 1855. It would culminate and assume its final form with the "Enfans d'Adam" poems of 1860 (called "Children of Adam" in 1867 and thereafter). Certainly, "Unfolded out of the Folds" ("Poem of Women" in 1856)—even though it never belonged to the Adam poems—celebrates the sex act, if only from the eugenic point of view: "Unfolded out of the strong and arrogant woman I love, only thence can appear the strong and arrogant man I love . . . / First the man is shaped in the woman, he can then be shaped in himself." What is shaped, of course, is Character or identity; it subsequently becomes suppressed by society until the man comes to himself.

"A Woman Waits for Me" ("Poem of Procreation" in 1856) is more direct, in its assertion that "all were lacking, if sex were lacking." The poet promises (in a line later dropped) to "fetch bully breeds of children yet!" Indeed, as the sexual version of representation (of "what I assume you shall assume"), the poem speaks of draining "pent-up rivers" of identity across the land. This was bold and shocking language for 1856, but Whitman went even further in "Spontaneous Me." Called "Bunch Poem" in 1856 (a reference to the seminal seed), the poem celebrates "love-thoughts, love-juice, love-odor, love-yielding,"[31] and so on—prompting such responses as E. P. Whipple's observation to Emerson that the author of *Leaves of Grass* "had every leaf but the fig leaf" (*JMN*, 14:74).

"There should not be infidelism about sex, but perfect faith," Whitman had said to Emerson in the open letter. He viewed sexuality as the central aspect of any person's identity or Character, including his own. Notwithstanding Emerson's public disapproval of the poet's "too frequent mention of the organ of generation," he may have inwardly applauded Whitman's treatment of the subject. Joel Porte, for example, sees Emerson as using the physiology of things as the central structure of the lectures that formed the essays in *The Conduct of Life* (1860). "Here was Emerson's fundamental question," he writes. "How could life be *conducted* without the unimpeded circulation of vital energies? Which was more *natural*, control or release?"[32] Whitman's program reflected the Emersonian idea of Character, expressed now in bolder terms. Emerson's interest in Whitman might have flagged after 1860, but it was acute during the period between the second and third editions. In 1859 he sent the poet a complimentary copy of *The Conduct of Life* (*JMN*, 14:367). And when Whitman came to Boston in the winter and spring of 1860 to see his third edition through the press, Emerson was one of the first to visit him. He took the initiative as he had in 1855, for he was probably curious to see how Whitman's "cause" had grown.

The years that passed between the second and third editions proved to be the most fruitful period of the poet's life. At first he intended to add only sixty-eight poems to his new edition, to make a round hundred, but the Thayer and Eldridge edition contained 146 new pieces as well as the thirty-two of 1856.[33] Just when Whitman found the time for this poetic unfolding is hard to say; for he also worked as editor of the Brooklyn *Daily Times* between 1 May 1857 and 26 June 1859. As in his earlier days as a journalist, he covered a wide range of topics, writing over two hundred editorials on subjects from the legalization of prostitution to the use of the death penalty (two issues he supported). But the routine of editing a daily newspaper must also have stimulated his progress in working out his sexual theme, which took its final form, more or less, in the 1860 "Enfans d'Adam" poems. A number of his editorials, for instance, took up subjects that were considered too delicate by most of his colleagues of the fourth estate. On one occasion he went so far as to suggest that women who did not marry (because of ugliness) need not necessarily remain ignorant of the pleasures of sexual intercourse. Unmarried men, he thought naively, could content themselves with "the counteracting resources of bodily and mental exertion, against which the affections can make but little head." But with women it was different: "*They* can't always be resorting to any of *our* thousand and one safety-valves to superfluous excitement. Are crochet, or crossed letters [crossword puzzles], or Sunday schools, so entirely engrossing as to drown forever the reproaches of Nature, that will make herself heard? . . . They see others happy all around them. It is hard to fast when so many are feasting" (*SIT*, pp. 29, 120–22).

This editorial of 22 June 1859 must have shocked Brooklynites as much as "A Woman Waits for Me" and "Spontaneous Me" had shocked many readers of the 1856 edition. And it probably cost Whitman his job on the *Times*, just as its poetic translation in the 1860 poems cost him his clerkship in the Bureau of Indian Affairs five years later. Nevertheless, the public response from local church and civic leaders did not deter him from adding the twelve new poems that constituted the "Enfans d'Adam" section of his new edition. For the poet was persistent in advancing his theme that the sex act represented human catharsis or rebirth. "After the child is born of woman," he had already announced in "I Sing the Body Electric" of 1855, "man is born of woman." In other words, it is through the sex experience, not by suppression of it, that man as a child of Adam finds his way back to the Garden of Eden.[34]

There were many new titles (some final) given to the old poems in the 1860 edition. Whitman abandoned the titles he had given to the sexual pieces in the 1856 edition, assigning them numbers instead. But like the book as a whole, the Adam poems were organized on a thematic plan. The opening piece ("To the Garden the World") introduces the grown child of Adam awakening in the garden of the world, "Curious, here behold[ing] my resurrection, after slumber." The Adamic figure awakens to his own sexuality. Like "the caresser of life" in "Song of Myself," he becomes aware of "potent mates, daughters, sons, preluding." As the child of Adam and nature he feels his limbs quiver in anticipation of his rejuvenation through the sex act.

In no. 2 ("From Pent-Up Aching Rivers") he sings the "phallus" with the realization that he were "nothing" without it. The

New Eden figure celebrates himself through the sexual act and in doing so "strikes up" for the New World: "Singing the song of procreation, / Singing the need of superb children, and therein superb grown people." Taken out of context, several lines seem too blunt even today for a public reading. But Whitman's intention, quite clearly, was to sing "the true song of the Soul" by focusing upon the aspect without which change and growth would cease. It was the Platonic version of the "body correlative attracting," and it possessed not only man but all of nature: "Renascent with grossest Nature, or among animals." Thoreau, after reading the 1856 edition (which Whitman had presented to him), thought that the poet did "not celebrate love at all [but that it was] as if the beasts had spoke."[35] Since that pronouncement, critics have generally viewed the poems as hedonistic—love poems only in the sense that Whitman expresses love for the senses. But "Enfans d'Adam" merely expands the theme of endless evolution that runs through the whole of *Leaves of Grass*. Earlier, in section 32 of "Song of Myself," Whitman had hinted that the act of sexual intercourse had come down to man from the animals: "They bring me tokens of myself, they evince them plainly in their possession."

The next three poems in the series were slight revisions of "I Sing the Body Electric," "A Woman Waits for Me," and "Spontaneous Me"; and they continued the theme of procreation and its formation and release of character. The poet may well have been celebrating sex without love, for nos. 6 through 9 concentrate on "libidinous joys only." In the last ("Once I Pass'd through a Populous City"), the poet makes love to a woman "casually met." Yet the assignation is not necessarily without true affection; instead, it is love during a "native" or spontaneous moment. In other words, it is meant to be by some higher law. To resist this force ("the body correlative") is to deny the functions of nature and the realization of one's own identity. No. 10 ("Facing West from California's Shores") is only vaguely connected with the procreation and liberation theme. The poet stands at the bow, as it were, of the New World and longs for his passage "home," to Adam's home. In nos. 11 and 12 ("In the New Garden" and "Ages and Ages, Returning at Intervals"), it is clear that the New

Garden lies in the American cities and the West. The Garden will
be the scene of the future ("You, born years, centuries after me, I
seek"). Each age in America, beginning with his own, Whitman
celebrates in songs of sex. The future is fixed and certain, and
there is no use denying the phallic aspect of its evolution.

Accordingly, "Enfans d'Adam" closes with a warning not to
resist the "sting" of sex, for its purpose is as worthy of notice as
the earth's gravitation. "Does not all matter, aching, attract all
matter?" he asks in no. 14 ("I Am He That Aches"). "So the body
of me to all I meet, or that I know." In the closing line of no. 15 he
urges: "Be not afraid of my body." These poems were crucial to
the thematic integrity of Whitman's book, for they reinforced the
theme of Body and Soul. Without them, he believed, the book
would have been as effective as a man without his virility. "I
might just as well have cut everything out—the full scheme
would no longer exist—it would have been violated in its most
sensitive spot" (*WWC*, 1:51). Moreover, sex was as important as
birth and death in the amelioration of mankind toward the "Elder
Brother." It was part of the cycle that would eventually take
Whitman on what he would too consciously call a "passage to
more than India!"[36] In spite of the public reaction to his "courage
of *treatment*," the poet grew stronger in his conviction that these
songs played a major role in *Leaves of Grass*. In fact, by the time
of the Osgood edition, when he finally found the structure that
satisfied him, he had placed the "Children of Adam" pieces
prominently after his first and greatest poem, "Song of Myself."

Whitman arrived in Boston on 15 March 1860 to supervise the
printing of his third edition. Two days later Emerson visited him
in the offices of Thayer and Eldridge. Evidently, the publishers
had consulted Emerson about the forthcoming edition, and he
may well have seen the manuscript before his visit. Otherwise, it
is difficult to understand why he urged Whitman to leave out the
"Enfans d'Adam" poems. Twenty years later Whitman recalled
his confrontation with Emerson on Boston Common, which may
have taken place on 17 March. "During those two hours," he
wrote, "he was the talker and I the listener. It was an argument-

statement, reconnoitring, review, attack, and pressing home . . . of all that could be said against that part (and the main part) in the construction of my poems, 'Children of Adam.' " He continued to say that Emerson's argument was "unanswerable" and that Emerson finally asked for a response. Whitman answered, "Only that while I can't answer them at all, I feel more settled than ever to adhere to my own theory and exemplify it" (*PW,* 1:281–82).

Later Whitman clarified the nature of Emerson's argument, insisting that it had nothing to do with the morality expressed in the Adam poems. "Always understand, Mr. Whitman," Emerson was quoted, "that my idea is not that there is evil in the book: my idea is that by taking certain things out of the book you are likely to be instrumental in removing some evil out of people" (*WWC,* 3:453). According to Whitman, he also thought that *Leaves of Grass* would be denounced as part of the free-love movement, thereby preventing the book from enjoying a healthy sale: "He wanted my book to sell—thought I had given it no chance to be popularly seen, apprehended: thought that if I cut out the bits here and there that offended the censors I might leave a book that would go through editions—perhaps many editions." During their conversation, Whitman asked Emerson: "You think that if I cut the book there would be a book left?" When Emerson answered affirmatively, he then asked: "But would there be as good a book left?" Whitman remembered the grave look on Emerson's face: "This seemed to disturb him just a bit. Then he smiled at me and said: 'I did not say as good a book—I said a good book'" (*WWC,* 3:439).

Emerson's position, Whitman insisted to Traubel on at least two other occasions, had been misunderstood: "He offered absolutely no spiritual arguments against the book exactly as it stood. . . . Emerson didn't say anything in the Leaves was bad: no: he only said people would insist on thinking some things bad" (*WWC,* 1:50; 3:321). Of course, we have only Whitman's account of the famous conversation; Emerson left no record of the meeting in either his journals or letters. And the critic, trying to be objective, naturally suspects that Whitman's recollections tended to be self-serving. Yet the descriptions appear to fit the pattern of

Emerson's behavior in controversial matters. Throughout his life, he seldom forced upon his auditors what he knew would be completely untenable. For example, his letter to President Van Buren in 1838 protesting the expulsion of the Cherokee nation from Georgia is considerably toned down from the fiery draft in his journal. Later that year he also agreed to minor changes in the printing of his Divinity School Address.[37] In his biography of Emerson, James Elliot Cabot described his friend as having "a characteristic slowness to take sides."[38] Emerson seldom argued; instead, he said what he had to, never going beyond the limits of suggestion. Afterwards he was content to let the world think what it would.

It may appear that Whitman in contrast was more daring in his prime, but the difference really lay in the subject matter. Emerson may have been attacked as a Christian heretic for a time, but Whitman was repeatedly dismissed as vulgar and reckless, insanely enveloped in the celebration of sexuality. Furthermore, in the 1830s Emerson was not alone in his religious dissent. But Whitman emerged alone with his "programme" during the heyday of censorship in America, the age of Noah Webster's *Family Bible* and Bowdler's expurgated Shakespeare. America was better prepared for Emerson's theological insights than it was for Whitman's libidinous songs. Emerson must have thought so in 1860 and sought to protect Whitman as well as himself from further ridicule. But the poet was implacable, and Emerson knew his friend would have to pay a high price for his exploration into areas that were taboo. The review of the 1860 *Leaves* in the Boston *Post* probably summed up the reaction Emerson feared the inclusion of the "Children of Adam" pieces would ensure. The editors wrote, "The most charitable conclusion at which we can arrive is that both Whitman's *Leaves* and Emerson's laudation had a common origin in temporary insanity."[39]

The personal relationship between Emerson and Whitman can be said to have ended with the publication of the third edition of *Leaves of Grass*. There may have been further meetings[40]—at least one when Whitman returned to Boston in 1880 to see his book through the press at James Osgood and Company. And Emerson provided the wound dresser with letters of introduction to the secretaries of state and the treasury in 1863. After the war, Emerson was also instrumental in placing "Proud Music of the Storm" in the *Atlantic Monthly*. As two journal entries show, he kept track of Whitman as late as 1876. In fact, the June entry for that year contains directions to Whitman's home in Camden and suggests that Emerson may have intended to visit the poet during his stay in Philadelphia for the centennial celebration.[41] However, he had really done all he could for Whitman before the war. He had inspired the journalist in the 1840s to write "the American Poem," and he had been the first to recognize Whitman as its author a decade later. Furthermore, his letter of 21 July 1855 had stimulated Whitman at the height of his poetic powers, inspiring a burst of literary genius that continued uninterrupted for the next five years. Although Emerson may have doubted the practicality of including the Adam poems in the 1860 edition, he could privately assure Whitman that they belonged to the spirit and theme of *Leaves of Grass*. Later, disciples of the poet complained that Emerson had been neglectful of Whitman after 1855, never publicly repeating his private endorsement of 21 July. But this was not Emerson's way. He served his "disciple" in ways more subtle. And he realized that he could do nothing more for him after 1860. Indeed, by ignoring Whitman's discipleship and by refusing to speak out in the poet's defense, he may have helped Whitman to establish his own literary identity. For unlike Thoreau's literary reputation, which was diminished by its association with Emerson's until the 1920s, Whitman's identity as a major American writer was almost a fact before his death in 1892.

Part Two

5. The Latest Form of Infidelity

When I read the North American Review,
or the London Quarterly, I seem to hear the
snore of the muses, not their waking voice.
Emerson, *JMN*, 7:18

Literary accomplishments, skill in grammar,
logic & rhetoric can never countervail the want
of things that demand voice.
Emerson, *JMN*, 7:308–9

The facts of the Emerson-Whitman relationship put us in a position to see a correspondence of a larger order. That is, their establishment allows us to focus on the "strong poetry" of each writer, Emerson's major works in this chapter and Whitman's in the next. Our examination of Emerson's best work must open, of course, with a continuation of the discussion of *Nature* that concluded Chapter 2. Although it is not Emerson's greatest achievement, it does mark his emergence from the psychological-social cage in which he had paced relentlessly since the early 1820s, perhaps earlier. Jonathan Bishop has told us how Emerson, between his graduation day from Harvard and his ordination as a Unitarian minister in 1829 ("execution day," he called it), was filled with anxiety over the direction in which his life was moving. Vision (seeing, not looking) would become his achievement in *Nature* and many of the lectures and essays, but his eyes were in fact weak during his study at the Harvard Divinity School, forcing him at one point to retreat to St. Augustine, Florida. Bishop conjectures that the malaise was psychosomatic. But weak lungs were a reality (and also a reason for the retreat), the family disease that would remove from his life in the 1830s those he loved most intensely. Indeed, it seems that the labyrinth in which he found himself after 1829 boded his own demise, as he watched one after another of his family succumb to tuberculosis, the cancer of the nineteenth century. "Nothing but the most total revolution in his way of life," Bishop comments, "could save him from the destruction which loomed ahead."[1]

The impending destruction was certainly more psychological than physical, and for his release from a life that led him toward it Emerson needed a persona, a mask, a voice that would allow him the same plethora of options Whitman later claimed in declaring: "I harbor for good or bad, I permit to speak at every hazard, / Nature without check with original energy." As noted in Chapter 2, the sections in *Nature* through "Language" are a direct reflection of the sermons delivered between 1826 and 1836. Emerson's conception of language was paramount to his development because it led him to the discovery of the poetic voice that would be necessary to cross from the world of the Understanding to the world of Reason. "Discipline" also might have been included in Chapter 2, for this fifth section really serves to reinforce the difference between the two realms. Once the two worlds are defined in "Language" and "Discipline," however, Emerson's text can be said to have been presented, its narrative imparted, and its tropes explained. His final chapter "Prospects" has been compared to the "Application" in a puritan sermon, but actually the "Application" consists of the concluding three chapters: "Idealism," "Spirit," and "Prospects." For here the poet in Emerson emerges (if only partially) to express truths too bold and visionary for the former Unitarian minister. Here he begins to anticipate Whitman's concept of original energy. As Stephen Whicher writes: "Where expository prose [of the preacher], tied down to common sense, falters, the freer and more irresponsible speech of the poet can complete thought. And the thought the orphic poet expresses for his creator is the ideal identity of man and God."[2]

Most readers will perhaps agree that this voice is heard more clearly in the lectures and essays, in Emerson's prose-poetry and not in his verse. For in his poems Emerson often tried too hard to convey knowledge instead of meaning. David Porter has observed that the result of the poetry "is a language that is predominately addressed to the mind and concerned more with reporting than with creating meaning." We miss "the element of digression: a linguistic sweep that incorporates the irrelevant, explores for meaning in new relationships, and arranges the permutations that absorb a particular world."[3] Emerson's poetic voice, then, is most powerful in prose, and it is that voice that speaks most effectively in *Nature* and elsewhere. Turning "sermon" into lecture and essay, he sounds the voice of the Central Man that he had hinted at in his treatment of Milton in the 1835 lecture series on "Biography." Now fully matured, this voice animates not only *Nature* but also many of the lectures and essays presented through to the composition of "The Poet" in the early 1840s. Whitman was fortunate to have heard the voice in 1842 before it became exhausted and absorbed by the more public Emerson of *Representative Men*, *English Traits*, and *The Conduct of Life*. With the publication of *Essays: Second Series* in 1844, Emerson had clearly begun to drift from solitude to society. He became more concerned with the context in which the individual must live, no matter how much of an individual he was.

"Turn the eyes upside down, by looking at the landscape through your legs," Emerson writes in the chapter "Idealism," "and how agreeable is the picture, though you have seen it any time these twenty years!" (*CW*, 1:31). This rather boyish hyperbole is probably as much of a personal observation as it is a rhetorical device; for about twenty years earlier, Emerson, at the age of thirteen, began the long process of development that enabled him to view the world as fluid and not fixed. "Crossing a bare common, in snow puddles, at twilight, under a clouded sky, without having in my thoughts any occurrence of special good fortune," he had written in the first chapter of *Nature*, "I have enjoyed a perfect exhilaration" (*CW*, 1:10). The statement leads us to the "transparent eye-ball" passage. But if we forget for the moment this possible account of a mystical experience, the statement becomes even more important as evidence of Emerson's new vision. It suggests that he had found exhilaration in the ordinary matters of life. Nothing external keeps him from feeling good about himself.

He expresses here a solid sense of self-reliance, the result of a twenty-year lesson. In possibly the earliest extant letter, dated 16 April 1813, Emerson recorded for his Aunt Mary a Franklinesque "account of what I do commonly in one day." The young Emerson traces his day from rising "about five minutes before six" to eight o'clock that evening when he retires "to my private devotions, and then close my eyes in sleep, and there ends the toils of the day." In printing part of the letter, James Elliot Cabot remarks: "It must not be supposed, however, that the household, with all its austerities, was a gloomy one." To the contrary, it may indeed have been a gloomy life externally, with only a widowed mother as the mainstay of a family of five boys and one girl (who died that year). And the gloom was no doubt augmented by the competition Emerson faced from his siblings. "I confess," he told his aunt, "I often feel an angry passion start in one corner of my heart when one of my Brothers gets above me, which I think sometimes they do by unfair means."[4] That year he composed his first poem "Fortus," whose namesake single-handedly slays, along with two dragons, thousands of enemy soldiers. The victory brings him a magically guarded ring and an anonymous damsel.[5] The romantic poem suggests the embryonic voice of triumph that, persisting throughout his youth and his days as sermonizer and early lecturer, finally found its first full expression in *Nature*.

In responding to the voice within, Emerson more and more discovered Character: the very style and form of the voice itself. And when he allowed it to speak, it silenced the external world of petty jealousies, austerity, boredom, and even death, especially in the 1830s when he lost those on whom he may have relied for his sense of identity. In writing *Nature*, therefore, it was appropriate that Emerson introduce the Poet in "Idealism" with the hyperbole mentioned above. Looking at the landscape through one's legs, we are told, is merely a mechanical way of seeing nature anew; the image is still static. Real seeing, however, takes place only through the Poet's eyes, because he lives from within: "In a higher manner, the poet communicates the same pleasure [or different angle of vision]. By a few strokes he delineates, as on air, the sun, the mountain, the camp, the city, the hero, the maiden, not different from what we know them, but only lifted from the ground and afloat before the eye." Through the eyes of the Poet, "the refractory world is ductile and flexible; he invests dust and stones with humanity, and makes them the words of Reason" (*CW*, 1:31).

This statement illuminates Emerson's "transparent eye-ball" passage, which Bishop finds silly. For by seeing from within, the observer becomes part of the landscape, or nature, and therefore begins to control its effect on his inner life: "Standing on the bare ground . . . all mean egotism vanishes. I become a transparent eye-ball. I am nothing. I see all. The currents of the Universal Being circulate through me; I am part or particle of God." Nature, or the world of which the speaker is a part, is no longer refractory. In fact, it ceases to exist except as an emblem, as evidence of the speaker's identity. It is interesting that Emerson chose *particle* instead of *parcel* (its substitute after 1856).[6] The words were more or less synonymous even in 1836, yet in its context in *Nature* the first connotes a less significant part of the whole. Perhaps Emerson's reading in science prompted him to use *particle*. Whatever the case, it appears to have been a conscious choice, for its connotation here contrasts sharply with the ecstasy expressed in the "transparent eye-ball" passage. Indeed, the contrast introduces Emerson's concept of self-reliance. For its realization clearly depends upon the voice of the Poet. Only the Poet could seriously utter something so "silly"; only the Poet could announce the divinity of a particle. "Sillier" yet in the nineteenth century was Whitman's account of his mystical experience in section 5 of "Song of Myself," where Body and Soul engage in an encounter that is clearly sexual. Yet Idealism, as Emerson wrote in chapter 6 of *Nature*, keeps the "Olympus of gods" from laughing: "Idealism sees the world in God. It beholds the whole circle of persons and things, of actions and events, of country and religion, not as painfully accumulated atom after atom, act after act, in an aged creeping Past, but as one vast picture, which God paints on the instant eternity, for the contemplation of the soul" (*CW*, 1:36). Thus, for the Poet the particles cohere and embolden him to speak with "original energy."

In the "Limits of Self-Reliance," first preached on 31 July 1831, Emerson warned that man should love God " 'with all thy heart' not with thy neighbor[']s but with thy own." He was complaining about "religion by rote." Taking his text from Proverbs 14:14 ("A good man shall be satisfied from himself"), he said that the "distrust of human reason that cries out so loud upon infidelity, calls its own name; it is based on infidelity. It fears the light." The only limit to self-reliance was man's knowledge that he did not make himself. Otherwise, man could, indeed must, trust his own responses to organized religion. For without this self-trust, he would never perceive "*the origin of self*" (Emerson's italics). Seeing this origin as the doorway to God, he wrote in his sermon: "To reflect—to use & trust your own reason, is to receive truth immediately from God *without any intervention*" (italics mine). The final phrase is canceled in Emerson's manuscript, but by including it in the original draft, he was anticipating his "blasphemy" in the Divinity School Address seven years later. Here Emerson was already straining at his theological leash, straining to declare that the only medium through which man may know God is solitude. ''The only way for a man to become religious is to be so by himself'' (MH).

In the next chapter of *Nature*, ''Spirit,'' he also anticipated his attack upon organized religion by saying, ''When we try to define and describe [God], both language and thought desert us, and we are as helpless as fools and savages.'' Therefore, God could no longer, if ever, be found in the language of organized religion, or scripture, but only ''in the coarse, and, as it were, distant phenomena of matter'' (CW, 1:37). But to experience delight of God in nature, as Emerson does in the ''transparent eye-ball'' passage, is nevertheless difficult within the community. Even the poet in Emerson confesses how society can intimidate him and thus stand between himself and his creator. At the conclusion of ''Spirit'' he asserts that ''even the poet finds something ridiculous in his delight, until he is out of the sight of men'' (CW, 1:39).

It is thus significant that when Emerson brings his poet on stage in ''Prospects,'' he uses the third person. ''I shall therefore conclude this essay,'' he wrote, ''with some traditions of man and nature, which a certain poet sang to me'' (CW, 1:41). Some critics have thought this to be a reference to Bronson Alcott, whose draft of ''Psyche'' Emerson had read and criticized in 1836. But since he found the manuscript ''deficient in variety of thought & illustration,'' it is unlikely that the ''orphic philosopher'' served as a model for the orphic poet (L, 2:5). Rather, the orphic poet is the self or voice Emerson was still trying to bring forth in his writing.[7] In *Nature* the essayist and the poet are not quite one, but they become so in many of the lectures and essays that followed between 1837 and 1842. Here Emerson the poet would act out the ''prospects'' set down at the conclusion of *Nature*. Without hesitation or embarrassment, he would speak boldly now from the premise that ''man is a god in ruins,'' ''a dwarf of himself.'' *Nature*, then, was the last occasion for self-consciousness, the last time, until 1842, that Emerson would require the third person to declare: ''Build, therefore, your own world'' (CW, 1:42, 45). This declaration is spoken by a caricature of Emerson in one of Christopher Pearse Cranch's satirical sketches from *Nature*; yet Cranch erred in fusing the voices of Emerson and the orphic poet. It would be another year, in the American Scholar Address, before Emerson was able to fully liberate himself from society's intimidation. Yet *Nature* provided the catharsis. With it, the lecturer and essayist became the Poet.

———————————

"When I read the North American Review, or the London Quarterly," Emerson confided to his journal in 1838, "I seem to hear the snore of the muses, not their waking voice" (*JMN*, 7:18). There was no sound of Orpheus there, he thought. According to R. A. Yoder, this orphic voice "animates Emerson's prose after *Nature*, during his years of assertion and challenge."[8] Its first full emergence occurs in the American Scholar Address of 1837, where the Whole or Central Man announces the close of America's "day of dependence, [its] long apprenticeship to the learning of other lands." No longer tied to the past, free from the rote effect of books, Emerson now had eyes firmly planted "in his forehead, not in his hindhead" (*CW*, 1:52, 57). The American Scholar, or "single man," plants himself "indomitably on his instincts" and confidently waits for the world to come to him. Holmes's remark about the address aside, the Phi Beta Kappa oration was really Emerson's own intellectual declaration of independence. As he spoke of the "old fable" of One Man, he was speaking of himself as representative of "Man *Thinking*." Like Orpheus, whose songs tamed the beasts of the wilderness, Emerson envisioned an American society not fragmented by details but one in which things were tied together. "Would we be blind?" he asked. "Do we fear lest we should outsee nature and God, and drink truth dry? I look upon the discontent of the literary class as a mere announcement of the fact that they find themselves not in the state of mind of their fathers, and regret the coming state as untried; as a boy dreads the water before he has learned that he can swim" (*CW*, 1:67).

Once again we find, as we did in *Nature*, an analogy harking back to childhood. In 1850 Emerson recalled the fright he had experienced when his father—the man whose Unitarian doctrine he would formally challenge a year later—forced him into the water for a swimming lesson. The Reverend William Emerson, he told his brother, "put me in mortal terror by forcing me into the salt water off some wharf or bathing house, and I still recall the fright with which, after some of this salt experience, I heard his voice one day, (as Adam that of the Lord God in the garden,) summoning us to a new bath, and I vainly endeavouring to hide myself" (*L*, 4:179). In the American Scholar Address, Emerson summoned his countrymen to "a new bath." Like Ahab, who consecrated his harpooners in the name of revenge, this nineteenth-century Orpheus boldly exhorted his listeners toward the same "paste-board mask"—to the brink of self-discovery. "In yourself," he told them, "slumbers the whole of Reason." Yet "young men of the fairest promise . . . are hindered from action by the disgust which the principles on which business is managed inspire, and turn drudges, or die of disgust,—some of them suicides" (*CW*, 1:69).

Emerson's comments remind us of "the bright boys & girls in New England," who, he told Carlyle in 1842, confessed their dislike for trade and "morning calls & evening parties." But at the time of the address, Emerson was probably thinking of Jones Very, the mad poet and tutor of Greek at Harvard who was present for the oration. A year later he wrote in his journal of Very's "peculiar state of mind and his relation to·society" (*J*, 5:98). Society had driven Very to conclude that the self had to become obliterated, purged, in order to bridge the distance between man and God. Nature was just as much a barrier as its more artificial manifestation in society. Very sought identification with Christ, he wanted to become the newborn Christ-ian man.[9] Emerson, on the other hand, sought and extolled the possibility of the individual. "Is it not the chief disgrace in the world," he asked in the American Scholar Address, "not to be an unit;—not to be reckoned one character;—not to yield that peculiar fruit which each man was created to bear?" (*CW*, 1:69). Old models, even the model of Christ, would no longer suffice.

This was more directly the message of the Divinity School Address of 1838. Doubtless, Andrews Norton, who was present for the 1837 address as well, could not have been surprised to hear "the latest form of infidelity" in 1838. For the spirit of the

American Scholar had taken hold almost immediately. The edition of five hundred copies, issued 23 September 1837, sold out in a month, while it took thirteen years to exhaust the first edition of *Nature*. Henry David Thoreau, a graduate of Harvard the day before, went home to Concord and the life of the scholar. James Russell Lowell, a Harvard junior, declared that Emerson had "cut the cable [to British thought] and [given] us a chance at the dangers and glories of blue water."[10] Upon reading the address, Carlyle announced, "and lo, out of the West, comes a clear utterance, clearly recognisable as a *m[an's]* voice, and I *have* a kinsman and a brother" (*CEC*, p. 173). Orpheus was now free of the psychological-social cage of the early 1830s. Full voiced, he was coming full circle back to the half-muted message of 1831, that Unitarianism "fears the light."

In the Divinity School Address, after describing the "refulgent summer" in a passage whose charm is certainly orphic, Emerson quickly advocated transcending the material world to ask "What am I? and What is?" His quest was the origin and identity of man constantly dazzled by the laws of nature. He urged his auditors of 15 July, "Behold these outrunning laws, which our imperfect apprehension can see tend this way and that, but not come full circle" (*CW*, 1:76–77). The idea of *completion* animates the address. Emerson's complaint was that organized religion—Unitarianism, on this occasion—had cut short the human quest for identity by dwelling on "the *person* of Jesus" (Emerson's italics). Although he called Christ a true prophet that day, he was also aware of his shortcomings as a thinker: a lack of humor, a lack of appreciation for natural science and art (*JMN*, 5:72). And since no *man* was perfect in response to his character, worship of one particular example produced stasis in the growth of other individual characters. The Soul, Reason had taught Emerson, "knows no persons. It invites every man to expand to the *full circle* of the universe" (*CW*, 1:82; italics mine).

Joel Porte has observed that the "doctrine" of the Divinity School Address is that the preacher should be a poet in the fashion that Christ had been a poet. Emerson's true preacher, he writes, was "a version of himself, the Christ/Preacher/Poet."[11] Yet this assumption may be in error, for Christ (or the Unitarian conception of Christ) is really the whipping boy in Emerson's address to the Divinity School Class of 1838. According to Unitarian teachings, Christ had encouraged not whole men, but disciples; not individuals who would "expand to the full circle of the universe," but followers who caused the once spontaneous "sallies of admiration and love" for Christ to become "petrified into official titles." Christianity, as a result, had "defrauded" man of the right of "coming into nature." Adherence to its principles required that "you must subordinate your nature to Christ's nature" (CW, 1:82). In other words, Christianity encouraged the outward rather than the inward look.

It is doubtful, therefore, that Emerson identified himself or the ideal preacher with Christ or, for that matter, any messiah. Emerson's role in the Divinity School Address, as in all the lectures and essays between 1836 and 1842, was clearly that of teacher. His sublime tone, the voice of Orpheus, misleads us if we suspect Emerson of seeing himself, however vaguely, as a Christ figure. Whitman may have been so deluded (but only briefly) in the wake of his second edition,[12] but Emerson's purpose, like that of the books he both praised and condemned a year earlier, was only *to inspire*—in this case, to inspire the new graduates of the Harvard Divinity School to throw off the "Cultus" and "to go alone." He urged them to become *new* teachers, so that they might reacquaint men with God firsthand. "I look for the new Teacher," he concluded, "that shall follow so far those shining laws, that he shall see them come full circle" (CW, 1:93). The new teacher would not follow the preacher of Christ's example, like the preacher who had "sorely tempted" Emerson "to go to church no more." In commenting that the snowstorm outside the church was real, "the preacher [inside] merely spectral," Emerson called for teachers of the doctrine that nature in all its flux is man's only reliable spiritual guide.

Porte is correct in arguing that Emerson wished to restore poets to the pulpit. In anticipation of "The Poet," Emerson described this individual as one who "perceives that this homely game of life we play, covers, under what seem foolish details, principles that astonish" (CW, 1:77). Yet the roles of poet and teacher are synonymous for Emerson: neither is useful as the gatherer of disciples but only as the inspirer of *self*-reliance. Emerson's method was to push man toward himself. He was therefore intentionally vague at critical junctures in the address in order to allow his audience to fill in the answers.[13] Convers Francis, a Unitarian minister and member of the Transcendental Club, described Emerson's method of lecturing: "Mr. E. is not a philosopher, so called, not a logic-man, not one whose vocation it is to state processes of argument; he is a *seer* who reports in sweet and significant words what he sees . . . if you see it as he does, you will recognize him for a gifted teacher."[14] If Emerson "preached" any doctrine in the address, it was self-reliance. He urged the young ministers to understand that man's "being is without bound; that, to the good, to the perfect, he is born, low as he now lies in evil and weakness. That which he venerates is still his own, though he has not realized it yet. *He ought*" (*CW*, 1:77). Christianity directed that veneration toward another, the *person* of Christ. But as Quentin Anderson reminds us, "the personal God was one person too many for the soul which sought its authority in an exploration of its own consciousness."[15]

Generally, it has been thought that the main thrust of the Divinity School Address lay in its calling into question the value of miracles as evidence of the divine mission of Christ. This was, of course, Andrews Norton's conclusion a year later in *A Discourse on the Latest Form of Infidelity*. "Nothing is left that can be called Christianity," Norton complained, "if its miraculous character be denied. Its essence is gone; its evidence is annihilated."[16] He was partly correct, but Emerson was not only challenging the validity of past miracles as the source of faith, but also the validity of the argument that Christ's mission was more divine than any other man's. "I do not wonder that there was a Christ," he wrote in his journal; "I wonder that there were not a thousand" (*JMN*, 7:458). In the address he called upon Christ himself as a witness against the rote religion he had created: "He spoke of miracles; for he felt that [every] man's life was a miracle, and all that man doth, and he knew that this *daily miracle* shines, as the man is diviner" (italics mine). But, as Emerson insisted in a rather mocking tone, "The understanding [i.e., the rote religion Christ had fostered in his followers] caught this high chant from the poet's lips, and said in the next age, 'This was Jehovah come down out of heaven. I will kill you, if you say he was a man'" (CW, 1:81). Emerson was well aware by this time that his assault upon Christianity made him a pariah of sorts: that year he stopped attending church regularly and he preached his last sermon on 20 January 1839.

Emerson's place in the front rank of American literature and as prophet of the American Renaissance lies with the addresses and essays he wrote between 1836 and 1842. This is the Emerson we appreciate most, not the Emerson of the 1840s and 1850s who saw nature as no longer penetrable, the Emerson who, after the death of his first son, concluded in "Experience" that the "mid-world is best."[17] With this essay his orphic muse is displaced by the voice of experience: his vision becomes wisdom. This is not to denigrate the later works, but to identify the years in which Emerson's art is totally Transcendental and therefore a precursor to Whitman's best poetry. And that poetry, as we shall see in Chapter 6, is also limited to a five-year span, 1855–60.

After *Nature*, the American Scholar Address, and the Divinity School Address, Emerson's orphic legacy is found in *Essays* (1841) and, in at least one sense, in "The Poet" of *Essays: Second Series*. In order to appreciate the Neoplatonic force of these works, however, it is necessary also to examine an address and two lecture series that Emerson presented between the Divinity School Address and his "connection" with Whitman in 1842.[18]

On 24 July 1838, hardly a week after his Cambridge address, Emerson presented "An Oration Delivered before the Literary Societies of Dartmouth College" (later reprinted as "Literary Ethics"). Thirty-four years later the graduating class of Dartmouth would also invite Walt Whitman to read "As a Strong Bird on Pinions Free." Like Whitman, Emerson continued to advance ideas at Dartmouth that had been introduced in his earlier works, in *Nature* and the American Scholar and Divinity School Addresses. The attempt at Hanover, in fact, was to come full circle. In *Nature* he had said that ethics and religion "may be fitly called, —the practice of ideas" (CW, 1:35). In the American Scholar he had defined the education and duties of the scholar and in the Divinity School Address, the education and duties of the minister. What was more appropriate, therefore, than to use the Dartmouth occasion to describe with less intensity but more latitude the conduct of this Central Man?

Having "reached the middle age of man," Emerson said, he was not less sanguine about the possibilities of this individual, for his divine impulses led "him directly into the holy ground where other men's aspirations only point." Once again, society was castigated for perverting "the image of this great duty," but he still saw nothing but hope. Through the biographies of such men as Milton, Shakespeare, and Plato, history had demonstrated that "the power of character" was undeniable in healthy minds, unapproachable by the mediocrity of society (CW, 1:99, 100, 102). Although "Literary Ethics" was more of a reiteration than an expansion of previous themes, Emerson drove home more directly the need for solitude (to be embraced "as a bride") and independence of action. He warned: "Do not go into solitude only that you may presently come to the public. Such solitude denies itself" (CW, 1:109). In other words, street dwelling defrauds the individual of his Neoplatonic vision. Of course, Emerson meant independence of spirit and not necessarily isolation of place. As he would say in "Self-Reliance," mechanical isolation left out the elevation of the Soul. Thus he told the Dartmouth boys, "The youth, intoxicated with his admiration of a hero, fails to see, that it is only a projection of his own soul, which he admires" (CW, 2:41; 1:103). Out of repudiation of the false in society, he finds the hero in his own character.

In "Human Life," Emerson's third lecture series under his own management, we find the lecturer moving even more relentlessly toward the apex of his orphic philosophy. Indeed, in such overlooked lectures as "The Doctrine of the Soul," "Home," "The School," "Genius," and "The Protest," there is an appeal equal in sublimity if not eloquence to the American Scholar and the Divinity School Addresses. The sustained power of his thought may lie in the occasion. Emerson was on home ground with his radicalism for the first time. He was in control, even to the point of distributing many of the tickets to his own lectures. He was also beyond the stage of having to worry about shocking his audience. Andrews Norton had already branded him as a heretic in the *Daily Advertiser*, and Emerson now saw himself solidly in the tradition of Martin Luther and George Fox, two religious rebels he had celebrated in his 1835 series on biography. Shortly before giving his first lecture on "Human Life" in Boston on 5 December 1838, he wrote in his journal: "The same thing has happened so many times over, (that is, with the appearance of every original observer) that if people were not very ignorant of literary history they would be struck with the exact coincidence." And he warned his adversaries privately, "And whilst I see this[,] that you must have been shocked & must cry out at what I have said[,] I see too that we cannot easily be reconciled[;] for I have a great deal more to say that will shock you out of all patience" (*JMN*, 7:105).

It might be said that Emerson approached this lecture series with almost the same zeal and self-confidence that Whitman felt as he prepared his 1856 edition. Both men believed they were speaking boldly and originally. Surely it is not often that we find Emerson describing himself as an "original observer." Accordingly, he set out in "Doctrine of the Soul" to consider "the great question of primary philosophy, Who lives? What is life?" (*EL*, 3:5). In printing the lecture, the editors of *The Early Lectures* point out that a large part of it was revised for "The Over-Soul" (*Essays: First Series*); yet an equal amount of its thesis also went into "Self-Reliance" (*Essays: First Series*). For 1838 marked the zenith of Emerson's confidence in his direct relation to God.

"There is a great responsible Thinker and Actor moving wherever moves a man," Emerson observed (*EL*, 3:7). In "Self-Reliance" he would write that man "is attended by a visible escort of angels" (*CW*, 2:35). When the individual surrendered himself to his "Unconscious Nature," he achieved a "just publication" of his Soul: "From within or from behind [he wrote in "Doctrine" and later in "The Over-Soul"] I may say a light shines through us upon things and makes us aware that we are nothing but the Light is all" (*EL*, 3:16, 20). Without this force, "we are beasts or boxes at once." Society and Unitarianism, he implied, were nothing but "busy Interference" with the Soul's attempt to shine through the trivia of life and achieve its singular effect on Character. In anticipation of "The Over-Soul," he urged: "If we will not interfere with our thought but will act entirely or see how the thing stands in God we know the particular thing and every thing and every man. For the Maker of all things and all persons stands behind us and casts his dread omniscience through us over things" (*EL*, 3:17). Like Whitman's message in the first three editions of his book, the shibboleth is *freedom* in "Doctrine of the Soul."

In "Home," first delivered at the Masonic temple on 12 December 1838, Emerson established the central metaphor for his course and one of the themes for "Self-Reliance": that man is "at home" with himself whenever he is following the urgings of his Soul. "He is at home in markets, in senates, in battles, at home with Man, at home with God, and learns to look at sea and land, at nations and globes as the moveables and furniture of the City of God" (*EL*, 3:29). Unfortunately, part of this lecture is lost, but from working notes in Emerson's journal we have a fair idea of its content. He would voice a similar theme in "Domestic Life" (a lecture, incidentally, that Whitman may have heard in New York City on 28 February 1843): "Will not man one day open his eyes and see how dear he is to the soul of Nature,—how near it is to him? Will he not see, through all he miscalls accident, that Law prevails for ever and ever; that his private being is a part of it; that its home is in his own unsounded heart" (*W*, 7:132).

It was this "Homesickness of the Soul," he said in "Home," that man had to accept and satisfy (*EL*, 3:30). The message is somewhat muted in "Domestic Life," where Emerson is more concerned with living in *this world*; "Home," on the other hand, is decidedly Neoplatonic. "Genius" (9 January 1839) expresses the thought that the essence of any man's genius is spontaneity: "There is no halfness about genius" (*EL*, 3:70). It responds instinctively to its spiritual whole because it must. Or, as he wrote in his journal for 1839, "A man must consider what a rich realm he abdicates when he becomes a conformist" (*JMN*, 7:179). Conformity keeps man from knowing himself. Under the influence of society, a man finds himself abroad from himself and lost in the streets of his mind.

In "Experience" Emerson would feel compelled to ask the question, "Where do we find ourselves?" There man has to ask for further directions; he is no longer sure of the way home. This essay marks the fading point in Emerson's Neoplatonic vision. But in the series "Human Life" he still thought that he knew his way home, that the shadow of the Soul was still visible in nature. Accordingly, he continued to shock his auditors "out of all patience" in "The School" (delivered only once, on 19 December 1838). He asked if the teaching of Christ was less effective now than when it was first taught. The answer, of course, was clearly affirmative, for "the things we now esteem fixed shall one by one detach themselves like ripe fruit, from our experience." The Soul, he said, is always moving forward, "leaving worlds always behind her. She has no dates nor rites nor persons nor specialities nor men. The soul knows only the soul" (*EL*, 3:39). He would say almost the same thing in "The Over-Soul"; then and now Emerson insisted that no middle man—such as Christ, who was stationary in history—was acceptable. Only "high primary instincts" could provide spiritual insights.

Emerson's vision was confidently sublime in "Human Life." "The Protest" (16 January 1839) condemned society as evidence of the Fall of Man. "Society loves the past; society desponds; sneers; serves; sits; it talks from the memory or from the senses and not from the soul." And such old age had led to the ossification of the Soul: "The fat in the brain; this degeneracy; is the Fall of Man." He maintained that man had to live from impulse instead of from memory. Only then, he concluded in a rather clear echo of Carlyle's *Sartor Resartus* (whose first American publication he had arranged in 1836), can the individual find his own path: "Losing his dread of society which kept him dumb and paralytic, he begins to work according to his faculty. He has done protesting: now he begins to affirm" (*EL*, 3:89, 100).

I have not touched upon all of the lectures in "Human Life" because the doctrine of the Soul runs relentlessly through the series, being applied to the various aspects of life. Emerson summed up the endeavor in "Demonology," the final lecture (20 February 1839):

> We have attempted *in the first lecture* to read a line of the
> Doctrine of the Soul . . . ; *in the next*, to describe the circum-
> stances and to deduce the law of Home . . . ; *then*, to sketch
> its School or its teachings by the Instincts . . . ; *then* in the
> two following lectures ["Love" and "Genius"] to sketch the
> natural history of Affection, and of Intellect; *then*, to describe
> [in "The Protest"] the position of antagonism in which each
> man finds himself . . . ; *then*, to consider [in "Tragedy"]
> the shades of life, the value and place of the tragic element;
> *then*, the nature of the Comic; *then*, the grand element of
> Virtue [in "The Comic" and "Duty," respectively]; and,
> *tonight*, the alleged exception to the law. [*EL*, 3:170–71]

The alleged exception to the law of the Soul, Emerson declared
in "Demonology," was found in dreams, omens, coincidence,
luck, phrenology, animal magnetism, and so on. Such "gypsy"
principles were not exceptions at all, only exaggerations that
misled man to think that nature chose favorites in revealing its
emblematic power. Indeed, they were as misleading as the Christian miracles he had criticized in the Divinity School Address. For
the man who took his nature for granted, who overlooked its
spiritual significance, such exceptions made him reconsider. Yet
the inquiry was hopelessly based on low principles. Animal magnetism, for example, he said, only peeps at the Soul. The fallacy
in supposing it, or another exception, to be a wonder at the
expense of the rest of nature was that it confined man to the
particular and denied him the knowledge of the general miracle
of his being. "The whole world is an omen and a sign," Emerson
concluded. "Why look so wistfully in a corner?" (*EL*, 3:170). Like
Christian miracles, demonology severely limited the Neoplatonic
vision.

During the winter of 1839–40, Emerson postponed work on his
book of essays to deliver ten lectures under the title of "The Present Age." Actually, the postponement enhanced the richness of
his *Essays*; for as he continued the Neoplatonic ascent that would
culminate in the book, he discovered and articulated concepts

that account for the originality and grace of such essays as "Self-Reliance," "Spiritual Laws," and "The Over-Soul." Grateful, as he told Carlyle, to learn from the success of "Human Life" that his "blasphemy" could still draw an audience (*CEC*, p. 217), Emerson continued to allow the orphic poet to investigate the usefulness of organized religion in the present age. The editors of *The Early Lectures* claim a more coherent theme for this series over that of the preceding one, but one has to doubt the claim as he wades through the first five lectures. There he finds Emerson still groping for conclusions about "the character, resources, & tendencies of the Present Age" (*EL*, 3:177).

In "Introductory" (4 December 1839) Emerson repeated his attack on society (which, he said, should exist for the individual), while also uttering vague epithets at commerce. If there is anything new, or even newly phrased, in the lecture, it is his advice to "trust the time" (*EL*, 3:200). The next two lectures on "Literature" (11 and 18 December) were equally labyrinthine in their attempts to find a thesis. Clearly, Emerson was stalled in his quest to articulate the spiritual value of the present age in a new way. His argument found ballast only when he renewed his attack on the church; and in "Literature" he touched only briefly on that theme by suggesting that the Bible was valuable as the source of inspiration but not as evidence of the divinity of Christ's mission.[19] "Politics" and "Private Life" (1 and 8 January 1840) did little to add coherence to the series as it stood thus far. The first lecture essentially repeated the theme of "Introductory" (that institutions are not superior to the citizen), and the other, although only fragments of it remain, probably formed the basis of "Friendship" in *Essays* (1841). Generally, the first half of the series bore out the fear that Emerson expressed on 4 November 1839 in a letter to Elizabeth Hoar: "I have advertised my new Course & shall call it the Present Age, but alas it is still the Future Age to me" (*L*, 2:231).

The future age became the present age, however, in the seventh lecture, called "Religion" (22 January). Here Emerson's remarks lived up to the title of his series as he announced the Transcendental position: "We have found out the mythical character of Christianity, and we are adopting a new manner of speech in regard to it" (*EL*, 3:274). Having warmed to his topic in "Reforms," delivered the preceding week, Emerson argued that first-century Christians, were they to be incarnated in the nineteenth century, "would never recognize their own work; the formal church has overlaid the real, and the creeds of the nations traverse and caricature [the original] perceptions" (*EL*, 3:273). Christ had allowed his own character to flower; but it was now enshrined in "a private and personal history," whereas his religious sentiment should have been recognized as representative of all individuals. Nevertheless, Emerson envisioned the advent of a new awareness. For the young men and women of New England now believed that "Character is the true Theocracy" (*EL*, 3:276).

The failure of Christianity, he believed, was its dependence on either the past or the future. It relied upon the past for evidence of revelation in the form of material miracles. Yet to allow a material miracle to abut a spiritual law in the present—that of the infinitude of the individual—was "intrinsically absurd and impossible." In every particular example in which Christianity looked to the past, he said, recalling the image used in the "Idealism" section of *Nature*, it was like "putting every fact as it were upside down" (*EL*, 3:278). To look to the future was equally fruitless and demoralizing. In other words, the concept of coming into God's kingdom after death denied man access to his soul, to his spiritual vision in the present. The disciples had erroneously taught the doctrine of "duration," the idea that divinity awaited the passing of the flesh; they had separated "duration from the moral element" in man in order to teach the immortality of the Soul. And in doing so they had effected the Fall of Man: "For the soul is true to itself, and the man in whom it is shed abroad, cannot wander from the present which is infinitude to a future which would be finite" (*EL*, 3:277). The argument had been used in "The Protest" and would become more lucid in "The Over-Soul." The moment we look to scripture for answers about the future, we confess our sin. For God has no answer "in words" to such a question. Rather, it is in the nature of man "that a veil shuts down on the facts of to-morrow: for the soul will not have us read any other cipher than that of cause and effect. By this veil [of nature] which curtains events, it instructs the children of men to live in to-day" (*CW*, 2:168). The Soul, then, has nothing to do with mortality, for the very concept implies a limitation of our vision in the present, which is the eternal.

The concept of the present age, as developed in *Nature* and publicized in "The Over-Soul," is surprisingly like Whitman's doctrine of the inseparability of the Body and Soul. Both spoke "from within the veil" of nature. And despite Emerson's complaint after 1860 that Whitman too often dealt with the physical, both poets at the zenith of their art extolled the doctrine of the Body (or nature) as the visible form of the Soul. "O my brothers, God exists," Emerson had exhorted in "Religion" (and again in "The Over-Soul"). "There is a soul at the centre of nature and over the will of every man so that none of us can wrong the Universe" (*EL*, 3:281). Near the close of "Song of Myself," Whitman exclaimed: "Do you see O my brothers and sisters? / It is not chaos or death. . . . it is form and union and plan. . . . it is eternal life. . . . it is happiness." Or, as he declared earlier in the poem:

> There was never any more inception than there is now,
> Nor any more youth or age than there is now;
> And will never be any more perfection than there is now,
> Nor any more heaven or hell than there is now.[20]

Whereas Whitman's faith enclosed "all worship ancient and modern," Emerson's vision required "a new manner of speech" with regard to Christianity. In anticipation of "Self-Reliance," he said that its dependence on scriptural authority made man timid and apologetic: "He is no longer upright: he dares not say, *I think; I am*; but quotes some saint or sage." Therefore, reliance on this authority instead of the self measured the decline of true religious sentiment; it measured "the withdrawal of the Soul." Emerson concluded in "Religion," "Now man is ashamed before the blade of grass and the blowing rose." For neither made reference to the past or future but existed in God in the present. Christianity was always either remembering or anticipating, and in the process creating "a gulf between the supple soul and its well being" in the present age (*EL*, 3:282–83).

"Religion" expanded the belief touched upon in "The Protest" of the preceding series of lectures (that society "loves the past") by suggesting that the church, the most influential force in society, misled man not only by looking to the past but also to the future for assurances of immortality. He returned to that theme in "Education" (5 February),[21] but not before attacking organized religion again. As with "Demonology," he cited the popularity of phrenology in "Education" as evidence that Christianity had not satisfied the soul of man. Its inadequate breadth worked to subdue the growth of every potentially unique character. In the same manner society had encouraged in the education of its youth a dependence on tradition. And it therefore failed to "call out God in man." Seeing every individual as his own poet, Emerson echoed Sampson Reed's philosophy that the mind is "a most delicate germ" which must be allowed to grow internally.[22] "Let us wait and see," Emerson advised, "what is this new creation, of what new organ the great Spirit had need when it incarnated this new Will. A new Adam in the garden, he is to name all the beasts in the field, all the gods in the sky" (EL, 3:290, 295).

Emerson's theme in "The Present Age" is that man, bred to society, tended to avoid the living order. Religion had encouraged man to avoid living in the present by preserving the facts of yesterday, "that having found a good man a thousand years ago he can embalm the corpse with amomum and spices." Yet it was nevertheless a corpse, and society fed on the same object in its tendency to interfere with the order of the present. It was "a foolish consistency" that violated the order of things in God's mind, he said in "Tendencies," the final lecture in the series (12 February). With such consistency "a great soul has simply nothing to do." The present age might intimidate man with its jagged voyage, but this was "only microscopic criticism." Seen from the distance that only self-reliance could provide, nature's clues became signs, and "the line of a hundred tacks" straightened itself out (EL, 3:304, 310–11).

In his study of Whitman's influence upon the personal epic in America, James E. Miller, Jr., credits Emerson with the idea of history as essentially biography. Quoting from "The Poet," he cites Emerson's statement that Dante's greatness lies in the fact "that he dared to write his autobiography in colossal cipher, or into universality."[23] But the idea for the "colossal cipher" had already been articulated in "The Present Age" with the doctrine of self-reliance. It was appropriate, therefore, that Emerson opened *Essays* (1841) with "History," which argued that "there is properly no history, only biography" (*CW*, 2:6). History had to be read and written in the light that nature is the correlative of the One Mind. The "colossal cipher" was but another name for nature, which reflected the unity of all men with that mind: "I am God in nature, I am a weed by the wall" (*JMN*, 7:362).[24] Published on 21 March, *Essays* is Emerson's own spiritual biography writ large. It is his most personal statement to the world, also the final one in which he "interprets the riddle of Orpheus." As Joseph Slater describes the volume, "The voice that speaks in these pages is that of 'an experimenter . . . an endless seeker with no Past at [his] back,' an enemy of imitation and interference, a scorner of those who quote from saints and sages. . . . It trusts only the flashes which come from within—instinctive, involuntary, and spontaneous" (*CW*, 2:xxiv). Indeed, *Essays* is Emerson's final unadulterated Neoplatonic statement. For after the death of Waldo on 27 January 1842, he is much like the forlorn Orpheus, who, while leading Eurydice back from the depths of Hades, looks back and loses her forever. Unlike the death of Ellen in 1831, this loss deprived him of the ability to find consolation and compensation in the changes of nature. No longer could he honestly say, as he had in "Compensation," that the "death of a dear friend, wife, brother, lover, which seemed nothing but privation, somewhat later assumes the aspect of a guide or genius; for it commonly operates revolutions in our way of life, terminates an epoch of infancy or of youth which was waiting to be closed . . . , [allowing] the formation of new ones more friendly to the growth of character" (*CW*, 2:73). Eight days after the death of his first son, he committed to his journal the question that would become the theme of "Experience": "Does it not seem as if the middle region of our being were the only zone of life & thought?" (*JMN*, 8:200).

His first book of essays culminates the lesson Emerson had begun to learn back in 1832, that the power of Character cannot be stifled by the voice of tradition. That power "ceases in the instant of repose," he declared in "Self-Reliance." "This one fact the world hates, that the soul *becomes*" (*CW*, 2:40). The Soul is forever traveling, and its movement is reflected in the growth of Character. Conjuring up the image from his lecture "Home," he said that the wise man stays at home where life's necessities take him. Any other kind of traveling is a "fool's paradise." If you would know the power of Character, Emerson had written in his journal during the early stages of composition for "Self-Reliance," "see how much you would impoverish the world if you could take clean out of history the life of Milton, of Shakespear, of Plato" (*JMN*, 7:13). Such figures avoided conformity or "travelling" with society and consequently allowed their character or genius to shape and define history.

In "Spiritual Laws" Emerson applied his ideas from "Education" to the problem of organized religion. The concepts of original sin, the origin of evil, predestination, and so forth were "the soul's mumps and measles, and whooping-coughs." This homage to the past was only as permanent on the mind guided by Character as the duration of a childhood disease on the body. Eventually, every man is asked to answer the call of his character: "As in dreams, so in scarcely less fluid events of the world, every man sees himself in colossal, without knowing that it is himself" (*CW*, 2:78, 86). The same idea is developed in "Compensation," that whole men know better than their theology or society. They refuse to gratify the senses at the expense of the demands of Character.

"Love" and "Friendship" are generally considered inferior to the foregoing essays in the volume, probably because Emerson's "reverence for the intellect," as he stated in "Love," made him "unjustly cold to the personal relations" (*CW*, 2:101). However, both pieces continue Emerson's Neoplatonic argument of the One Mind toward which all Character is drawn. "Love" shows the influence of Dante's *Vita Nuova*, which Emerson had first read in 1839 and finally translated (but never published) in 1843.[25] Love begins with "misplaced" satisfaction with the body, just as

Dante is first enamored of Beatrice's physical beauty. Eventually, as the lover accepts the "hint of these visions and suggestions which beauty makes to his mind, [his] soul passes through the body, and falls to admire strokes of character." In his Neoplatonic definition of love, Emerson also anticipates the image in "Circles" by saying that "this dream of love, though beautiful, is only one scene in our play. In the procession of the soul from within outward, it enlarges its circles, like a pebble thrown into a pond." Thus, as the physical objects of love are forever grouping themselves according to higher laws, the love itself, which is "a deification of persons," must become more impersonal in order to achieve its higher flight. Ultimately, the "soul is wholly embodied, and the body is wholly ensouled" (*CW*, 2:106, 108).

If this final line sounds more like Whitman than Emerson, "Friendship" is also suggestive of the New York poet's idea of Calamus, or a platonic, manly love. In fact, we might do well to compare his sequence of the "Children of Adam" and "Calamus" poems with the essays "Love" and "Friendship." In "Children of Adam" the male-female relationship is reduced to the level of sex in order to celebrate spontaneity, as, for example, in "Native Moments." There is something uplifting in this chance consorting with "Nature's darlings." Indeed, "Children of Adam," with its "misplaced" satisfaction, is quite the reverse of Emerson's concept of love; yet both poets eschew the conventional idea of personal love. Like Emerson's use of Dante's "Ladder of Love," Whitman's definition and exemplification of love appear to demand the impersonal. Each approach is ultimately democratic in its "deification of persons." The Transcendental catalyst is found in all of nature. If one may use an oxymoron, "Calamus" and "Friendship" are also intimately impersonal. For Whitman there are many objects of his "manly love." The same freedom abounds in Emerson's "Friendship," in which he calls a friend one with whom we "may think aloud. . . . [We] may deal with him with the simplicity and wholeness, with which one chemical atom meets with another." Both argue for spontaneity in relationships to the degree and fortuitousness of a chemical interaction. The attraction is impersonal, for without the impersonal nature the friend would compromise his separate identity: "Let me be alone to the end of the world, rather than that my friend should over-step by a word or a look his real sympathy. . . . Let him not cease an instant to be himself. The only joy I have in his being mine, is that the *not mine* is *mine*" (*CW*, 2:119, 122). Conventional love, on the other hand, commingles identities and is therefore transitory and quotidian. Although Emerson and Whitman approach the Neoplatonic ideal from different origins, both nevertheless find this higher flight of love in the "simple, separate person."

"Every man alone is sincere," Emerson says in "Friendship." "At the entrance of a second person, hypocrisy begins." This statement provides a natural transition to the next essay, "Pru-dence." For the friend, or "simple, separate person," recognizes three levels of knowledge in "Prudence": (1) the utility of nature, (2) the beauty of nature, and (3) the meaning of nature (*CW*, 2:119, 132). The observer can enjoy the third level only by himself, just as the lover must climb from the personal to the impersonal on the "Ladder of Love." Prudence is but another name for self-reliance. The same can be said for "Heroism," which argues for persistency in the quest for individual character: "All men have wandering impulses, fits and starts of generosity. But when you have chosen your part, abide by it, and do not weakly try to reconcile yourself with the world" (*CW*, 2:153–54).

It is in "The Over-Soul," however, that we find Emerson at the very height of his Neoplatonism in the *Essays*. Here his orphic voice is clear and resonant. Life is measured in each divine im-pulse, which comes in rare moments of faith. As noted earlier, the essay bears a strong resemblance to "Religion." In that lec-ture, which, like "The Over-Soul," is the Neoplatonic center of its series, he saw man "in transition from the worship which enshrined the law in a private and personal history to worship which recognizes the true eternity of the law." In "The Over-Soul" the transition is defined in terms of ceaseless growth: "By every throe of growth, the man expands there where he works, passing, at each pulsation, classes, populations of men. With each divine impulse the mind rends the thin rinds of the visible and finite, and comes out into eternity" (*CW*, 2:163). The ideal man speaks from Character, not from his tongue—from within and not wholly from talents gained in his *public* education.

Throughout the essay Emerson is sublimely optimistic, seeing nothing but an infinite expansion of the soul that responds to itself.

If there is any sign of pessimism in *Essays*, it can be found in "Circles." This is perhaps because "Circles" was the latest of the essays in terms of composition and therefore the closest in time to his loss of the Neoplatonic spirit after 1842. In his study of "The Skeptic" (a poem that Emerson composed in 1842), Carl F. Strauch finds a discrepancy between the inner Emerson of the journals and the outer Emerson of the lectures and essays. "Paradoxically enough, the pessimism [between 1838 and 1842] received unrestrained expression in private verse and prose jottings in the very period when Emerson was establishing his reputation as chief of the Transcendental optimists, author of 'Self-Reliance' and 'The Over-Soul.' " But Strauch concludes that this negativism manifested itself merely as a preparation for his acknowledgment of the problem of evil in *The Conduct of Life* (1860).[26] One might argue that it surfaced earlier, in "Experience," for like the period in Emerson's life during his ministry, this period of Neoplatonism also contained the seeds of the next stage in Emerson's thought.

Strauch's thesis is further clarified by another critic who notes Emerson's awareness of the paradox he presents in "Circles." Emerson calls life a "self-evolving circle . . . [that] rushes on all sides outwards to new and larger circles, and that without end." Yet inherent in this statement is the concept of the unachieved, which has two poles: it is both the "inspirer and condemner of every success."[27] The idea is fully articulated in "Experience" and later works, when Emerson's soul had perhaps wearied of drawing another circle. In "Circles," however, the quest for the unachieved is still the source of optimism. Here Emerson's weariness can still be resisted. What resists this weariness, this blurred vision of the Soul, is the voice of the Poet: "The field cannot be well seen from within the field. The astronomer must have his diameter of the earth's orbit as a base to find the parallax of any star. Therefore, we value the poet" (*CW*, 2:185). "Literary accomplishments, skill in grammar, logic, & rhetoric," he had clearly understood by 1839, "can never countervail the want of things that demand voice. Literature is but a poor trick when it busies itself to make words pass for things" (*JMN*, 7:308–9).

———

Emerson intended thirteen essays for the volume, but proof sheets for the first twelve arrived before he could finish what became "Nature" in *Essays: Second Series*. It was just as well, for "Intellect" and "Art" combined to close the book with a statement about literature that suggested how the truths of the other ten might be perceived. The intellect pieces together the forms of nature, and art reconstructs the form for those too weary to draw another circle. The statements are also penultimate to "The Poet," which combines them to produce a theory of poetry that influenced Whitman and, through him, such twentieth-century poets as Wallace Stevens and William Carlos Williams. The Poet is "the timely man" (originally suggested in "The Present Age") who "dares to write his autobiography in colossal cipher" (*W*, 3:37).

The essay celebrates the process of the orphic voice and in this sense it belongs to Emerson's Neoplatonic period and therefore to *Essays*; it also brings together many of his thoughts on character, genius, art, and religion. Yet there is a strain of pessimism in "The Poet" that seems to bridge the gap between Emerson's two points of view; although the essay celebrates the role of "the timely man," it simultaneously hints at the more pessimistic mood of "Experience." Certainly there is evidence of despair in Emerson's admission, "I look in vain for the poet whom I describe." His description of the scholar and the minister back in 1837 and 1838 had no such sour notes. "The Poet," on the other hand, serves as both "the inspirer and the condemner" of the Neoplatonic dream.

The pessimism is also suggested by Emerson's need for the first time since *Nature* to evoke the third person in order to describe the origin of poetry. Reporting again what "a certain poet" told him, he compares the emergence of poetry to the botanical process in which an agaric produces countless spores. Almost all are subject to the ravishment of time, as are most human acts in history. But one

> atom of seed is thrown into a new place, not subject to the accidents which destroyed its parent two rods off. [Nature] makes a man; and having brought him to ripe age, she will no longer run the risk of losing this wonder at a blow, but she detaches from him a new self, that the kind may be safe from accidents to which the individual is exposed. So when the soul of the poet has come to ripeness of thought, she detaches and sends away from it its poems or songs,—a fearless, sleepless, deathless progeny, which is not exposed *to the accidents of the weary kingdom of time* [italics mine]; a fearless, vivacious offspring, clad with wings (such was the virtue of the soul out of which they came) which carry them fast and far, and infix them irrecoverably into the hearts of men. These wings are the beauty of the poet's soul. The songs, thus flying immortal from their mortal parent, are pursued by clamorous flights of censures, which swarm in far greater numbers and threaten to devour them; but these last are not winged. At the end of a very short leap they fall plump down and rot, having received from the souls out of which they came no beautiful wings. But the melodies of the poet ascend and leap and pierce into the deeps of infinite time. [*W*, 3:23–24]

"So far the bard taught me," Emerson writes, "using his freer speech." Emerson here reminds us of the earthbound poet in Poe's "Israfel," who laments that the flowers of his world "are merely—flowers." And we must ask why Emerson no longer feels capable of this "freer speech." The answer, I think, is that he now believes, in his own case, at least, that such a voice is too lofty in the face of life's disappointments. Therefore the only way in which he can render this emphatically Romantic description of the origin of poetry is to find a seraph like Poe's, "whose heart-strings are a lute."

The Emerson of 1843–44 (when "The Poet" was finished) was simply too weary of the world to invoke the orphic voice. Hence, we have in the essay a duality of belief: both a celebration and a lament of the possibility of the poetic vision. This is due, of course, to the fact that the essay was begun during the height of his Neoplatonism and concluded in the wake of his son's death. There is a feeling, too, of exhaustion at the end of "The Poet," not merely when Emerson hints that he has looked in vain for the poet he describes, but also in the exhortation to this individual to "doubt not . . . but persist. . . . Stand there, balked and dumb, stuttering and stammering, hissed and hooted" (W, 3:40). It is as if the poet in Emerson is now "balked and dumb, stuttering and stammering," exposed again "to the accidents of the weary kingdom of time." He can no longer write with abandon of the possibilities of transcendence either in himself or in others. On the other hand, in "Nature and the Powers of the Poet" (the lecture Whitman heard in 1842), there is absolutely no doubt in the speaker's words about the possibility of the poet he describes: "To doubt that the poet will yet appear is to doubt of day and night" (EL, 3:363).

Of course, it is just as much of an oversimplification to say that Waldo's death changed Emerson as it is to suggest that Ellen's death effected an equally dramatic change back in 1832. Both were merely catalysts for changes that would have occurred more gradually. As noted in the discussion of "Circles," Emerson was already drifting toward the philosophy articulated in "Experience" and later essays. The pessimism was confined to the journals (just as his skepticism about Unitarianism was in the 1820s), but from them it is clear what was coming. In 1841 he thought it the worst feature of our biography that we are condemned to "a sort of double consciousness, that the two lives of the Understanding & of the Soul . . . never meet & criticize each other, but one prevails now all buzz & din, & the other prevails then, all infinitude & paradise, and with the progress of life the two discover no greater disposition to reconcile themselves" (JMN, 8:10).

In "The Poet" Emerson also confessed that "adequate expression" of these moments of the Soul was rare: "There is some obstruction or some excess of phlegm in our constitution, which does not suffer them [the phenomena of nature] to yield the due effect. Too feeble fall the impressions of nature on us to make us artists" (*W*, 3:6). The Poet was an individual without this speech impediment, but he was also perhaps beyond solid belief for Emerson in 1843–44. This may explain why he never sustained a permanent belief in many he found so promising—Alcott, Thoreau, Fuller, Ellery Channing, Cranch, and Newcomb. Even his faith in Whitman wearied after 1860. Yet with Whitman at least, Emerson's faith lasted the longest. He found no speech defect, no excess of phlegm in the first three editions, or, as he wrote in his famous letter of 1855, no excess of "lymph in the temperament [that made] our western wits fat & mean."

Emerson found in these editions of *Leaves of Grass* the poetic vision that he had described as almost unachievable in "The Poet." And it is therefore one of the great ironies in American literary history that this essay, which inspired Whitman and became one of the central doctrines in our poetic theory, should also be Emerson's lament, signaling the end of his boundless faith in the possibilities of language to charm the Understanding out of its fear of death. Read separately from the lectures and essays that immediately preceded it, "The Poet" is an affirmation of the value of language to transcend the limits of time and space. In the context of Emerson's five-year period of unabated Neoplatonism, however, it must also be read as an admission of defeat. For it brought him full circle, back to earth and the "stuttering and stammering" of *Nature*. Yet, just as Emerson's orphic voice was abating in the 1840s, another was already "simmering."

6. A Jetblack Sunrise

Hear now the tale of a jetblack sunrise.
Whitman, *Leaves of Grass*, 1855

Sometimes with one I love, I fill myself with rage,
for I fear I effuse unreturned love.
Whitman, "Calamus"

At sixty-four Walt Whitman sat for a photograph while vaca-
tioning at Ocean Grove, New Jersey. The year was 1883, and the
poet had just weathered the "banning" of his *Leaves of Grass* in
Boston; yet his pose betrayed none of the frustration he had en-
dured during the national debate over the merits of his "indecent" poems. The camera eye caught him sitting on a rustic
bench holding his right hand aloft, with a butterfly balanced on
the forefinger. Actually, "caught" is the wrong word here, for the
camera eye caught no one in the nineteenth century; the scene is
quite literally a pose—all the way down to the cardboard butterfly
wired to fit on the finger. The photograph was used as a frontispiece in an 1889 issue of *Leaves*, and for years it was thought by
many to have portrayed a real butterfly, as if the poet were "so
close to nature that he could draw a butterfly to him and induce it
to light on his finger."[1] The discovery that the butterfly was fake
was made by Esther Shephard, who found the paper object
among Whitman's notebooks in the Library of Congress. No
doubt it helped to suggest the title of her study, *Walt Whitman's
Pose* (1938), in which she set out to debunk what she considered
the Whitman myth, to expose Whitman's career as one long pose
and a calculated attempt to deceive his readers. And her mission,
had it been carried out with less zeal and more respect for Whitman's originality as a poet, would not have been far from the
mark, at least in its focus on the period after 1860 and the third
edition of *Leaves of Grass*. For after his five-year interpenetration
with the self, Whitman had to satisfy himself more or less with
living out the legend he had created in the first three editions of
his book. After 1860, with the Civil War under way, he was no
longer the "solitary singer" suggested in the 1883 photograph
but the Good Gray Poet, who moved Christ-like from bedside to
bedside, from hospital to hospital, in Washington, D.C., cheering
up the wounded and sick soldiers from both the North and the
South.

But just as Emerson was Christ-like by resisting the Christic
identification as the prophet of self-reliance in the New World,
Whitman needed no model in 1855 to embolden him to speak,
to act out the character he had discovered during his literary
apprenticeship. Indeed, before Whitman there had been no

American poet quite like him, no bard who had dared to celebrate *himself* in such candid and "aboriginal" terms. The steel
engraving that served as the frontispiece for the 1855 and 1856
editions was also of a pose, but a more accurate depiction of the
man who came to himself in the poetry of this period. Standing
erect, hand on hip, hat cocked to one side, the man in the picture
is the "Me myself" of what came to be called "Song of Myself"
in 1881. The figure projects and represents the inner voice of
the Poet.

Chapters 3 and 4 have already covered various aspects of the
first three editions of *Leaves of Grass*, including the 1855 preface
and the "Enfans d'Adam" poems. Here I would like to examine
what Roy Harvey Pearce has called the "complete sequence [the
poetry of the first three editions] in which the poet invents modern poetry, explores its possibility as an instrument for studying
his role in the world at large, and comes finally to define, ex-
pound, and exemplify his vocation."[2] Unlike Pearce, however, I
do not want to argue for the superiority of the third edition over
the other two; nor do I want to second the opinion of Malcolm
Cowley and others that the first edition marks the high point of
Whitman's work. Rather, I see the three editions as "a complete
sequence" in which Whitman acts out the drama of becoming in
a world of what Poe called "sweets and sours."

Edwin Haviland Miller is one of those closest to the truth in his
assessment of Whitman's work as a poet. He writes that from
1855 to 1860 Whitman "explored and depicted a new inner landscape in an extraordinary series of poems, in an extraordinary
outburst of creativity." Although he seems bothered by the "confessional" nature of the "Calamus" sequence, Miller sees the 1860
edition as the "culmination of Whitman's poetic career."[3] I would
argue, in fact, that the "culmination" lasted five years (from 1855
to 1860) and during that period, a period like that of Emerson's
literary outpouring, Whitman confronted the fact of his existence.
The period is the culmination and centerpiece of a literary life
that began and ended in journalism: an existence in which he
observed the exterior of life, first in the lives of others and finally
in the self-serving articles about himself planted in various newspapers around the country. At the center of this life we have the

heart of Whitman's vision. From "I celebrate myself" in 1855 to "In paths untrodden" in 1860, Whitman expressed both the exhilaration of loving oneself and the agony of loneliness that ultimately comes from discovering that the self is really the only "comrade" or "lover" in life. Like Emerson, who announced self-reliance in *Nature* but defeat of the orphic voice in "The Poet," Whitman expressed an unabated sense of self-sufficiency in "Song of Myself" but confessed his inability to feel completely "happy in himself" in "Calamus" and other poems of 1860.[4]

As noted in Chapter 3, there is enacted in Whitman's foreground a process of simultaneously rejecting the "corrupt" political leaders and reaching out to the American average. The political undertone is not a minor aspect but the animus of Whitman's first book of poetry. In reaching out, however, he had to reach inward to know the average and to celebrate it. Accordingly, "Song of Myself" (as Whitman later insisted) expressed above all else his "own physical, emotional, moral, intellectual, and aesthetic Personality" (*PW*, 2:714).[5] In Whitman's poetry, as in Emerson's best essays, Personality or Character is discovered or is yet to be revealed. Hence, "Song of Myself" is most representative when it is most personal, when it celebrates the self, or the act of being. "Re examine all you have been told at school or church or in any book, dismiss whatever insults your own soul," Whitman advises in the preface, "and your very flesh shall be a great poem."[6]

This passage signals the celebration of the Body along with the Soul, as well as such jarring passages as "the scent of these armpits is aroma finer than prayer" (Furness, p. 29). Further along, the poet confesses: "I dote on myself. . . . there is that lot of me, and all so luscious" (Furness, p. 30). The central poem in the 1855 *Leaves* had no title, of course. Yet "Song of Myself" was quite appropriate. For Whitman was echoing Emerson's truth that ultimately one has only the self to celebrate. Between 1855 and 1860 the poet follows a cycle that begins and ends with the self, and his byword is *intimacy*—first with himself and then with others. The first attempt succeeded but could not be sustained beyond the 1856 edition; the second succeeded too, in that it produced the confessional poetry of "Calamus," yet it brought the poet to an emotional impasse that only his hospital work during the Civil War could overcome (if not resolve). This may account for the sense of loss that pervades *Drum-Taps* (1865) and its sequel, especially "When Lilacs Last in the Dooryard Bloom'd" (possibly Whitman's greatest poem after "Song of Myself"). The love that first celebrated "myself" and then "the need of comrades" was displaced by a mourning for the kind of political leader Whitman had sought back in the early 1850s during the composition of the first *Leaves of Grass*. Yet it was not for Lincoln alone but a mourning for all deaths, even death itself:

> (Nor for you, for one alone,
> Blossoms and branches green to coffins all I bring,
> For fresh as the morning, thus would I chant a song for you
>   O sane and sacred death.
>
> .   .   .   .
>
> For you and the coffins all of you O death.)[7]

In the poetry of 1855 death is celebrated rather than mourned. The poet is defiantly unafraid: "And as to you death, and you bitter hug of mortality. . . . it is idle to try to alarm me / . . . . / And as to you corpse I think you are good manure, but that does not offend me" (Furness, p. 54). Death's work as a midwife delivering the Soul into the next cycle is celebrated. There is, in fact, no death. "I know I am deathless," the poet exclaims earlier in "Song of Myself." "I know this orbit of mine cannot be swept by a carpenter's compass" (Furness, p. 26). Speaking from the grave to future generations, he departs "as air," effusing his flesh into the "lacy jags" of clouds. In such a context or frame of mind, the poet is without limit in his vision of himself. Like Emerson, who until the death of his son saw death as effecting "revolutions in our way of life," the poet of "Song of Myself" is confident that his existence is without end.

Whitman addresses the reader directly several times in "Song of Myself," but the poem is more clearly realized as a colloquy with oneself, a conversation with one's soul. Indeed, the "you" in the line "And what I assume you shall assume" can be likened to the "you" in "The Love Song of J. Alfred Prufrock." Unlike

T. S. Eliot's object, however, the "you" is not the better half that Prufrock seeks to bring out in his character but simply the *other* half: "Clear and sweet is my soul. . . . and clear and sweet is all that is not my soul. / Lack one lacks both" (Furness, p. 14). In 1860 Whitman opened his book with the autobiographical poem "Starting from Paumanok" (final title), but this version rings a little hollow when compared to the "trippers and askers" passage of "Song of Myself." "Starting from Paumanok" marks the birth and growth of Walter Whitman, the man; the "trippers and askers" passage invokes the fable of poetry to dismiss the quotidian background and announces the birth of Walt Whitman, the poet—the "Me myself." Thus he clearly states: "Apart from the pulling and hauling stands what I am" (Furness, p. 15).

"What I am" is dramatically described in what became section 5 of the poem: a man who can embrace only himself, his soul. In the passage that follows, the poet is clearly done with trying to embrace others. Remembering "how it stings to be slighted" (Furness, p. 17), he is no longer afraid to "merge" with himself. He feels sorry for those who continue to search for fulfillment in others, such as the woman who bathes vicariously with the twenty-eight young men but actually hides herself "aft the blinds of the window" (p. 19). He now believes in "winged purposes," in the elevation that comes from self-reliance and self-love: "The press of my foot to the earth springs a hundred affections, / . . . . / What is commonest and cheapest and nearest and easiest is Me" (Furness, p. 21).

"Song of Myself," then, is "the thoughtful merge" of the poet's Body and Soul. Each dotes on the other. "Who goes there!" asks the Soul, "hankering, gross, mystical, nude?" "How is it," asks the Body, "I extract strength from the beef I eat?" (Furness, p. 25). In his recent biography of Whitman, Justin Kaplan argues that "sexuality as sexuality—'the desire to copulate'—is a force in *Leaves of Grass*, a work that celebrates the democratization of the whole person, the liberation of impulse and instinct from involuntary servitude."[8] Whitman's "merge" does indeed release "forbidden voices," but it is the copulation of Body and Soul that animates "Song of Myself." Sexuality as sexuality, of course, is fully acknowledged and celebrated in the poem, but as a previously uncelebrated function of life. And its emphasis as such is lighter in the first edition. For example, in alluding to "the procreant urge of the world" in 1855, Whitman wrote: "Out of the dimness opposite equals advance. . . . Always substance and increase" (Furness, p. 14). It was not until the second edition that he added "always sex."[9]

To say that sexuality is not an important part of Whitman's poetry, of course, is to contradict the poet himself, who told Emerson in 1860 that cutting sex out of *Leaves of Grass* would be the same as castrating a virile man (*WWC*, 3:321). Yet the poet of "Song of Myself" is neither fully heterosexual nor homosexual but, as it were, androgynous. No relationship is ever really consummated. As Edwin Haviland Miller points out: "Although many people appear in the poem, no one converses with the protagonist, who is, in the final analysis, as thwarted as the old maid who in her fantasy caresses the bodies of twenty-eight swimmers."[10] The poet might think of himself as "fleshy and sensual," but he is in fact held back from others by an unwanted but unavoidable sense of chastity.

"I think I will do nothing for a long time but listen," he concludes halfway through the poem. He can do little else but listen for other voices. His own "voice goes after what [his] eyes cannot reach" (Furness, p. 31). Insisting that his "is no callous shell," that he possesses "instant conductors" all over his body (Furness, p. 32), he is nevertheless resigned to himself and the touch of his own skin, which overwhelms him: "You villain touch! what are you doing?. . . . My breath is tight in its throat; / Unclench your floodgates! you are too much for me" (Furness, p. 33). All attempts to reach out to others in the catalogs before and after this passage are useless; the only outlet for his feelings, he discovers, is through autoeroticism. As Emerson's representative man and poet, he can assimilate all that he sees, hears, touches, and smells, but he can *speak* to no one but himself.

"The sun shines today also," Emerson had written in *Nature*. In "Song of Myself," however, it is "a jetblack sunrise," under which the speaker's hopes for requited love are mourned along with the 412 Texas soldiers massacred at Goliad during the Mexican War (Furness, pp. 40–41). The second half of the poem finds the poet totally alone now and loving only himself: "Man or woman! I might tell how I like you, but cannot" (Furness, p. 44). He tramps "a perpetual journey" into himself. And it is the "gum" from his eyes, not another's, that he now washes away. He may wish to lead another "upon the knoll" or down the "plain public road," but he knows now that all such journeys must be solitary ventures. As he confesses to the reader (once considered a potential lover and fellow traveler), "Not I, not any one else can travel that road for you, / You must travel it for yourself" (Furness, pp. 51–52).

The road must be traveled alone, for it is the road within one-self: "It is not far . . . it is within reach, / Perhaps you have been on it since you were born, and did not know, / Perhaps it is every where on water and land." The poet can give the reader-traveler "biscuits to eat" and "milk to drink," but he must also give him the "goodbye kiss and open the gate for [his] egress hence." The imagery of the road gives way to the imagery of the sea in what becomes section 46 of the poem. Like Emerson's young swimmer trembling at the thought of a "new bath," Whitman's reader has "timidly waded, holding a plank by the shore." "Now I *will* you to be a bold swimmer," he exhorts, "To jump off in the midst of the sea, and rise again and nod to me and shout, and laughingly dash with your hair" (Furness, p. 52; italics mine). The reader, like the twenty-eight swimmers, will "not think whom [he] souse[s] with spray" (Furness, p. 20). On this swim, however, the poet is left behind, as is the woman "aft the blinds," unable to do anything but observe. Like the woman in the poem, he cannot find true reciprocal love in anyone but himself.

But unlike the woman, the protagonist in "Song of Myself" is not frustrated by this circumstance. Here separation is seen as an opportunity to reach the pinnacle of self-sufficiency or self-reliance. To be a teacher is quite enough—"the teacher of athletes" who muscularly "jump off in the midst of the sea" (Furness, pp. 52–53). The teacher Emerson envisioned, the poet teaches "straying from me." All men are alone except for the company of God. Appropriately, he sees God in "the faces of men and women" and "in my own face in the glass." The poem ends on this note of ecstasy. "There is that in me," he tells us joyously, "I do not know what it is . . . but I know it is in me" (Furness, pp. 54–55). In many ways "Song of Myself" is a deeply personal poem, one in which the poet embraces himself and finds not a "particle of an inch . . . vile." But ultimately his auto-eroticism is transcended, for God had come to him as "a loving bedfellow" (Furness, pp. 14–15). By the end of the poem, the protagonist is fully convinced that to know and love onself is to know and love God.

The other eleven poems in the first edition have been described as "cuttings" from "Song of Myself."[11] In some cases, especially with "The Sleepers," this may have been literally true. However, the effect achieved makes the other poems different, for they generally lack the affirmation of the self so evident in the first poem. The other poems signal the poet's outward search for love that will be more earnestly sought in "Calamus." Ivan Marki observes that these poems spend much more time with "you" the reader than does the first one. He notes: "The poet turns full face to 'you' and stays with his listener this time. In the first 30 or so lines of ['A Song for Occupations'] there are more lines consecutively spoken to 'you' than in the 1,330 or so lines of ['Song of Myself']."[12]

The poet in these pieces is starting to reach out, as he will in "Calamus," but is finding the task immensely frustrating. "Come closer to me," he urges in "A Song for Occupations," yet finds himself separated from his reader by "the cold types and cylinder and wet paper" that produced his book (Furness, p. 57). A clearer anticipation of "Calamus" is found in "The Sleepers." This dream sequence has a pleading tone in which the persona asks to "let me catch myself with you and stay. . . . I will not chafe you" (Furness, p. 72). We also encounter the swimmer again, "swimming naked through the eddies of the sea." But the swimmer no longer "nods" to the poet as he had in "Song of Myself"; instead he leaves him "confused." The scene, as he tells us, is a "pastreading" from "Song of Myself." The difference is that the swimmer (now the ship) "helplessly leads on." There is now a separation of the man on the beach and the object in the water: "I hear the burst as she strikes / I hear the howls of dismay. . . . they grow fainter and fainter'' (Furness, p. 73). Fifty or more lines later we have the ''beautiful [but] lost swimmer.''

In the closing lines of ''The Sleepers,'' the poet asks: ''Why should I be afraid to trust myself to you?'' He says he is not afraid, but the truth is that he can mingle himself in the dreams of others, he can absorb their conflicts and conquests, but he cannot, as Emerson had taught him in ''Friendship,'' commingle his identity with that of another.[13] The lesson is probably best expressed in ''There Was a Child Went Forth,'' which is an autobiographical account of a young mind absorbing all that it perceives: ''These became part of the child who went forth every day, and who now goes and will always go forth every day'' (Furness, p. 91). He can filter through himself everything but retain nothing. ''The mother at home quietly placing the dishes on the suppertable / The father strong, *selfsufficient*, manly, mean, angered, unjust / . . . / Men and women crowding fast in the streets . . . if they are not *flashes and specks* what are they?'' (Furness, p. 91; italics mine). What are they, indeed, but ''flashes and specks'' of self-sufficiency? Or, more accurately, self-containment?

The idea that the progress of the Soul is anything but a solitary pilgrimage is also presented in ''Great Are the Myths,'' the final poem in the 1855 edition. Taken as an assertion that ''everything is good,'' it is doubtless one of the weakest in the volume (rejected by Whitman in the 1881 edition). Attempting to say something favorable about the poem, Gay Wilson Allen writes: ''Possibly it does serve as a general summary of the themes in the edition, though in no systematic manner, and it contains nothing to suggest new interpretations. Worst of all, it is anticlimactic.''[14] The poem is loosely organized and anticlimactic, but it works well as a closing of the first *Leaves* because it reinforces the idea that all the poet has celebrated (except the self) are illusions. It is a summary of the myths about life, and hence it is appropriately anticlimactic. Whether his intent was conscious or not, the celebration is appropriately hollow.

In the second or third issue of the first edition, Whitman included reviews of his book. Several of these reappeared in the 1856 edition, but one self-review that he did not include was

"Walt Whitman and His Poems." Since the review alluded specifically to the 1855 text of twelve poems, it would have been out of place in the 1856 text. However, Whitman may have had another reason for excluding the review, one perhaps as unconscious as his use of "Great Are the Myths." The review suggests his uneasiness about the other eleven poems, which, he said, had "distinct purposes, curiously veiled." In these, he admitted, it was "his pleasure to elude [the reader] and provoke [him] for deliberate purposes of his own." He was indeed elusive, for after introducing the subject of the eleven poems in the review, he proceeded to quote not from any of them but from "Song of Myself." Rather than cite from one of the "you" poems, he reverted to another "pastreading," which includes the line, "What is commonest and cheapest and nearest and easiest is Me." He is clearly more secure in limiting his celebration to the self, and it is only after steeling himself with lines about the self that he can turn to the other poems. He quotes from "A Song for Occupations," and the selection reveals much about his purpose and his fear:

> When the psalm sings instead of the singer,
> When the script preaches instead of the preacher,
> When the pulpit descends and goes instead of the carver
>   that carved the supporting desk,
> When the sacred vessels or the bits of the eucharist, or the
>   lath or plast, procreate as effectually as the young
>   silversmiths or bakers, or the masons in their overalls,
> When a university course convinces like a slumbering
>   woman and child convince,
> When the minted gold in the vault smiles like the night-
>   watchman's daughter,
> When the warantee deeds loafe in chairs opposite and are
>   my friendly companions,
> I intend to reach them my hand and make as much of them
>   as I do of men and women.

[Furness, p. 64]

Although the poet strains to find cosmic significance in the occupations of mankind, in the lives men lead, he has to admit that outside the self, life is filled not with real and loving people but with functions—mere "flashes and specks" of humanity. "Who then *is* that insolent unknown?" he asks in the review after quoting the lines (italics mine). He states in the last line taken from "A Song for Occupations" that he intends to extend "my hand and make as much of them as I do of men and women." Make much of *what*? we must ask. The psalm? The pulpit? The leavings of lives? The attempt, then, is to celebrate a void, a vacuum. Although Whitman changed many lines in "Occupations" between 1856 and 1881, those that he quoted in the review survived without change. On the other hand, the first seven lines in the poem (beginning with "Come closer to me, / Push close my lovers and take the best I possess") were dropped by 1881. With the original opening lines, the poem was a forerunner of the search for lovers in "Calamus."[15] The lines left in place, however, more clearly anticipate the failure of the search in "Calamus." The change reflects Whitman's realization in 1881 that such a search had been futile. It represents the poet's backward glance over traveled but rocky roads.

In summing up his discussion of the 1856 edition, Gay Wilson Allen observes that "the greatest importance of the second edition is the testimony it bears to the courage and fortitude of Walt Whitman in the face of literary failure. Nearly every poem in the book radiates his faith in himself, in his ideas, and in his newly-invented technique."[16] Of course, the second *Leaves* failed commercially (with possibly as few copies being sold as the first), but the book succeeded immensely as Whitman's celebration of the love cycle. In poems whose final titles are "Salut au Monde!" "Crossing Brooklyn Ferry," "Song of the Open Road," and "Song of the Rolling Earth," the poet follows the course of love from universality back to the self. In these poems, perhaps the strongest compositions of the 1856 edition, he attempts to overcome the obstacles to reciprocal love by embracing the world. For in 1856 he had not yet fully confronted (as he would in the 1860 edition) the doubts that had surfaced briefly in the "cuttings" from the 1855 "Song of Myself."

In "Salut au Monde!" the poet takes his own hand, which is

joined in "unended links, each hooked to the next!" The world widens within him as he first hears the sounds of the globe and sees the multitudes from Asia, Africa, Europe, and America. "Within me latitude widens, longitude lengthens." After hearing and seeing, he salutes the inhabitants of the world, "You, inevitable where you are!" His "spirit has passed in compassion and determination around the whole earth." He has "looked for brothers, sisters, lovers, and found them ready . . . in all lands." Doubtless, the Emerson letter had something to do with Whitman's persistent optimism; his brother George reported that Whitman had been "set up" by the epistle.[17] Amid the cries of derision at the publication of the 1855 *Leaves* had come this one assent and approval. And it had been issued from the individual most responsible for Whitman's spontaneous celebration of self-reliance.

The same celebration is found in "Crossing Brooklyn Ferry." It too is directed to the world but to the world of future generations, fifty and a hundred years hence. Just as distance loses significance in "Salut au Monde!" so time in "Crossing Brooklyn Ferry" "avails not." We also find the idea of mankind linked hand in hand not only around the globe but throughout existence. All are "struck from the float forever held in solution" (Allen, pp. 212, 216). In section 44 of "Song of Myself," where the poet records his evolution from the "huge first Nothing," the solitary self is celebrated. Here the evolution of mankind is celebrated, and it is the celebration of a common existence:

> It is not you alone, nor I alone,
> Not a few races, not a few generations, not a few centuries,
> It is that each came, or comes, or shall come from its
> due emission, without fail, either now, or then, or
> henceforth.

> [Allen, p. 218]

Time is significant only in that it marks the passage of the "me into you," in this case, the pouring of the poet's meaning into future generations. "Just as you stand and lean on the rail, yet hurry with the swift current," the poet reminds his future readers, "I stood, yet was hurried." Whitman seems to be saying that time is an illusion, that nothing separates past, present, and future generations. One future reader, T. S. Eliot, agreed and perhaps clarified Whitman's observation by expanding it:

> Fare forward, travellers! not escaping from the past
> Into different lives, or into any future;
>
> .   .   .   .
>
> [While] on the deck of the drumming liner
> Watching the furrow that widens behind you,
> You shall not think "the past is finished"
> or "the future is before us."[18]

To be deceived by Whitman's "swift current" or Eliot's widening "furrow" is to have the experience of life but to miss its meaning. To look to the future for change, that is, change in the human condition, is to separate the past and the future from the present. Time is but a deceiver, and "Crossing Brooklyn Ferry" denies time by celebrating its illusion. The poem therefore denies the concept of a separate past, present, and future; it denies the separation of generations.

After celebrating the illusion of time, the poet of the 1856 *Leaves* takes to the public road. "Song of the Open Road" attempts to celebrate "the profound lesson of reception." In doing so, it marks the first time Whitman used the word *adhesiveness* in his poetry. He says "it is not previously fashioned, [but] it is appropos." Adhesiveness became the theme of his androgynous poetry in "Calamus"; here it is used in the sense of the instinctive and unconscious love that all men and women hold for each other. "Do you know what it is as you pass to be loved by strangers?" he asks. "Do you know the talk of those turning eye-balls?" Yet this affinity is more spiritual than physical and possible only on the open road, which the Soul must travel alone after a certain point: "The body does not travel as much as the soul, / The body has just as great a work as the soul, and parts away at last" (Allen, pp. 224, 229, 236). And for its part along the road, the body, like that of the common prostitute, must be "worthy" of the journey:

> Come not here if you have already spent the best of
>   yourself!

Only those may come who come in sweet and determined
  bodies,
No diseased person—no rum-drinker or venereal taint is
  permitted here.

[Allen, p. 232]

In poem after poem of this edition, Whitman attempts to tear
down the barriers that separate mankind: distance in "Salut au
Monde!" time in "Crossing Brooklyn Ferry," and the limitations
of the body in "Song of the Open Road." Up to this point, there
is no indication, as there is in "The Sleepers," that man is ultimately alone. Only one more barrier remains to be leveled, and
that is language, the subject of "Song of the Rolling Earth." But
with this barrier falls also the concept of community along the
road. Originally called "Poem of the Sayers of the Words of the
Earth," it announces that "amelioration is one of the earth's
words," but the language that communicates this truth is un-
heard. Human language, furthermore, can articulate only hints
of the truth:

Were you thinking that those were the words—
  those upright lines? those curves, angles, dots?
No, those are not the words—the substantial words are in
  the ground and sea,
They are in the air—they are in you.

[Allen, pp. 322–23]

The earth does not exhibit these "substantial" words but keeps
them beneath "the ostensible sounds, the august chorus of heroes, the wail of slaves, / Persuasions of lovers, curses, gasps of
the dying, laughter of young people, accents of bargainers." For
the best of the earth remains untold. The truth is that mankind
moves together on a voyage that "does not fail," but the paradox is that we are all together in our loneliness along the public
road: "Each man to himself, and each woman to herself" (Allen,
p. 325). In other words, Whitman now acknowledges that we are
spiritual deaf-mutes throughout the journey home. We travel
together but cannot speak to one another. We must grow or make
our passage alone:

Not one can acquire for another—not one!
Not one can grow for another—not one!
[Allen, p. 328]

And yet "Song of the Rolling Earth" continues to sound the theme of the other three poems discussed, for it is a celebration, not a lamentation. If the "earth remains broken and jagged," it is such "only to him or her who remains broken and jagged," to him or her who tries to speak to or love another. Whitman is saying that there is a more substantial speech that calls up a "love with sweeter spasms than that which responds love! / It is *that which contains itself*" (italics mine). All other speech, the "audible words," contain nothing "substantial." As in "Song of the Open Road," the message here is Neoplatonic. Togetherness or wholeness is possible only at the end of the public road, where all men are made one again with God. In the meantime, it is fruitless, indeed baneful, to look for "that which responds love." The only love possible during the voyage of the Soul is "that which contains itself."

With "Song of the Rolling Earth" (the penultimate poem in the 1856 sequence and the final new poem), Whitman came full circle back to the celebration of the self in "Song of Myself." Like a house of cards, his concept of community collapsed before him. With the book and its attempt at cosmic love behind him, he entered one of the most painfully lonely periods of his life. The literary consequence was the 1860 edition and "Calamus," in which Whitman, for the last time in his poetry, endeavored to become the personal lover.

––––––––––––

The third edition of *Leaves of Grass*, published in Boston by Thayer and Eldridge, reflects a significant change in Whitman. He appears more aware of his role as a poet, less intent upon being one of nature's "roughs." He discarded the steel engraving that had adorned the frontispiece of the first two editions for a sketch that suggested the stereotype of the poet in the nineteenth century. With his beard well cropped and hair attractively coifed, he even resembles Byron slightly—with his necktie and coat neatly fitted about his frame. Although I do not agree with Roy Harvey Pearce that the 1855 and 1856 editions were only "collections of poems,"[19] I do think that this edition presents a more "organized" theme than either of the others. The 1860 theme certainly covers a wider range of Whitman's experience. That Whitman was conscious of a greater poetical breadth is seen in the new opening poem, "Proto-Leaf" (later called "Starting from Paumanok"). Perhaps he was too conscious of his aims, for "Proto-Leaf" is far more literal in its intent than that of the portrait drawn in "Song of Myself." The poet introduces himself to America and urges the nation to return the love he offers:

> Take my leaves, America!
> Make welcome for them everywhere, for they are your own
>   offspring.

> [Pearce, p. 8]

Much of the poetry in the third edition was probably written shortly after the publication of the 1856 edition and before 1857 when Whitman started editing the Brooklyn *Daily Times*. This would include "Proto-Leaf" and would thus account for its optimism, which was carried over from the mood that produced the second edition. "Calamus," on the other hand, was most likely composed in 1858 or 1859,[20] and it reflected the years when Whitman gave full range to his feelings. These were the years of Whitman's "slough," when he found himself a lonely and unrequited lover. In his late thirties, he found himself fearfully alone but all the while trying to fill the void he felt. An Eriksonian would say that he was in his period of "intimacy," in which the "need to develop a true and mutual psychological intimacy with another person" can be overwhelming.[21] Justin Kaplan suggests that one of the objects of Whitman's intimacy may have been his younger brother, Thomas Jefferson Whitman. The poet's favorite sibling and clearly the only family member who understood *Leaves of Grass*, Jeff had accompanied Walt to New Orleans in 1848 and had grown up to share his brother's fondness for the opera and, to a lesser extent, his interest in literature. "When Jeff was born I was in my 15th year," Whitman wrote after his brother's death in 1890, "and [I] had much care of him for many years afterward, and he did not separate from me. He was a very hand-some, healthy, affectionate, smart child, and would sit on my lap or hang on my neck half an hour at a time. . . . O, how we loved each other—how many jovial good times we had!" (*PW*, 2:693). It may be significant, therefore, that Walt's "slough" and Jeff's mar-riage in 1859 coincided, thus removing Jeff to separate Brooklyn quarters and Walt from the object of his affection. As Kaplan puts it, "After the marriage Jeff was Walt's ward and companion no longer."[22]

Further evidence of Whitman's longing for intimacy and its resulting crisis is found in notebooks written during the period of his editorship of the *Times*.[23] "Why be there men I meet, and others I know," he asked himself, "that while they are with me, the sunlight of Paradise expands my blood—that when I walk with an arm of theirs around my neck, my soul scoots and courses like an unleashed dog—that when they leave me the pennants of my joy sink flat and lank in the deadest calm?" "Adhesiveness" was the term Whitman borrowed from phrenology to explain the compelling need for intimacy he found inescapable and baffling.[24] "What is the meaning, any how, of my adhesiveness toward others?" he asked. "What is the cause of theirs toward me?—Am I loved by them boundlessly because my love for them is more boundless?" (*DN*, 3:764–65). Whitman's attempt to answer these questions is found in "Calamus," where his crisis is acted out with tenderness and fear. Whereas the "Enfans d'Adam" se-quence reveals only his sensual love, the "Calamus" poems "ex-pose me more than all my other poems" (Pearce, p. 377).

Whitman makes it clear in no. 1 of the series that he intends "to celebrate the *need* of comrades" (italics mine), not their abun-dance. He wants to escape "from the life that exhibits itself" in order to celebrate "the Soul of the man I speak for, [who] feeds, rejoices only in comrades." This can be taken to mean an escape from the life of a heterosexual to that of a homosexual, but it may also be read in the context of the 1856 poems discussed above. Having tried to embrace the world but ultimately discovering himself isolated on the public road, he once again tries to escape from "the life that exhibits itself," that is, a life of solitude and loneliness. Floyd Stovall was one of the first to point out that after

1859 Whitman's "barbaric yawp is silenced, and in its place are heard the softer song of love and the melancholy chant of death."[25] I would argue against the idea that the "barbaric yawp" or the theme of freedom is dominant in the earlier editions, of course, but I do think Stovall is correct in finding love and death inextricably bound together in the 1860 edition. For one of his examples, he cites "Out of the Cradle Endlessly Rocking"; however, I find the same chant in "Calamus." Indeed, "Out of the Cradle," which was very possibly composed after "Calamus,"[26] sings of the loss of love through death. More important, it reinforces the theme of "Calamus," that of the failure of the personal lover's pilgrimage. "Calamus" reflects the poet's looking down the public road of *this* life and seeing clearly for the first time the inevitability of his own death. Death may have been celebrated or dismissed as the divine midwife in 1855, but in 1858–59 it took on a different, highly personal aspect. In "the secret of [his] nights and days" Whitman therefore recorded his attempt to climb out of his "slough," his effort to blot out the loneliness of life and the inevitability of death through a quest for reciprocal love.

"I will escape from the sham that was proposed to me," the poet promises in no. 2. "I will sound myself and comrades only —I will never again utter a call, only their call." But as he already suspects, the call of self "and comrades only" reflects an attempt to retreat in the face of oncoming death. The "sham" is the truth that love and death are "folded together above all"; therefore the only love worth seeking is that which makes "death exhilarating." Accordingly, he warns his lover in no. 3 that "all is useless without that which you may guess at many times and not hit —that which I hinted at." He is speaking of the realization that personal love makes death ominous, not exhilarating. As a result, the "way is suspicious—the result slow, uncertain, may-be destructive." It may be destructive, he is suggesting, because personal love makes the object of intimacy "God, sole and exclusive." Such a love, Emerson would have said, "leaves God out of me." Its rapture merely temporary, the love is soon thwarted and the lover is left frustrated by the resulting loneliness. Here Whitman is echoing Emerson's discovery in "Friendship" that the only joy in a friend's "being mine, is that the *not mine* is *mine*" (*CW*, 2:122). They both realized that there is only one love and one God. "Therefore," Whitman tells his lover, "release me now, before troubling yourself any further—Let go your hand from my shoulders, / Put me down, and depart on your way" (Pearce, no. 3).

   Although the leaves of love are seen as "Tomb-leaves" early in "Calamus," the quest for personal love is nevertheless undertaken; for though the truth may be realized, it is not yet accepted. In highly sexual imagery, the poet offers "this calamus-root" as the token of interchange between comrades. By no. 7, "He ahold of my hand has completely satisfied me." The coitus or love is "enough," but like any personal love, the rapture cannot last. The moments of ecstasy give way to "hours discouraged, distracted" (no. 9), as he sees his lover "content himself without me." In these hours of torment he wonders whether there exists another with the same sense of loss:

> Is there even one other like me—distracted—his friend, his
>   lover, lost to him?
> Is he too as I am now? Does he still rise in the morning
>   dejected, thinking who is lost to him? and at night
>   awaking, think of who is lost?
>
>   [Pearce, no. 9]

As his lover returns to him in no. 11, the relationship improves, only to be dampened again by misunderstanding in no. 12. The sequence thus far resembles a lovers' quarrel in which each doubts the other's sincerity. (In his old age Whitman would relive the drama with the young Harry Stafford—as they passed a ring back and forth.)[27] At one extremely depressed moment in "Calamus," the speaker, angered and embittered, even declares his lover "dead" to him. The act also suggests a wish to push his lover forward into the region where all lovers are satisfied through their reunion with God. For in this life the quest for love results in the discovery that "every place was a burial-place" (Pearce, no. 17).

   Promiscuity follows this failed attempt at a mutually satisfying and lasting relationship. The poet goes "cruising" through Manhattan and then out across the nation and the world in search of "continual lovers":

> Passing stranger! you do not know how longingly I look
>   upon you,
> You must be he I was seeking, or she I was seeking, (It
>   comes to me, as of a dream).

[Pearce, no. 22]

Metaphysically, the experience may be fulfilling in the sense that it is reminiscent of the poet's attempts at cosmic love in the 1856 edition. Personally, it is unsatisfying, because variety prevents intimacy. He finds himself filled with envy at those who appear to have found meaningful and permanent relationships. "When I read of the brotherhood of lovers, how it was with them, / . . . / Then I am pensive—I hastily put down the book, and walk away, filled with the bitterest envy" (Pearce, no. 28). Disheartened, he nevertheless continues his song, for he now believes that his attempt to sing of personal love, regardless of its imperfections, will be the only part of him he can leave behind. No discovery he has made, machine invented, or book written can immortalize him in the minds of future generations: "Only these carols, vibrating through the air, I leave / For comrades and lovers" (Pearce, no. 33). And so he proceeds to sing of "the new City of Friends," a new nation of which "the main purport . . . is to found a superb friendship, exalté, previously unknown" (Pearce, nos. 34, 35).

This respite from the awful truth about personal love, however, is short-lived; for he knows his "Calamus" song must ultimately confront the superiority of self-love over personal love, that it must confront the Emersonian fact that reciprocal love is found only in the "Me," or on the other side of death. Thus he confesses:

> Sometimes with one I love, I fill myself with rage, for fear I
>   effuse unreturned love;
> But now I think there is no unreturned love—the pay is
>   certain, one way or another.

[Pearce, no. 39]

The "pay" is certain only in the sense that the search for the "Not-Me" has led him to the "Me." At the close of "Calamus," therefore, his plight remains unresolved. Something more remains to be said about the tensions between Body and Soul; the poet is not yet fully committed (as he was in "Song of Myself") to the quest of the self-lover. At this juncture in the composition of the 1860 edition, he does not completely accept the fact that "I effuse unreturned love." Yet the growing suspicion about the impossibility of personal love allows for little hope. He is left, it appears, with little more than his shadow, and even this external object may be separate from the self: "How often I find myself," he admits in no. 40, "standing and looking at it where it flits, / How often I question whether that is really me."

In truth, the only thing—and the very thing—he has gained from the "Calamus" quest is the memory of the particular infatuations and its expression in the "Calamus" poems. The defeat of personal love, the discovery in "Calamus" that adhesive action is nothing more than a momentary distraction from the relentless pace of life down the road, produces a spiritual catharsis. The memory and the song are enough: "In these, and among my lovers, and carrolling my songs, / O I never doubt whether that is really me" (Pearce, no. 40). Without his attempts at personal love, he now realizes that he could not have completely fulfilled his vocation as a poet. The memory and the song are deathless in his hands. Thus his message in the final "Calamus" chant is addressed not only to a contemporary lover or reader but also "to one a century hence, or any number of centuries hence, / To you, yet unborn, these seeking you" (Pearce, no. 45). Yet "Calamus," it should be said, was only the dress rehearsal for Whitman's greatest achievement of the 1860 edition, the poem subsequently entitled "Out of the Cradle Endlessly Rocking." For it is here that the memory and the song, love and death, are ultimately fused.

By the time Whitman composed "A Word Out of the Sea" ("Out of the Cradle Endlessly Rocking"), he was coming out of his "slough"; he was beginning to accept the inadequacy of personal love and death as the ultimate consoler. To quote Stovall again, he now saw death as "the clue to man's destiny, because it is the divine complement to human perfection, through which love is made complete and immortal."[28] Armed now with the memory on record in the song, he was thus prepared to act out the ultimate vocation of the poet: to celebrate and lament at once the fusion of love and death. The poem, which first appeared in the *Saturday Press* for Christmas 1859 as "A Child's Reminiscence," is not concerned so much with a child's reminiscence as it is with that point in Whitman's life when the recollection of a childhood experience served as a catalyst in his transformation from a belief in "adhesiveness" to a mild form of nihilism. The "reminiscence," whether of an actual or imaginary event, concerns "two guests from Alabama—two together":

> And every day the he-bird, to and fro, near at hand,
> And every day the she-bird, crouched on her nest, silent,
>   with bright eyes,
> And every day I, a curious boy, never too close, never
>   disturbing them,
> Cautiously peering, absorbing, translating.
>
> [Pearce, p. 270]

The he-bird becomes the "solitary guest from Alabama" when his mate vanishes among the "white arms out in the breakers tirelessly tossing." As the "lone singer" stands before the sea and pours forth his lament, the "peaceful child" listens. The cry is one of loneliness, and though the boy listened passively, the poet that the boy has finally become knows what it feels like to be halted at the land's edge in pursuit of love. The speaker is a "man—yet by these tears a little boy again, / Throwing myself on the sand, confronting the waves."

At the time of the childhood experience recalled, the boy basked emotionally in the warmth of the sun as did the two lovers before their separation. "*Shine! Shine!*" they exclaim. "*Pour down your warmth, great Sun! / While we two bask together.*" And yet the crucial moment in the event remembered—hearing the solitary mate's aria ("*Loved—but no more with me, / We two together no more*") —takes place at midnight under the "yellow half-moon, late-risen, and swollen as if with tears." The *late-risen* moon clearly man's version of "Experience." Both the poem and the essay reenact the discovery that *true* love is fused with death. Thus Emerson writes, "We dress our garden, eat our dinners, discuss the household with our wives, and these things make no impression, are forgotten next week; but, in the solitude to which every man is always returning, he has a sanity and revelations which in his passage into new worlds he will carry with him" (*W*, 3:85).

With "A Word Out of the Sea," Whitman followed the Emerson of 1844 "out of the rocked cradle," out of the youthful illusions about perfect health and personal love. But the greatness of the poem lies in its success in resolving the conflict between personal love and self-love through the fusion of love and death. In this regard, it may be compared to Emerson's "The Poet," which can be read as a glorification and a bemoaning of the powers of the poet. Like Emerson's orphic poet, Whitman's child-man lulls the Understanding out of its fear of death. Unfortunately, this illumination is fleeting and is as precarious as Emerson's "agaric"; thus the ultimate vocation of the poet is short-lived. With this poem Whitman comes full circle. As in "Song of Myself," he is once again fully committed to the quest of the self-lover; but like the poet of 1855 in "The Sleepers" and the other "cuttings," he slips back into the mortal abyss. This time, however, there is no chance of recovery. Orpheus is gone forever—his departure recorded and dramatized in "As I Ebb'd with the Ocean of Life."

That this poem precedes both "Calamus" and "A Word Out of the Sea" in the third edition is of little importance, for the 1860 arrangement is appropriately "inexact and elastic but consonant with the depiction of the self."[29] Indeed, it was probably an unconscious depiction, consonant with the years of confusion and fear that preceded the 1860 publication. In all likelihood, "As I Ebb'd" was written as a sequel to Whitman's "Reminiscence." The poem was first published as "Bardic Symbols" in the *Atlantic Monthly* for April 1860, a full three months after "A Child's Reminiscence" had appeared in the *Saturday Press*. "As I Ebb'd" should have concluded the 1860 edition, therefore, because it was a most appropriate conclusion to Whitman's period of strength as a poet.

The poem is Whitman's farewell to the poetry of self-reliance, as "Experience" is Emerson's. More exactly, it is his farewell to Transcendental self-reliance itself, the very conceit upon which all great poems are constructed. Unlike "A Word Out of the Sea," this poem reveals *nothing* but paradox, the paradox of self-reliance. Its subject is the tension that self-reliance produces between the mortal self and its lover on the other side of death. For self-reliance effectively blurs the mortal vision, dissolves the impact of death. It sees beyond or through death to the other half. As Emerson had told Whitman back in 1842, in his lecture on "Nature and the Powers of the Poet," the man is only half himself; the other half is his expression (*EL*, 3:349). The Understanding told Whitman who he was not; the Reason taught him who he *was*. But paradoxically, to attempt to cross that line—to walk the shores of Paumanok, as Whitman does in the poem, "with that eternal self of me, seeking types"—is at the same time to deny the mortal self. Such abnegation, of course, calls for the denial of personal love as well. We thus find in the poem Whitman's version of "The Poet." Both are ambivalent. Poetry not only enables one to overcome the limitations of his mortality, but demonstrates by its very success those limitations or the inadequacy of the mortal self.

This paradox is most dramatically rendered in "As I Ebb'd." For the poem records the collapse of "bardic symbols." The poet walks the shores of Paumanok, "the shores I know," in search of "the shores I know not." And yet he walks in fear: "Alone, held by the eternal self of me that threatens to get the better of me, and stifle me." The "eternal self," the offspring of self-reliance, is the villain that threatens to expose life for what it is—shallow. To yearn for it, as Emerson realized in "Experience," is to "pay the costly price of sons and lovers." The price is grief, which had taught Emerson only "how shallow it is" (*W*, 3:48). *Shallow* or empty because it longs for what was never really there. It is a longing at best for halfness, for the fragments of life ("little corpses" in Whitman's poem) that relentlessly drive man into the hands of death.

Probably no American poet was more sensitive to the fragmentary nature of life than Emily Dickinson, who, after the death of yet another "lover," exclaimed rhetorically, "Is God Love's Adversary?"[30] But, as is demonstrated in Chapter 7, this was an attitude that Whitman would ultimately reject. He would not allow its nihilism to stifle his ability to write poetry, as it did Dickinson's. To continue in the vocation, however, he had to make the ultimate compromise, the same that Emerson made in "Experience": he was forced to turn from self-reliance to God-reliance. In doing so he exchanged the "vision" of the orphic poet for the "wisdom" of the national poet best visualized in "Passage to India." This poem and others simply avoid the tragic vision of "As I Ebb'd with the Ocean of Life." Ever afterward, the poetry of self-reliance is regarded as a fable that dangerously inflates the ego and lulls man into the arrogant belief that he can experience the elusive identity of his source. As Stephen Whicher observes, the poet seeks "types" on the shores of Paumanok; "Nature ironically offers him the trash on the water's edge, and with a shock of recognition he finds in it the emblem of his present state, namely his inability any more to see saving emblems."[31] In the poem Whitman finally admits that his poems are "insolent poems," "that the real Me still stands untouched, untold, altogether unreached." It is not only unreached but withdrawn "with peals of distant ironical laughter at every word I have written or shall write, / Striking me with insults till I fall helpless upon the sand." Like the grown child of "A Word Out of the Sea," the persona of this poem lies helpless and ridiculed on the eternal shore. Joining him this time is the humanity he would speak for, lying like "drowned corpses" at the feet of God: "We, capricious, brought hither, we know not whence, spread out before You, up there, walking or sitting, / Whoever *you* are—we too lie in drifts at your feet" (Pearce, pp. 197–99).

I have supplied the emphasis on "you" because the statement now acknowledges Whitman's rejection of the arrogance of self-reliance in favor of the humility of God-reliance. In "Song of Myself" he could boldly ask:

> Listener up there! Here you. . . . what have you to confide
>   to me?
> Look in my face while I snuff the sidle of evening,
> Talk honestly, for no one else hears you, and I stay only a
>   minute longer.
>
> [Furness, p. 55]

There he was on personal terms with the creator. This poet was indeed privileged, the only one who could hear God. In "As I Ebb'd," however, the poet no longer dares to believe (as Emerson could no longer believe) that he is "part or particle of God." It might be said that "Song of Myself" acts out the whole cycle of the paradox of self-reliance: it opens with a celebration of the "I" and closes in pursuit of the "you." It sets the stage, if not for the entire cycle, for the "you" (or personal lover) poems found in the 1856 poems and "Calamus." These in turn take him back to self-love and its collapse in "As I Ebb'd with the Ocean of Life." For on the one hand, self-reliance denies the possibility of personal love in its insistence on transcendence; on the other, it denies self-love in its failure to experience ultimately the "real Me." It was the hoax, therefore, that led Whitman up Emerson's spiral "stair" to nowhere.

7. The Muse as "Wisdom"

It is very unhappy, but too late to be helped,
the discovery we have made that we exist.
That discovery is called the Fall of Man.
Ever afterwards we suspect our instruments. . . .
Once we lived in what we saw; now,
the rapaciousness of this new power, which
threatens to absorb all things,
engages us.
Emerson, "Experience"

"The fate of my books is like the impression of my face," Emerson remarked shortly after the publication of *Representative Men* in 1850. "My acquaintances, as long back as I can remember, have always said, 'Seems to me you look a little thinner than when I saw you last.'" He may have been alluding to an all-too-brief review in the British *Eclectic Review*, published in February. The editors had written: "The 215 pages before us contain the essence of many a 'folio'; but how far such matter is wholesome, or calculated to sustain the life and vigour of the spiritual man, is, alas! quite another question" (*JMN*, 11:214–15). Althouth it is true (as Emerson also noted) that the British in general had never "admitted the claims" of his first two volumes of essays, the response from across the Atlantic was more discerning this time. What the English reviewers correctly found lacking in *Representative Men* was spontaneity, or the voice that arose from the heart of the subject it embraced. Indeed, Emerson himself had probably rehearsed the tenor of their remarks in his journal the year before when he wrote: "It is no matter how fine is your rhetoric, or how strong is your understanding, no book is good which is not written by the Instincts. A fatal frost makes cheerless & undesireable every house where animal heat is not" (*JMN*, 11:145). In *Representative Men* the "animal heat" that produced the essays and lectures written between *Nature* and "The Poet" had clearly waned. Not since "The Poet" could Emerson wholeheartedly believe in the possibility of the Central Man. No longer either could he believe himself to be that individual. Now he stood aside and confessed that "no man, in all the procession of famous men, is reason or illumination or that essence we were looking for." Hence, in his third volume of essays, his great men are partial men, "an exhibition" merely of how we might demonstrate in our own lives one or more of the qualities manifest in the Ideal or Central Man (*W*, 4:32).

The orphic poet of *Nature*, the Whole Man of the American Scholar and Divinity School Addresses, even the friend of *Essays* (1841)—all were now impossible for Emerson. He could no longer inhabit the persona of his essays. Now he had to become the scholar or "literary man" and sing the praise not of heroes but of representative or partial men: Plato, who had "clapped copyright on the world . . . [but could] be quoted on both sides of every question"; Swedenborg, who penetrated "the science of the age with a far more subtle science . . . [but] could never break the umbilical cord which held him to nature"; Montaigne, who scoffed at the extremes of the "abstractionist" and the "materialist" and found satisfaction only in the statement, "There are doubts"; Shakespeare, whose genius made him the world's "most indebted man"; and finally, Bonaparte and Goethe, representatives of the external and internal worlds, but neither able to represent his sphere fully because the first was "an intellect without conscience," the second a "lawgiver of art [but] not an artist."

For Emerson these were *representative* men, for he now found the term *great men* "injurious." "A new danger," he warned, "appears in the excess of influence of the great man. His attractions warp us from our place. We have become underlings and intellectual suicides" (*W*, 4:27). This sounds like Emerson's old caveat against imitation or discipleship, but in the context of *Representative Men* it must be taken as an admission that the possibility of the ideal or great man overwhelms our sense of self-reliance. He would intimidate us with his success, make us doubt our own power. As a consequence, we could no longer imagine our selves at the center of life's drama. In a real sense, this is what happened to Emerson the artist. Unable to square his experience after 1842 with the vision he had apprehended in his earlier work, he stopped writing about himself as the hero of his essays. He became the intellectual "underling" who would never again, not even in "Fate," be able to repress the aspects of the past which now tyrannized his ability to create the drama of his own identity.

A strong poet, writes Harold Bloom, "must divine or invent himself, and so attempt the impossibility of *originating himself*."[1] Bloom points out, of course, that the task is impossible, or that the drama cannot be sustained, and the only evidence of its honest endeavor is the poem itself. Long after his own powers of "original energy" had vanished, Whitman could still define the endeavor: "Camerado, this is no book, / Who touches this touches a man."[2] To become a strong poet, therefore, one must throw himself into the role of the Central Man. Since culmination of the task is beyond the reality of the human condition, a partial repression of the past is necessary. Or to cite Bloom again, all language, especially poetic language, is necessarily a revision of previous language, all poetry a revision of previous poetry: "Any poet (meaning even Homer, if we could know enough about his precursors) is in the position of being 'after the event,' in terms of literary language. His art is necessarily an *aftering*, and so at best he strives for selection, through repression, out of the traces of the language of poetry; that is, he represses some traces, and remembers others."[3]

The strong poet, asserts Bloom, is always about to become his own father (though "son" is perhaps more accurate). This "is the distinguishing mark of a specifically American Sublime, that it begins anew not with restoration or rebirth, in the radically displaced Protestant pattern of the Wordsworthian Sublime, but that it is truly past even such displacement, despite the line from Edwards to Emerson." It is not merely rebirth but "the even more hyperbolical trope of self-begetting"[4] that distinguishes Emerson and Whitman from their Romantic precursors. The "hyperbolical trope" is based upon the concept of the New World, the idea that the American rebirth is not simply a continuation of the Old World generations or literary traditions but the emergence of a new breed. In the American Scholar Address, Emerson called for the Americanization of his country's literary men; they were no longer to remain displaced Englishmen but were now to become naturalized citizens of the New World: "Our day of dependence, our long apprenticeship to the learning of other lands, draws to a close. . . . Events, actions arise, that must be sung, that will sing themselves. Who can doubt that poetry will revive and lead in a new age, as the star in the constellation Harp which now flames in our zenith, astronomers announce, shall one day be the polestar for a thousand years?" (*CW*, 1:52).

As noted in Chapter 5, the Phi Beta Kappa oration was not only America's "intellectual declaration of independence" (as Holmes described it), but Emerson's as well. For in announcing his nation's day of intellectual independence, he was declaring his own by envisioning himself as a personification of the New World. "What I assume you shall assume," Emerson might just as well have announced that day, because his life and the life of his nation became one; and appropriately, they were lives writ large. For the hyperbole they produced resulted from the selective repression of America's literary past in England and on the continent. Whitman would agree that "America does not repel the past or what it has produced under its forms or amid other politics or the ideas of caste or the old religions." Like Emerson in his *strong* work, Whitman at his own literary zenith took from the traces of the past what was necessary and repressed what was not to create his own dual biography. Emerging as his country's poet-priest, he could therefore calmly announce: "The Americans of all nations at any time upon the earth have probably the fullest poetical nature. The United States themselves are essentially the greatest poem."[5] Such a proclamation in the face of a British literary tradition so fresh in the minds of Americans was akin to Emerson's dismissal of "the courtly muses of Europe" in the wake of the English Romantics. Both statements were hyperbolic because they called for a self-begetting. And it is in this light that we can consider Emerson and Whitman the "fathers" of the American sublime. At their literary pinnacles, they cast off the limitations of the human condition and invented the American experience, the exaltation of a spiritual manifest destiny.

———————

"Experience," however, marks the sober point in Emerson's art. This essay is one of his best, for it is indeed autobiography in the sense that the writer's character emerges from the heart of the matter under discussion. It is the matter, though, that keeps the writer from the sublime. He cannot now escape the full impact of the past but must admit defeat of the voice of Orpheus. "All history becomes subjective," Emerson had written in *Essays* (1841); "in other words, there is properly no History; only Biography" (*CW*, 2:6). At that time he was committed to the invention of self, or self-begetting. But with "Experience" he had to confess that "nothing is left us now but death. We look to that with a grim satisfaction, saying There at least is reality that will not dodge us" (*W*, 3:49). Having pursued the hypothetical life through all its illusions, he could no longer elude the truth of history. He thus acknowledged in "Experience," "It is very unhappy, but too late to be helped, the discovery we have made that we exist. That discovery is called the Fall of Man. Ever afterwards we suspect our instruments. . . . Once we lived in what we saw; now, the rapaciousness of this new power, which threatens to absorb all things, engages us" (*W*, 3:75–76).

This new power is "wisdom," the knowledge of human limitation that replaces the "vision" of the self-begetting Poet. The instruments of vision are now suspect, and the drama of self now becomes low comedy: "Do you see that kitten chasing so prettily her own tail? If you could look with her eyes you might see her surrounded with hundreds of figures performing complex dramas, with tragic and comic issues, long conversations, many characters, many ups and downs of fate,—and meantime it is only puss and her tail." He then asks, "How long before our masquerade will end its noise of tambourines, laughter, and shouting, and we shall find it was a solitary performance?" (*W*, 3:80). Puss and her tail. Man is little more than nature's playmate and fool: "We may have the sphere for our cricket-ball, but not a berry for our philosophy" (*W*, 3:49).

"Experience" can be read as a statement of willed optimism in the face of life's adversity. Emerson states at its outset that our "life is not so much threatened as our perception." But to all of us, and particularly the artist, perception is everything. When it finally sees through all the illusions of life to reveal the naked and solitary self, the only reality is death. With "Experience" Emerson becomes the preacher again, trying ever and anon to explain away the limitations of life. He consoles in an often-quoted passage: "Life is a train of moods like a string of beads, and as we pass through them they prove to be many-colored lenses which paint the world their own hue, and each shows only what lies in its own focus" (*W*, 3:45, 50). Temperament, not vision, is everything now. We find not the exaltation of a spiritual manifest destiny but "good advice" under the circumstances. We have, then, in *Essays: Second Series*, *Representative Men*, *English Traits*, *The Conduct of Life*, and beyond, Emerson's bardic wisdom. "Never mind the ridicule, never mind the defeat," he exhorts in "Experience"; "up again, old heart! . . . the true romance which the world exists to realize will be the transformation of genius into practical power" (*W*, 3:85). There is little left that is visionary, for, in the words of Carlyle, "To *know*; to get into the truth of anything is ever a mystic act,—of which the best logics can but babble on the surface."[6]

The quotation comes from *On Heroes and Hero-Worship* (1841), a work that celebrates the concept of the great man, the divinely inspired, unpredictable hero. Emerson's individuals after 1841, however, are neither heroes nor great men but partial men who put their limitations to the best use in an imperfect world. They make allowances and accordingly reflect the spirit of "Experience." Beginning with this essay, Emerson's world view becomes increasingly naturalistic, his concerns more worldly. "The question of the Times is to each one a practical question of the Conduct of Life," he wrote in 1850 and later in "Fate." "How shall I live?" (*JMN*, 11:218). That year, while returning from his first lecture tour in the western states, he met John Murray Forbes, the railroad industrialist. In 1865 Forbes's son married Emerson's younger daughter. Forbes himself was both a successful businessman and a civic-minded American. He brought to the problem of railroad building sound business judgment and a broad view of the relation of the railroad to the public interest. During the Civil War he helped put the state of Massachusetts on a war footing and unselfishly aided his country in a number of other ways. Indeed, Forbes combined the best part of talent and virtue to survive in and contribute to a nation that valued action above all else. Emerson recalled in *Letters and Social Aims* (1875) that "it was my fortune not long ago . . . to fall in with an American to be proud of. . . . never was such force, good meaning, good sense, good action, combined with such domestic lovely behavior, such modesty and persistent preference for others. Wherever he moved he was a benefactor" (*W*, 8:102–3). Forbes and other successful individuals that Emerson came to know through the Saturday Club in the 1850s, for example, must have impressed him with their abilities to survive with dignity in a world of which he wrote in "Wealth": "As soon as a stranger is introduced into any company, one of the first questions which all wish to have answered, is, How does that man get his living?" The question must be entertained, Emerson insisted, for "He is no whole man until he knows how to earn a blameless livelihood" (*W*, 6:85).

At one time the Whole Man was Man Thinking, the man for whom action was essential but subordinate. Now action is equal to thought, for the world operates on polarities of good and evil. "We can only obey our own polarity," Emerson wrote in "Fate." "Nature is no sentimentalist,—does not cosset or pamper us. We must see that the world is rough and surly, and will not mind drowning a man or woman, but swallows your ship like a grain of dust. . . . The way of Providence is a little rude. The habit of snake and spider, the snap of the tiger and other leapers and bloody jumpers, the crackle of the bones of his prey in the coil of the anaconda,—these are in the system, and our habits are like theirs" (*W*, 6:3, 6–7). The Whole Man of "Fate" has no chance for survival until he takes into account the defects of his nature. The concept of Character becomes what the naturalist Dreiser (who read Emerson)[7] called chemism, the condition under which man is a victim mainly of his heredity. As Emerson observes in "Fate," "Jesus said, 'When he looketh on her, he hath committed adultery.' But he is an adulterer before he has yet looked on the woman, by the superfluity of animal and the defect of thought in his constitution. Who meets him, or who meets her, in the street, sees they are ripe to be each other's victim" (*W*, 6:11). Emerson's view of humankind is no longer balanced by the power of spontaneity or Character (as it is in "Self-Reliance," for example),[8] or considered in the light of one of Whitman's "native" moments (first described in the edition that addressed Emerson as "Master"). Instead, it is viewed as a disorder of "digestion and sex" that saps the individual's "vital force." Man is too often the victim of the baser instincts from which only the actions (or the example) of such men as Forbes can protect him.

Emerson's gradual shift from Man Thinking to Man Acting in the 1850s makes his admiration of *Leaves of Grass* all the more remarkable. We could perhaps understand it so much the better had Whitman issued his book in the 1830s. For then Emerson still sought out and encouraged "thinkers"—Alcott, Thoreau, Ellery Channing, Charles Newcomb, and Margaret Fuller—individuals who would have been hard-pressed to answer the worldly question of how they got their living. There were many in Concord, for example, who never quite forgave Thoreau for quitting his teaching post in the midst of the Panic of 1837, for becoming an "idler" when he had been one of the few in the town fortunate enough to receive a university education. Emerson, on the other hand, remained beyond reproach as to the manner in which he earned his living.[9] Indeed, the role of gentleman-lecturer gradually replaced that of "infidel," convincing even the conservative elders at Harvard College more than thirty years after the Divinity School Address that it was safe to have him back as a lecturer.

Yet it is at this point in Emerson's career that he enjoys his most daring and prescient moment as a critic—his recognition of Whitman's genius. We might speculate, therefore, that Emerson's more worldly view was in some way responsible for his perception, that *Leaves of Grass* might have gone unnoticed by him in the 1830s. In Chapter 2 it was noted how the young minister's interest in geology and evolution led him to the theory of amelioration. Still, the very concept confined man to the world of thought and kept him from the world of action, just as it anticipated the platonic return of the Soul to its origin. In 1855, when Emerson began to admire men of action (without the hesitation of the Transcendentalist), he found in *Leaves of Grass* a poet with a "blameless livelihood." Here was a poet who combined the *Bhagavadgita* and the New York *Herald*.

The theory helps to explain not only Emerson's enthusiasm for *Leaves of Grass*, but also its brevity. "I find it the most extraordinary piece of wit & wisdom America has yet contributed," Emerson wrote in 1855. "Wit" and "wisdom" have always struck me as strange terms for the father of American Romanticism to use in greeting his son. Nevertheless, as he opened the volume and encountered the steel engraving of this "workingman" and read his sublime thoughts, he must have discovered the supreme Yankee, one who had indeed written the new "edition" of *Nature*, the "practical" application of Transcendentalism. It appeared that Whitman's "vision," with its emphasis on the *Body* as well as the Soul, was Emerson's "wisdom." In this context it echoed the theme of "Fate" (in lecture form since the early 1850s): "One key, one solution to the mysteries of human condition, one solution to the old knots of fate, freedom, and foreknowledge, exists; the propounding, namely, of the double consciousness. A man must ride alternately on the horses of his private and his public nature" (W, 6:47). No better example, surely, of the private man and his public soul could Emerson find than in Whitman's blend of "wit & wisdom" in *Leaves of Grass*.

To put the matter another way, the Emerson of "wisdom" could appreciate Whitman's "vision" because *Leaves of Grass* was true to the senses, to the Body to which Emerson had returned in "Experience." Unlike Emerson's strong work, which cut him off from the Body and allowed the work to control the life, Whitman's work was almost totally experiential, a fact Emerson could clearly see. Whereas the Emersonian "vision" became an ameliorative quest of the Soul, Whitman's refused to let the Body go; once the poet was dead, it would fill the forms of his readers, "filter and fibre [their] blood." Emerson may have held his nose when he read the 1856 edition, as he told Moncure Conway,[10] but this was not the case in 1855. Nor are his negative comments to Conway and others[11] indicative of more than his embarrassed reaction to Whitman's printing of his letter and to the public response to *Leaves of Grass*. Emerson's admiration for not only the first edition but the second and third of Whitman's book was sound, notwithstanding his banter about "deodorizing the illustration," because those editions contained the best part of Emerson's early and late philosophy. Thus, when Whitman after 1860 eventually blurred his doctrine of the private body and the public soul in order to become more Emersonian, Emerson saw his mistake. Orpheus had come to each in different guises. Therefore, Whitman's becoming the poet of the Soul (as he does in such later poems as "Proud Music of the Storm" and "Passage to India") made the orphic flight a sham. It was a sham because he no longer invents himself, but instead clones another Emerson. Out of the pieces of his own shattered "vision," Whitman constructed the mosaic that became Emerson's "wisdom."

"Vision" becomes "wisdom" the moment the artist's work comes into conflict with truth and nature. This juncture in Emerson's work is characterized by pessimism and compromise, first evident in "Experience." Whitman's later phase is somewhat different because he fights off the pessimism as his art now reflects a *conscious* attempt to ignore and hence transcend the "trash" of nature's shores. And it was because of this difference that Emerson generally disapproved of Whitman's later poetry.

The clash between the later Emerson and the later Whitman is best appreciated in an examination of their respective definitions of culture. At the outset of this study, I dismissed this difference in the context that the term is a synonym for "background." However, with Emerson and Whitman beyond their *strong* periods, the distinction is useful and illuminating in the sense that culture is the "link" that draws both men back into the fold of society. Emerson, no longer holding a belief in the ability of Character to do more than mitigate the surly antagonism of nature, now saw man as isolated by his own self-love. The admission that transcendence was not fully possible was judicious, he thought. At the same time, he realized that the acceptance of isolation, or the ineffectuality of spiritual growth in a world of ruthless change, could also lead to provinciality or egotism. That is, man cut off from the community of souls throughout time and cut off from most of the living would naturally seek out only those who nourished his sense of self-love; he would confine his conversation to "his family, or a few companions,—perhaps with half a dozen personalities that are famous in his neighborhood." In his essay on "Culture" (in *The Conduct of Life*), he therefore defined his subject as that which "kills [man's] exaggeration; his conceit of his village or his city" (*W*, 6:135, 137). Culture, then, is an antidote to self-love or egotism in a world in which compromise or balance is always necessary. "We go to Europe to be Americanized," he wrote, qualifying his long-standing caveat on traveling "as a fool's paradise." For Emerson, culture is an admission of the fact of our limitations, of the truth that Knowledge resides in the Old World of necessity, too: "And thus, of the six or seven teachers whom each man wants among his contemporaries, it often happens that one or two of them live on the other side of the world" (*W*, 6:147).

Like the Whole Man of "Fate," the man of "Culture" is whole

only when he can admit his limitations, only when he considers
the spontaneous and sole reliance upon Character as ultimately
provincial and egotistical. Whitman, however, refused to give up
the concept of Character even when his poetry was no longer
capable of celebrating it. With the persona of the early *Leaves*
totally dissipated, he tried relentlessly to turn his ideas into a
program for America. Evidence of this effort is first seen in the
essay "Personalism," which was published in the *Galaxy* in 1868.
It was Whitman's answer to Emerson's version of culture. "The
quality of B E I N G, in the object's self, according to its own central
idea and purpose, and of growing therefrom and thereto—not
criticism by other standards, and adjustments thereto—is the
lesson of Nature," Whitman argued.[12] As to the kind of culture
advocated in "the rich pages of old-world Plutarch and Shakespeare, or our own Emerson," he asked: "Are not the processes
of Culture rapidly creating a class of supercilious infidels, who
believe in nothing?"[13] He thought such a culture tended to "sys-
temize" the products of American "fertility" in order to bring
them into line with European models. "I should demand a programme of Culture, drawn out, not for a single class alone, or for
the parlors or lecture-rooms, but with an eye to practical life, the
West, the workingmen, the facts of farmers, and jackplanes and
engineers, and of the broad range of the women also of the
middle and working strata of the States, and with reference to
the perfect equality of women, and of a grand and powerful
motherhood."[14]

Whitman's culture was hardly short of a national program of
eugenics. "Will the time hasten when fatherhood and motherhood shall become a science—and the noblest science?" he in-
quired.[15] In "Song of Myself" the protagonist sees himself as
starting "bigger and nimbler babes . . . jetting the stuff of far
more arrogant republics." There he is speaking in the hyperbolical context of self-begetting; here it is a "programme." We have
clearly in the later Whitman the Good Gray Poet, a bard who has
lost the spontaneity of being and become a tireless preacher. In
his second act, so to speak, he even removes the sex from his
poetry in order to become *the* poet, the bard of transcendence for
America. On the surface of things, we might expect Emerson to

think better of Whitman's sex-less poetry because he had urged the excision of the "Children of Adam" poems from the 1860 edition. In fact, it was Emerson who placed "Proud Music of the Storm" in the *Atlantic Monthly* a year after Whitman's "Personalism" had appeared. But in the light of the later Emerson's appreciation of Whitman's combination of sense and spirit, we must accept Whitman's assertion that Emerson's objections on Boston Common were practical instead of aesthetic or philosophical. Possibly, Emerson hoped to find in Whitman's "new rhythmus," which promised to produce "poems bridging the way from life to Death," a development of the "vision" he had admired in the first three editions of *Leaves of Grass*.[16]

Whatever the case, there is no further evidence to suggest that Emerson found in the later poetry what he looked for. The publication of "Proud Music of the Storm" was the last occasion when he intervened on Whitman's behalf. More likely, he grew tired of the poet's "second act." In 1870 he spoke of Whitman to the Englishman James Bryce "very amusingly, [as one] from whom he evidently does not expect much more now, thinking he has not improved in his later productions." Emerson added that Whitman had "an immense estimate of his own performances, and does not desire criticism."[17] It was doubtless Whitman's "immense estimate" of his poetry that led Emerson to lose interest in the man he had once called his literary "benefactor." Full of "wisdom" now, Whitman was playing *the* poet, posing as *the* poet in countless photographs in his later phase. Taking in, without qualification perhaps, William O'Connor's generous comparisons of him with Homer, Dante, Shakespeare, and other great national poets, he set out on his program of eugenics. His "second act," however, was really no more than an encore. Unlike the poetry of the first three editions in which he traveled the public road by himself, the later poetry contained his endeavor to lead a nation down that road. This undertaking is perhaps most clearly exemplified in "Passage to India."

Richard Chase is probably the most perceptive of those few critics who do not consider the poem a masterpiece. With "Passage to India," he writes, "Whitman has given up poetry and become a speechmaker."[18] We look in vain for the tensions that mark the earlier poetry—the loneliness, the insecurity, the search for identity, indeed, the rhythms of American vernacular. Rather, we now have the messiah leading his people on "a passage to more than India!" Roy Harvey Pearce observes that Whitman was asking more of poetry that it could give.[19] First published in 1871, it surveys three feats of engineering[20] in order to sail forth on "the seas of God." But the language is flaccid, the philosophy vague. To quote Chase again, "The deft and flexible wit [of the earlier poetry] disappears along with the contraries and disparities which once produced it. The pathos, once so moving when the poet contemplated the disintegration of the self or felt the loss which all living things know, is now generalized out into a vague perception of the universal."[21] In short, with his new theory of personalism, the poet suffers from the excesses of "mean egotism," as Emerson termed it in *Nature*.

In the essay on personalism, Whitman had defined culture as the emergence of New World Character, a development that would take America on a voyage back to what he called the Elder Brother in "Passage to India." Personalism was "not physically perfect only—not satisfied with the mere mind's and learning's store, but Religious, possessing the idea of the Infinite. . . . Personality of mortal life is most important with reference to the immortal, the Unknown, the Spiritual, the only permanently real, which, as the ocean waits for and receives the rivers, waits for us each and all."[22] In the poem the narrator hails Columbus: "Dominating the rest I see the Admiral himself." The poet now is identified with Columbus, the ultimate voyager because he discovered the New World. No longer the solitary explorer of "Song of Myself," the poet is the captain of the ship that takes his crew to a New World beyond all previous worlds:

> After the seas are all cross'd, (as they seem already
>   cross'd,)
> After the great captains and engineers have accomplish'd
>   their work,
> After the noble inventors, after the scientists, the chemist,
>   the geologist, ethnologist,

> Finally shall come the poet worthy that name,
> The True son of God shall come singing his songs.[23]

Of course, this is not Emerson's poet of compromise, the Whole Man of "Fate"; neither is he who worries about being worthy of the name poet the man of the American Scholar Address or "The Poet." Instead, he is the leader of the people, the savior of all men who have come into conflict with truth and nature. This poet culminates the deeds of lesser but nevertheless "worthy" individuals—voyagers, scientists, inventors—who apprehend only *part* of the New World. But in the wake of the Poet: "Nature and man shall be disjoined and diffused no more, / The true son of God shall absolutely fuse them." The "true son of God"? Whitman was accused of playing Christ in "Song of Myself," whereas actually he was playing himself. In "Passage to India," however, he has fallen back on conventional Christian ideas and is obviously guilty of trying to play God.

In this passage and throughout the poem generally, the problem is that Whitman simply tried too hard or too consciously to become the poet Emerson had described before "Experience," a liberating god that leads men to find "within their world another world" (*W*, 3:30). As a result, the ideas in the poem are not sufficiently Whitman's. "Swiftly I shrivel at the thought of God, / At nature and its wonders, Time and Space and Death," the poet exclaims sententiously. The confession pales beside the spontaneity and native swagger of such lines as "Be not curious about God" or "I hear and behold God in every object, yet understand God not in the least, / Nor do I understand who there can be more wonderful than myself." In "Song of Myself" and "A Word Out of the Sea," Body and Soul are inexplicably bound together, without a conscious thought for Emerson's distinction between the "Me" and the "Not-Me." In "Passage to India" Whitman forces his thoughts into the old Emersonian form. The Body is now discarded for the Soul, "thou actual Me."[24]

"When I commenced, years ago, elaborating the plan of my poems . . . ," Whitman claimed in 1872, "one deep purpose un-

derlay the others, and has underlain it and its execution ever
since—and that has been the religious purpose." This fabrication
was compounded in 1876 when he announced that his *original*
intention was, "after chanting in 'Leaves of Grass' the songs
of the body and existence, to then compose a further, equally
needed volume, based on those convictions of perpetuity and
conservation which . . . make the unseen soul govern absolutely
at last" (*PW*, 461, 466). Although he insisted that he was not
denying the "physical and the sensuous," he nevertheless violated the very nature of *Leaves of Grass* in his attempt to become
Emerson's poet of "transcendence," a poet who would be "respectable" because his art transcended the physical in its "passage to more than India." He announced in his 1872 preface: "I
will see . . . whether there is not, for my purposes as poet, a
religion, and a sound religious germanency in the average human
race, at least in their modern development in the United States
. . . a germanency that has too long been unencouraged, unsung,
almost unknown" (*PW*, 2:462). In such a role, however, Whitman
was a Transcendentalist who had missed the movement. Besides
the fact that his poetry now appeals to a nation and not to the
individual, it attempts to call forth the "Slumbering Giant" in a
nation whose self-reliance has been shattered by civil war. His
appeal is addressed to a nation so disillusioned by events that it
now seeks refuge in Emerson's conception of culture.

Emerson was no philosopher in the true sense of the word. He
originated no philosophy—only a language or metaphor with
which American intellectuals could embrace the principles of English Romanticism and thereby experience the *American* sublime.
Whitman was no philosopher either, and when he attempted to
become one in his poetry, his vision was conceptualized rather
than imagined (as in "Passage to India"). It was also bad philosophy because it hopelessly diluted and distorted the "vision" that
made him a strong poet in the first three editions of *Leaves of
Grass*. Both writers, then, cease to write at their best when they
abandon language and its ability to clothe the invisible world
with original and exotic tropes for the vernacular of the philosopher and its inevitable failure to transcend the limits of empirical
knowledge. To say it another way, their passage from "vision" to

"wisdom" is the path from individualism to institutionalism. With particular reference to their art, it is the way back from gnosticism to faith. Both, finally thrown back by the harshness of the individual pilgrimage in their strong poetry, retreat to rally the nation behind them. Here Emerson proceeds with caution and turns to culture; Whitman develops an inflated sense of ego that Emerson's culture warns against. But in both cases, self-reliance is now nothing unless it be institutionalized and called culture or personalism. They come full circle in their later periods. Indeed, they return to a form of Christianity in which the law of the group is more important than the freedom of the individual.

Their ultimate destination is Society, a landing place most clearly suggested by Emerson in "Poetry and Imagination." This essay was begun in the 1850s but not published until 1875 in *Letters and Social Aims* (a volume largely pieced together from Emerson's lectures by James Elliot Cabot). Poetry is defined as "the perpetual endeavor to express the spirit of a thing, to pass the brute body and search the life and reason which causes it to exist" (*W*, 8:17). It is the attempt to look beyond "the brute body" of this world for a second set of facts, and this is accomplished through the imagination, or man's "second sight." But Emerson concedes that the poet merely *observes* these higher laws; he does not transgress them. The best the poet can hope for is a "union of the first and second sight," or the Understanding and the Reason. For men may be imaginative, "but are not overpowered by [this second sight] to the extent of confounding its suggestions with the external facts" (*W*, 8:22).

"We live in both spheres, and must not mix them" (*W*, 8:22). Death forever separates the realms of the Understanding and the Reason. This definition of poetry is, of course, not the one that led either Emerson himself or Whitman to the brink of self-discovery, to the American sublime that so confounded its suggestions with "the external facts" as to make them fade into oblivion. Nor is this the same poet who wrote: "With what joy I begin to read a poem which I confide in as an inspiration! And now my chains are to be broken; I shall mount above these clouds and opaque airs in which I live,—opaque though they seem transparent,— and from the heaven of truth I shall see and comprehend my relations" (*W*, 3:12). In "Poetry and Imagination" the poet is no longer envisioned as the Whole or Central Man; he is not a *hero* but a *representative* man. "When we describe man as poet, and credit him with the triumphs of art," Emerson now confessed, "we speak of the potential or ideal man,—*not found in any one person*" (italics mine). As he had done in *Representative Men* (which was published about the time this essay was conceived), Emerson shrank from allowing any one individual to possess *all* of the heroic characteristics: "You must go through a city or a nation, and find one faculty here, one there, to build the true poet withal. Yet all men know the portrait when it is drawn, and it is part of religion to believe its possible incarnation" (*W*, 8:26). "Poetry and Imagination" is Emerson's textbook version of his earlier "vision"; its message is not that all poetry "was written before time was," but that "poetry is faith" (*W*, 8:31). Its vision is now "part of religion." The essay contains Emerson's "wisdom" that the institution is stronger than the individual. It also anticipates Whitman's theme in "Passage to India" and other poems. Like Emerson in this essay and other later works, Whitman came to forsake self-reliance for the composite strength of a nation. Indeed, one might say that in both cases pluralism marked the departure of the orphic muse. No longer could their songs pretend to tame the beasts of the wilderness.

Abbreviations

The following abbreviations are used parenthetically in the text and notes:

EMERSON

CW   *The Collected Works of Ralph Waldo Emerson*, ed. Alfred R. Ferguson et al., 2 vols. to date (Cambridge: Harvard University Press, 1971–).

CEC   *The Correspondence of Emerson and Carlyle*, ed. Joseph Slater (New York: Columbia University Press, 1964).

EL   *The Early Lectures of Ralph Waldo Emerson*, ed. Stephen E. Whicher, Robert E. Spiller, and Wallace E. Williams, 3 vols. (Cambridge: Harvard University Press, 1959–72).

J   *Journals of Ralph Waldo Emerson*, ed. Edward Waldo Emerson and Waldo Emerson Forbes, 10 vols. (Boston: Houghton, Mifflin and Co., 1909–14).

JMN   *The Journals and Miscellaneous Notebooks of Ralph Waldo Emerson*, ed. William H. Gilman et al., 15 vols. to date (Cambridge: Harvard University Press, 1960–).

L   *The Letters of Ralph Waldo Emerson*, ed. Ralph L. Rusk, 6 vols. (New York: Columbia University Press, 1939).

MH   Houghton Library, Harvard University.

W   *The Complete Works of Ralph Waldo Emerson*, ed. Edward Waldo Emerson, 12 vols. (Boston: Houghton, Mifflin and Co., 1903–4).

YES   *Young Emerson Speaks*, ed. Arthur C. McGiffert, Jr. (Boston: Houghton Mifflin Co., 1938).

WHITMAN

C   *The Correspondence of Walt Whitman*, ed. Edwin Haviland Miller, 6 vols. (New York: New York University Press, 1961–77).

DN   *Walt Whitman: Daybooks and Notebooks*, ed. William White, 3 vols. (New York: New York University Press, 1978).

EPF *Walt Whitman: The Early Poems and the Fiction*, ed. Thomas L.
       Brasher (New York: New York University Press, 1963).
GF   *The Gathering of the Forces by Walt Whitman*, ed. Cleveland Rodgers
       and John Black, 2 vols. (New York: G. P. Putnam's Sons, 1920).
PW   *Walt Whitman: Prose Works 1892*, ed. Floyd Stovall, 2 vols. (New
       York: New York University Press, 1963–64).
SIT *I Sit and Look Out: Editorials from the Brooklyn "Daily Times" by
       Walt Whitman*, ed. Emory Holloway and Vernolian Schwarz (New
       York: Columbia University Press, 1932).
UPP *The Uncollected Poetry and Prose of Walt Whitman*, ed. Emory
       Holloway, 2 vols. (New York: Doubleday, Doran & Co., 1921).
WWA *Walt Whitman of the New York "Aurora,"* ed. Joseph Jay Rubin
       and Charles H. Brown (State College, Penn.: Bald Eagle Press,
       1950; reprint ed., Westport, Conn.: Greenwood Press, 1972).
WWC *With Walt Whitman in Camden*, ed. Horace Traubel, 6 vols.: vol. 1
       (Boston: Small, Maynard & Co., 1906); vols. 2 and 3 (New York:
       Mitchell Kennerley, 1914 and 1915); vol. 4 (Philadelphia: University
       of Pennsylvania Press, 1953); vols. 5 and 6 (Carbondale: University
       of Southern Illinois Press, 1964 and 1982).

Notes

1. James Elliot Cabot, *A Memoir of Ralph Waldo Emerson* (Boston: Houghton, Mifflin and Co., 1887), vol. 1, pp. 280–81.

2. *The Transcendentalists: An Anthology*, ed. Perry Miller (Cambridge: Harvard University Press, 1950), p. 151.

3. See also *J*, 9:401: "*Thoreau*. Perhaps his fancy for Walt Whitman grew out of his taste for wild nature, for an otter, a woodchuck, or a loon." In other words, Thoreau often celebrated nature as much for its own sake as for its use as a Transcendental emblem.

4. See William M. Moss, " 'So Many Promising Youths': Emerson's Disappointing Discoveries of New England Poet-Seers," *New England Quarterly* 49 (1976): 46–64.

5. Trowbridge claimed that Whitman had admitted to him: "I was simmering, simmering, simmering; Emerson brought me to a boil." See his "Reminiscences of Walt Whitman," *Atlantic Monthly* 89 (1902): 163–75; the anecdote is repeated in *My Own Story* (Boston: Houghton, Mifflin and Co., 1903), pp. 360–401.

6. Eleanor M. Tilton, ed. "*Leaves of Grass*: Four Letters to Emerson," *Harvard Library Bulletin* 27 (1979): 337–39.

7. For the opposition of Lowell and the arguments by O'Connor and Burroughs, see Jerome Loving, *Walt Whitman's Champion: William Douglas O'Connor* (College Station: Texas A&M University Press, 1978), pp. 103–38 passim. Edward Emerson's comment regarding his father's attitude toward Whitman is found in his *Emerson in Concord* (Boston: Houghton, Mifflin and Co., 1889), p. 228n. The most useful study of the "Whitmaniacs" is Charles B. Willard, *Whitman's American Fame: The Growth of His Reputation in America after 1892* (Providence: Brown University Press, 1950), pp. 32–84.

8. John B. Moore, "The Master of Whitman," *Studies in Philology* 23 (1926): 77–89; and Clarence Gohdes, "Whitman and Emerson," *Sewanee Review* 37 (1929): 79–93.

9. Lawrence Willson, "The 'Body Electric' Meets the Genteel Tradition," *New Mexico Quarterly* 26 (1956–57): 369–86. Although Willson's argument is somewhat of a caricature of the pro-Emerson sentiment, it nevertheless represents the consensus, which is decidedly against

Whitman. Critics have persisted, it appears, to see Whitman as inferior to and thus the disciple of Emerson. For further arguments in this vein, see Emerson Grant Sutcliffe, "Whitman, Emerson and the New Poetry," *New Republic* 19 (1919): 114–16; Norman Foerster, "Whitman and the Cult of Confusion," *North American Review* 213 (1921): 799–812; Killis Campbell, "The Evolution of Whitman as an Artist," *American Literature* 6 (1934): 254–63; Hyatt H. Waggoner, *American Poets from the Puritans to the Present* (Boston: Houghton Mifflin Co., 1968); and Harold Bloom, *A Map of Misreading* (New York: Oxford University Press, 1975) and *Poetry and Repression: Revisionism from Blake to Stevens* (New Haven: Yale University Press, 1976). Few studies that confront the Emerson-Whitman connection directly argue convincingly for Whitman's originality: Leon Howard, "For a Critique of Whitman's Transcendentalism," *Modern Language Notes* 47 (1932): 79–85; F. O. Matthiessen, *American Renaissance: Art and Expression in the Age of Emerson and Whitman* (New York: Oxford University Press, 1941); Roy Harvey Pearce, *The Continuity of American Poetry* (Princeton: Princeton University Press, 1961); and Lawrence Buell, "Transcendentalist Catalogue Rhetoric: Vision versus Form," *American Literature* 40 (1968): 325–39, and *Literary Transcendentalism: Style and Vision in the American Renaissance* (Ithaca: Cornell University Press, 1973).

10. Stephen Whicher, *Freedom and Fate: An Inner Life of Ralph Waldo Emerson* (Philadelphia: University of Pennsylvania Press, 1953).

11. To his credit, however, Emerson first spoke out against slavery in 1838 in Concord. In 1844, on the anniversary of the emancipation of the slaves of the British West Indies, his protest grew stronger. Yet his attitude toward the abolition movement is probably best characterized by the following journal entry: "Does he not do more to abolish slavery who works all day steadily in his own garden than he who goes to the abolition-meeting and makes a speech?" (Cabot, *A Memoir*, vol. 2, p. 424). It was not until the passage of the Fugitive Slave Law in 1850 that Emerson's tone became more satisfying to the abolitionists. For Emerson's letter to Van Buren, see Cabot, *A Memoir*, vol. 2, pp. 697–702; evidence of his mixed feelings over the affair is found in *JMN*, 5:479.

12. The story of Whittier's response to *Leaves of Grass* may be apocryphal; see Lewis E. Weeks, Jr., "Did Whittier Really Burn Whitman's *Leaves of Grass?*" *Walt Whitman Review* 22 (1976): 22–30.

13. Hyatt H. Waggoner, *Emerson As Poet* (Princeton: Princeton University Press, 1975), p. 22.

14. Frederic Ives Carpenter, *Emerson Handbook* (New York: Hendrick House, 1953), p. 126.

15. *Walt Whitman's "Leaves of Grass": The First (1855) Edition*, ed. Malcolm Cowley (New York: Viking Press, 1959), p. 22.

16. Ibid., p. 34.

17. *Civil War Letters of George Washington Whitman*, ed. Jerome Loving (Durham: Duke University Press, 1975), p. 9.

18. The tales and poems mentioned above are found in *EPF*, pp. 110–15, 61–68, 21–24, 55–60, and 61–67.

19. See *UPP*, 2:35–37; and *EPF*, pp. 55–60.

20. *The First (1855) Edition*, pp. 31–32, 39.

CHAPTER 2

1. See Conrad Wright, *The Beginnings of Unitarianism in America* (New York: Archon Books, 1976), pp. 8–14.

2. Ibid., pp. 57–58.

3. See Alexander Kern, "The Rise of Transcendentalism," in *Transitions in American Literary History*, ed. Harry Hayden Clark (Durham: Duke University Press, 1953), pp. 252–53.

4. Perry Miller, "From Jonathan Edwards to Emerson" (*New England Quarterly*, 1940), in *American Transcendentalism: An Anthology of Criticism*, ed. Brian M. Barbour (Notre Dame: University of Notre Dame Press, 1973), p. 70.

5. See also Sheldon W. Liebman, "Emerson's Transformation in the 1820's," *American Literature* 40 (1968): 133–54.

6. See *The Transcendentalists: An Anthology*, ed. Perry Miller (Cambridge: Harvard University Press, 1950), pp. 23, 25.

7. Joel Porte, *Representative Man: Ralph Waldo Emerson in His Time* (New York: Oxford University Press, 1979), pp. 125–26.

8. Liebman, "Emerson's Transformation in the 1820's," p. 133.

9. Joy Bayless, *Rufus Wilmot Griswold; Poe's Literary Executor* (Nashville: Vanderbilt University Press, 1943), p. 66.

10. In a lecture entitled "The Head." Variations of this passage occur in *JMN*, 5:112; and in the essay "Intellect."

11. Gay Wilson Allen, "A New Look at Emerson and Science," in *Literature and Ideas in America: Essays in Memory of Harry Hayden Clark*, ed. Robert Falk (Athens: Ohio University Press, 1975), p. 69.

12. "The stars awaken a certain reverence" (*Nature*); "I once heard a preacher who sorely tempted me to say, I would go to church no more" (Divinity School Address).

13. Ralph L. Rusk, *Life of Ralph Waldo Emerson* (New York: Columbia University Press, 1949), p. 187.

14. The final clause was later amended to read: "But the language put together into a most significant & universal book."

15. Allen, "A New Look at Emerson and Science," p. 70; see also David Robinson, "Emerson's Natural Theology and the Paris Naturalists: Toward a Theory of Animated Nature," *Journal of the History of Ideas* 41 (1980): 69–88.

16. Frederic Ives Carpenter, *Emerson and Asia* (Cambridge: Harvard University Press, 1930), pp. 44–45.

17. Porte, *Representative Man*, p. 315.

18. Jerome Loving, *Walt Whitman's Champion: William Douglas O'Connor* (College Station: Texas A&M University Press, 1978), pp. 165–66.

19. Gay Wilson Allen, *Waldo Emerson: A Biography* (New York: Viking Press, 1981), p. 258.

20. Sanborn refused to allow Traubel to make his letter public, an action that seemingly challenges its validity; however, he did so to avoid offending the Emerson family. See Jerome Loving, "Emerson's 'Constant Way of Looking at Whitman's Genius,'" *American Literature* 51 (1979): 399–401.

CHAPTER 3

1. Charles I. Glicksberg, "William Leggett, Neglected Figure," *Journalism Quarterly* 25 (1948): 54.

2. Edward K. Spann, *Ideals and Politics: New York Intellectuals and Liberal Democracy* (Albany: State University of New York Press, 1972), p. 54.

3. William Cullen Bryant, "William Leggett," *United States Magazine and Democratic Review* 6 (1839): 18.

4. Thomas L. Brasher, *Whitman As Editor of the Brooklyn "Eagle"* (Detroit: Wayne State University Press, 1970), p. 20.

5. Joseph Jay Rubin, *The Historic Whitman* (University Park: Pennsylvania State University Press, 1973), p. 39.

6. Joseph Beaver, *Walt Whitman—Poet of Science* (Morningside Heights, N.Y.: King's Crown Press, 1951), pp. 124–25.

7. *Complete Writings of Walt Whitman*, ed. Richard Maurice Bucke et al. (New York: G. P. Putnam's Sons, 1902), vol. 10, p. 15.

8. Quoted from the *American Phrenological Journal* in Edward Hungerford, "Walt Whitman and His Chart of Bumps," *American Literature* 2 (1931): 370n.

9. The review was also included elsewhere; see Walt Whitman, *Imprints* (Boston: Thayer and Eldridge, 1860), pp. 38–41; and *In Re Walt Whitman*, ed. Horace Traubel et al. (Philadelphia: David McKay, 1893), pp. 27–30.

10. *Walt Whitman: "Leaves of Grass"; Comprehensive Reader's Edition*, ed. Harold W. Blodgett and Sculley Bradley (New York: New York University Press, 1965), p. 737.

11. *Complete Writings*, vol. 9, p. 3.

12. Walt Whitman, "Geology and the Scriptures," New York *Aurora*, 29 March 1842 (not included in *WWA*).

13. See Rubin, *The Historic Whitman*, pp. 3–136 passim; and Herbert Bergman, "Walt Whitman as a Journalist, 1831–January, 1848," *Journalism Quarterly* 48 (1971): 195–204.

14. Hungerford, "Walt Whitman and His Chart of Bumps," p. 360.

15. Ibid., p. 328.

16. See Arthur Wrobel, "Whitman and the Phrenologists: The Divine Body and the Sensuous Soul," *PMLA* 89 (1974): 19; and Justin Kaplan, "The Naked Self and Other Problems," in *Telling Lives: The Biographer's Art*, ed. Marc Pachter (Washington, D.C.: New Republic Books, 1979), p. 48.

17. John Burroughs, *Notes on Walt Whitman as Poet and Person*, 2d ed. (New York: American News Company, 1871), pp. 16–17. See also Frederick P. Hier, Jr., "The End of a Literary Mystery," *American Mercury* 1 (1934): 471–78.

18. For the most exhaustive survey of Whitman's reading of Emerson, see Floyd Stovall, *The Foreground of "Leaves of Grass"* (Charlottesville: University Press of Virginia, 1974), pp. 282–305.

19. Quoted from Richard Chase, *Walt Whitman Reconsidered* (New York: William Sloane Associates, 1955), pp. 50–51.

20. Whitman's clipping of the review is in the Trent Collection, Duke University Library; it is reprinted with the poet's marginalia in *Complete Writings*, vol. 9, pp. 158–59.

21. Chase, *Walt Whitman Reconsidered*, p. 48.

22. See Robert K. Martin, *The Homosexual Tradition in American Poetry* (Austin: University of Texas Press, 1979), p. 90. See also *UPP*, 2:90, 94–97; and Martin's discussion of it (*Homosexual Tradition*, p. 6).

23. Rubin, *The Historic Whitman*, p. 174.

24. Rollo G. Silver, "Whitman in 1850: Three Uncollected Articles," *American Literature* 19 (1948): 303.

25. *Walt Whitman's "Leaves of Grass": The First (1855) Edition*, ed. Malcolm Cowley (New York: Viking Press, 1959), pp. 5–6.

26. Ibid., pp. 16–17, 21.

27. Rubin, *The Historic Whitman*, p. 306.

28. Emerson's disenchantment is discussed in chap. 4.

29. See Rubin, *The Historic Whitman*, pp. 273–76, for additional background to this letter.

30. *The First (1855) Edition*, p. 8.

31. Rubin, *The Historic Whitman*, p. 272.

32. *The First (1855) Edition*, p. 121.

33. Ibid., p. 82.

34. Ibid., p. 68.

35. See James Elliot Cabot, *A Memoir of Ralph Waldo Emerson* (Boston: Houghton, Mifflin and Co., 1887), vol. 1, p. 306; *JMN*, 11:412; and "Song of Myself" (sec. 24). I am indebted to Gay Wilson Allen for calling the first parallel to my attention.

36. *Faint Clews & Indirections: Manuscripts of Walt Whitman and His Family*, ed. Clarence Gohdes and Rollo G. Silver (Durham: Duke University Press, 1949), p. 28.

37. D. H. Lawrence, *Studies in Classic American Literature* (New York: Viking Press, 1923), p. 171.

38. *The First (1855) Edition*, pp. x, xxviii.

39. Jerome Loving, " 'A Well-Intended Halfness': Emerson's View of *Leaves of Grass*," *Studies in American Humor* 3 (1976): 61–68. These poems are discussed briefly in chap. 7.

40. *The First (1855) Edition*, p. 5.

41. *In Re Walt Whitman*, pp. 13–14, 23–24, 27.

42. Bernard Bailyn et al., *The Great Republic: A History of the American People* (Lexington, Mass.: D. C. Heath and Co., 1977), pp. 624–30.

43. Clifton J. Furness, *Walt Whitman's Workshop: A Collection of Unpublished Manuscripts* (Cambridge: Harvard University Press, 1928), pp. 92–113, 227n. *Notes & Fragments* was edited by Richard Maurice Bucke in 1899 and printed for private distribution. Quotations from Whitman's tract, however, are taken from a later and more reliable text, *Walt Whitman: The Eighteenth Presidency!* ed. Edward F. Grier (Lawrence: University of Kansas Press, 1956), pp. 22, 21, 37.

44. Northern politicians who sympathized with the South.

45. Gay Wilson Allen, *The Solitary Singer: A Critical Biography of Walt Whitman*, rev. ed. (New York: New York University Press, 1967), p. 197.

46. *Walt Whitman: The Eighteenth Presidency!* p. 21.

47. Ibid., pp. 24–25.

48. Allen, *The Solitary Singer*, p. 198.

49. "1855 Preface," *The First (1855) Edition*, p. 15. Evidence of Whitman's desire to rally America into action may be found in what became "A Boston Ballad." "Clear the way there Jonathan!" the poet declares in the opening lines, thus suggesting that Americans are clearing the way for slavery in the North if they abide by Webster's compromise. The poem closes with this stinging remonstrance: "Stick your hands in your pockets Jonathan. . . . you are a made man from this day, / You are mighty cute. . . . and here is one of your bargains" (pp. 135, 137).

50. *The First (1855) Edition*, p. xxvii.

51. *Walt Whitman Reconsidered*, p. 23.

CHAPTER 4

1. See Ralph Admari, "*Leaves of Grass*—First Edition," *American Book Collector* 5 (1934): 150–52.

2. *Walt Whitman's "Leaves of Grass": The First (1855) Edition*, ed. Malcolm Cowley (New York: Viking Press, 1959), p. 13.

3. Ralph L. Rusk, *Life of Ralph Waldo Emerson* (New York: Columbia University Press, 1949), p. 373.

4. Theodore Bacon, *Delia Bacon: A Biographical Sketch* (Boston: Houghton, Mifflin and Co., 1888), p. 82.

5. Gay Wilson Allen, *The New Walt Whitman Handbook* (New York: New York University Press, 1975), p. 82.

6. Richard Maurice Bucke, *Walt Whitman* (Philadelphia: David McKay, 1883), p. 26.

7. John Burroughs, *Whitman: A Study* (Boston: Houghton, Mifflin and Co., 1896), p. 57.

8. Mary Elizabeth Burtis, *Moncure Conway, 1832–1907* (New Brunswick: Rutgers University Press, 1952), p. 49.

9. Moncure Daniel Conway, *Autobiography: Memories and Experiences* (Boston: Houghton, Mifflin and Co., 1904), vol. 1, pp. 215–16.

10. *The Shock of Recognition*, ed. Edmund Wilson (New York: Doubleday, Doran & Co., 1943), pp. 250–51.

11. Transcribed from the original in the Charles E. Feinberg Whitman Collection, Library of Congress, Washington, D.C.

12. Rusk, *Life of Ralph Waldo Emerson*, p. 372.

13. *Leaves of Grass by Walt Whitman: Reproduced from the First Edition (1855)*, introd. Clifton J. Furness (New York: Columbia University Press, 1939), p. xii.

14. *Records of a Lifelong Friendship*, ed. H. H. Furness (Cambridge, Mass.: Riverside Press, 1910), p. 107. Emerson also recommended the book to Sam Ward and mentioned its appearance to his brother William and to Thomas Carlyle. See Rusk, *Life of Ralph Waldo Emerson*, p. 372; *L*, 4:529n; and *CEC*, p. 509.

15. Eleanor M. Tilton, ed. "*Leaves of Grass*: Four Letters to Emerson," *Harvard Library Bulletin* 27 (1979): 339.

16. Rusk, *Life of Ralph Waldo Emerson*, p. 374.

17. See Jerome Loving, *Walt Whitman's Champion: William Douglas O'Connor* (College Station: Texas A&M University Press, 1978), pp. 112–13.

18. Burtis, *Moncure Conway*, p. 38.

19. M. D. Conway, "Walt Whitman," *Fortnightly Review* 6 (1866): 542–43.

20. See John Townsend Trowbridge, "Reminiscences of Walt Whitman," *Atlantic Monthly* 89 (1902): 166.

21. *Complete Writings of Walt Whitman*, ed. Richard Maurice Bucke et al. (New York: G. P. Putnam's Sons, 1902), vol. 9, p. 6.

22. Bliss Perry, *Walt Whitman: His Life and Works* (Boston: Houghton, Mifflin and Co., 1906), p. 115.

23. Emory Holloway, *Whitman: An Interpretation in Narrative* (New York: Alfred A. Knopf, 1926), p. 152.

24. Allen, *New Walt Whitman Handbook*, p. 83.

25. *Walt Whitman: "Leaves of Grass"; Comprehensive Reader's Edition*, ed. Harold W. Blodgett and Sculley Bradley (New York: New York University Press, 1965), pp. 734–35.

26. Ibid., p. 739.

27. Perry, *Walt Whitman*, p. 115.

28. Gay Wilson Allen provides the most useful discussions. See *The*

Solitary Singer: A Critical Biography of Walt Whitman, rev. ed. (New York: New York University Press, 1967), pp. 176–90; *New Walt Whitman Handbook*, pp. 81–88; and his introduction to *Leaves of Grass: Facsimile of the 1856 Edition by Walt Whitman* (Allentown, Penn.: Norwood, 1976)— reviews of the 1855 edition are included in the facsimile.

29. See Loving, *Walt Whitman's Champion*, pp. 109–23.

30. Allen, *New Walt Whitman Handbook*, p. 83.

31. *Facsimile of the 1856 Edition*, pp. 101–2, 240–42, 310.

32. Joel Porte, *Representative Man: Ralph Waldo Emerson in His Time* (New York: Oxford University Press, 1979), pp. 229, 236.

33. Allen, *New Walt Whitman Handbook*, pp. 88, 94.

34. For a persuasive discussion of this theme in the Adam poems, see James E. Miller, Jr., *A Critical Guide to "Leaves of Grass"* (Chicago: University of Chicago Press, 1957), pp. 36–51.

35. *Correspondence of Henry David Thoreau*, ed. Walter Harding and Carl Bode (New York: New York University Press, 1958), p. 444.

36. See my discussion of "Passage to India" in chap. 7.

37. Porte, *Representative Man*, pp. 97, 144.

38. James Elliot Cabot, *A Memoir of Ralph Waldo Emerson* (Boston: Houghton, Mifflin and Co., 1887), vol. 2, p. 390.

39. Reprinted from Bucke, *Walt Whitman*, p. 201.

40. See *C*, 1:64–66; 2:71n; and *WWC*, 2:22.

41. I am indebted to Ralph A. Orth, general editor of the *JMN*, and to Ronald A. Bosco and Glen M. Johnson, editors of *JMN*, vol. 16 (forthcoming in 1983), for this information.

CHAPTER 5

1. Jonathan Bishop, *Emerson on the Soul* (Cambridge: Harvard University Press, 1964), pp. 166–71.

2. Stephen Whicher, *Freedom and Fate: An Inner Life of Ralph Waldo Emerson* (Philadelphia: University of Pennsylvania Press, 1953), p. 54.

3. David Porter, *Emerson and Literary Change* (Cambridge: Harvard University Press, 1978), p. 29.

4. James Elliot Cabot, *A Memoir of Ralph Waldo Emerson* (Boston: Houghton, Mifflin and Co., 1887), vol. 1, pp. 35–37.

5. Ralph L. Rusk, *Life of Ralph Waldo Emerson* (New York: Columbia University Press, 1949), p. 38.

6. See *CW*, 1:288.

7. Doubtless, Emerson's idea for the orphic poet came from his reading of Plotinus (*Enneads*, vol. 5) and Proclus. See John S. Harrison, *The Teachers of Emerson* (New York: Haskell House Reprint, 1966), pp. 246–48.

8. R. A. Yoder, *Emerson and the Orphic Poet in America* (Berkeley: University of California Press, 1978), p. 33.

9. Edwin Gittleman, *Jones Very: The Effective Years* (New York: Columbia University Press, 1967), p. 179.

10. Bliss Perry, *The Praise of Folly and Other Papers* (Boston: Houghton Mifflin Co., 1923), pp. 107, 96.

11. Joel Porte, *Representative Man: Ralph Waldo Emerson in His Time* (New York: Oxford University Press, 1979), p. 115.

12. See chap. 4, p. 96.

13. Mary Worden Edrich, "The Rhetoric of Apostasy," *Texas Studies in Literature and Language* 8 (1967): 555–56.

14. Joel Myerson, "Convers Francis and Emerson," *American Literature* 50 (1978): 29.

15. Quentin Anderson, *The Imperial Self: An Essay in American Literary and Cultural History* (New York: Alfred A. Knopf, 1971), p. 6.

16. *The Transcendentalists: An Anthology*, ed. Perry Miller (Cambridge: Harvard University Press, 1950), p. 211.

17. See Yoder, *Emerson and the Orphic Poet*, p. 51.

18. As Glen M. Johnson points out, the sources of the *Essays* are also found in the lectures Emerson gave between 1836 and 1838 (*EL*, 2). However, my purpose here is not to present a comprehensive source study (for that, see Johnson's "The Making of Emerson's Essays" [Ph.D. dissertation, Indiana University, 1976] and his "Emerson's Craft of Revision: The Composition of the *Essays*," in *Studies in the American Renaissance*, ed. Joel Myerson [Boston: G. K. Hall, 1980]), but to trace Emerson's Neoplatonic development between his "heresy" in the Divinity School Address and the publication of "The Poet."

19. These two lectures were later combined and revised to become "Thoughts on Modern Literature," *The Dial* 1 (1840): 137–58.

20. *Walt Whitman's "Leaves of Grass": The First (1855) Edition*, ed. Malcolm Cowley (New York: Viking Press, 1959), pp. 85 (where the ellipses are Whitman's) and 26.

21. "Education" was the ninth lecture in the series; the eighth is lost but may have been the basis for "Ethics" in *Essays: Second Series*.

22. Sampson Reed, "Observations on the Growth of the Mind," in *The Transcendentalists*, p. 54.

23. James E. Miller, Jr., *The American Quest for a Supreme Fiction: Whitman's Legacy in the Personal Epic* (Chicago: University of Chicago Press, 1979), p. 37.

24. Also in "Circles," *CW*, 2:182.

25. See *L*, 2:180–84, and 3:183. Ralph L. Rusk discovered the translation among Emerson's papers in 1941; it was published by the Ralph Waldo Emerson Memorial Association in 1957.

26. Carl F. Strauch, "The Importance of Emerson's Skeptical Mood," *Harvard Library Bulletin* 11 (1957): 123, 139.

27. See David Robinson, "Emerson and the Challenge of the Future: The Paradox of the Unachieved in 'Circles.'" *Philological Quarterly* 57 (1978): 243–53.

CHAPTER 6

1. Gay Wilson Allen, "The Iconography of Walt Whitman," in *The Artistic Legacy of Walt Whitman*, ed. Edwin Haviland Miller (New York: New York University Press, 1970), p. 134.

2. Roy Harvey Pearce, *Leaves of Grass by Walt Whitman: Facsimile Edition of the 1860 Text* (Ithaca: Cornell University Press, 1961), p. xviii. This text is used for quotations from the third edition; references are given by either page or poem number in my text (e.g., Pearce, p. 45). See also Pearce, "Whitman Justified: The Poet in 1860," in *The Presence of Walt Whitman*, ed. R. W. B. Lewis (New York: Columbia University Press, 1962), pp. 72–109.

3. Edwin Haviland Miller, *Walt Whitman's Poetry: A Psychological Journey* (Boston: Houghton Mifflin Co., 1968), pp. 5, 134.

4. See Richard Lebeaux, "Walt Whitman and His Poems, 1856–1860: The Quest for Intimacy and Generativity," *Walt Whitman Review* 25 (December 1979): 150.

5. See also Ivan Marki, *The Trial of the Poet: An Interpretation of the First Edition of "Leaves of Grass"* (New York: Columbia University Press, 1976), p. 146.

6. *Leaves of Grass by Walt Whitman: Reproduced from the First Edition (1855)*, introd. Clifton J. Furness (New York: Columbia University Press, 1939), p. VI. Uppercase roman numerals indicate the pages of Whitman's 1855 preface. This text is used for quotations from the first edition, where page numbers are indicated parenthetically in my text (e.g., Furness, p. 29).

7. *Walt Whitman: "Leaves of Grass"; Comprehensive Reader's Edition*, ed. Harold W. Blodgett and Sculley Bradley (New York: New York University Press, 1965), p. 331.

8. Justin Kaplan, *Walt Whitman: A Life* (New York: Simon & Schuster, 1980), p. 193.

9. *Leaves of Grass: Facsimile of the 1856 Edition by Walt Whitman*, introd. Gay Wilson Allen (Allentown, Penn.: Norwood, 1976), p. 7. This text is used for quotations from the second edition, where references are given either by page or poem number in my text (e.g., Allen, p. 31).

10. Miller, *Psychological Journey*, p. 87.

11. See Frederik Schyberg, *Walt Whitman*, trans. Evie Allison Allen (New York: Columbia University Press, 1951), p. 123; and Bliss Perry, *Walt Whitman: His Life and Works* (Boston: Houghton, Mifflin and Co., 1906), p. 80.

12. Marki, *The Trial of the Poet*, pp. 232–33.

13. See chap. 5, pp. 136–37.

14. Gay Wilson Allen, *The New Walt Whitman Handbook* (New York: New York University Press, 1975), p. 81.

15. Ibid., pp. 77–78.

16. Ibid., pp. 87–88.

17. Ibid., pp. 104, 116, 120; "Notes from Conversations with George W. Whitman, 1893," *In Re Walt Whitman*, ed. Horace Traubel et al. (Philadelphia: David McKay, 1893), p. 35.

18. T. S. Eliot, "Four Quartets," in *T. S. Eliot: Collected Poems, 1909–1962* (New York: Harcourt, Brace, 1963), p. 196.

19. Pearce, *Facsimile Edition of the 1860 Text*, p. xiii.

20. See Fredson Bowers's introduction to *Whitman's Manuscripts: "Leaves of Grass" (1860), A Parallel Text* (Chicago: University of Chicago Press, 1955), pp. lxiii–lxxiv.

21. See Erik Erikson, *Identity, Youth and Crisis* (New York: W. W. Norton & Co., 1968), p. 135.

22. Kaplan, *Walt Whitman: A Life*, p. 236.

23. This notebook was written on the verso of City of Williamsburgh stationery. According to Bowers, such forms would probably not have been available to Whitman until after he started working for the Brooklyn *Times*; see *Whitman's Manuscripts: "Leaves of Grass" (1860)*, pp. xlii–xliii.

24. See Robert K. Martin, *The Homosexual Tradition in American Poetry*, (Austin: University of Texas Press, 1979), pp. 33–35.

25. Floyd Stovall, "Main Drifts in Whitman's Poetry," *American Literature* 4 (1932): 8.

26. I base this conjecture on the fact that the poem was first published and presented as a Christmas poem in the New York *Saturday Press* for 24 December 1859.

27. See *DN*, 1:48, 85; and Miller, *Psychological Journey*, p. 54.

28. Stovall, "Main Drifts in Whitman's Poetry," p. 10.

29. Miller, *Psychological Journey*, p. 134.

30. *Letters of Emily Dickinson*, ed. Thomas H. Johnson (Cambridge: Harvard University Press, 1958), vol. 3, p. 755.

31. Stephen Whicher, "Whitman's Awakening to Death: Toward a Biographical Reading of 'Out of the Cradle Endlessly Rocking,'" in *The Presence of Walt Whitman*, p. 13.

CHAPTER 7

1. Harold Bloom, *Poetry and Repression: Revisionism from Blake to Stevens* (New Haven: Yale University Press, 1976), p. 7.

2. Walt Whitman, "So Long," in *Walt Whitman: "Leaves of Grass"; Comprehensive Reader's Edition*, ed. Harold W. Blodgett and Sculley Bradley (New York: New York University Press, 1965), p. 505.

3. Bloom, *Poetry and Repression*, p. 4.

4. Ibid., p. 244.

5. *Leaves of Grass by Walt Whitman; Reproduced from the First Edition (1855)*, introd. Clifton J. Furness (New York: Columbia University Press, 1939), p. III.

6. Thomas Carlyle, *On Heroes and Hero-Worship and the Heroic History* (London: Chapman and Hall, 1903–4), p. 47.

7. Roger Asselineau, "Theodore Dreiser's Transcendentalism," in *English Studies Today: Second Series* (Bern: Francke Verlag, 1961), pp. 233–43.

8. "I remember an answer which when quite young I was prompted to make to a valued adviser who was wont to importune me with the dear old doctrines of the church. On my saying, 'What have I to do with the sacredness of traditions, if I live wholly from within?' my friend suggested,—'But these impulses may be from below, not from above.' I replied, 'They do not seem to me to be such; but if I am the Devil's child, I will live then from the Devil. . . . Be it known unto you that henceforward I obey no law less than the eternal law. I will have no covenants but proximities. I shall endeavor to nourish my parents, to support my family, to be the chaste husband of one wife,—but these relations I must fill after a new and unprecedented way. I appeal from your customs. I must be myself. I cannot break myself any longer for you, or you. If you can love me for what I am, we shall be happier" (*CW*, 2:30, 42).

9. Though he has been recently criticized for his worldliness, especially in his interest in his first wife's estate; see Joel Porte, *Representative Man: Ralph Waldo Emerson in His Time* (New York: Oxford University Press, 1979), pp. 160–63, 248–49.

10. Ralph L. Rusk, *Life of Ralph Waldo Emerson* (New York: Columbia University Press, 1949), p. 374.

11. To Carlyle he wrote: "One book, last summer, came out in New York, a nondescript monster which yet has terrible eyes & buffalo strength, & was indisputably American,—which I thought to send you; but the book throve so badly with the few to whom I showed it, & wanted good morals so much, that I never did" (*CEC*, p. 509). To Caroline Sturgis Tappan he described the poet as "our wild Whitman, with real inspiration but choked by Titanic abdomen" (*L*, 5:87).

12. Walt Whitman, "Personalism," *Galaxy* 5 (May 1868): 541.

13. Ibid., pp. 546, 542.

14. Ibid., p. 542.

15. Ibid., p. 543.

16. *Walt Whitman: "Leaves of Grass"; Comprehensive Reader's Edition*, p. 410.

17. Allan B. Lefcowitz and Barbara F. Lefcowitz, "James Bryce's Visit to America: The New England Sections of his 1870 Journal and Related Correspondence," *New England Quarterly* 50 (1977): 325.

18. Richard Chase, *Walt Whitman Reconsidered* (New York: William Sloane Associates, 1955), p. 147. Other such studies of the poem include Newton Arvin, *Whitman* (New York: MacMillan Co., 1938), pp. 225–26; Arthur Golden, "Passage to Less than India: Structure and Meaning in Whitman's 'Passage to India,'" *PMLA* 88 (1973): 1095–1103; Edwin Haviland Miller, *Walt Whitman's Poetry: A Psychological Journey*

(Boston: Houghton Mifflin Co., 1968), pp. 210–11; Roy Harvey Pearce, *The Continuity of American Poetry* (Princeton: Princeton University Press, 1961), p. 173; and Hyatt H. Waggoner, *American Poets: From the Puritans to the Present* (Boston: Houghton Mifflin Co., 1968), pp. 179–80.

19. Pearce, *The Continuity of American Poetry*, p. 173.

20. The opening of the Suez Canal, the junction of the Union and Central Pacific transcontinental railroads, and the laying of the Atlantic and Pacific cables.

21. Chase, *Walt Whitman Reconsidered*, pp. 148–49.

22. Walt Whitman, "Personalism," p. 547.

23. *Walt Whitman: "Leaves of Grass"; Comprehensive Reader's Edition*, p. 415.

24. Whitman, "Passage to India," in ibid., p. 419.

Selected Bibliography

This bibliography is restricted to items directly related to the personal and literary relationship of Emerson and Whitman. Annotations of the more important studies can be found in my essay on Whitman and the Transcendentalists in the *Transcendentalists: A Review of Research and Criticism*, ed. Joel Myerson (New York: Modern Language Association, 1983).

Adams, Richard P. "Whitman: A Brief Revaluation." *Tulane Studies in English* 5 (1955): 111–49.

Anderson, Quentin. *The Imperial Self: An Essay in American Literary and Cultural History*. New York: Alfred A. Knopf, 1971.

Baker, Carlos. "The Road to Concord: Another Milestone in the Emerson-Whitman Friendship." *Princeton University Library Chronicle* 7 (1946): 100–17.

Baker, Portia. "Walt Whitman and *The Atlantic Monthly*." *American Literature* 6 (1943): 283–301.

Baxter, Sylvester. "Walt Whitman in Boston." *New England Magazine* 6 (1892): 714–21.

Bernard, Edward G. "Some New Whitman Manuscript Notes." *American Literature* 8 (1936): 59–63.

Bloom, Harold. *A Map of Misreading*. New York: Oxford University Press, 1975.

———. *Poetry and Repression: Revisionism from Blake to Stevens*. New Haven: Yale University Press, 1976.

Bluestein, Gene. *The Voice of the Folk: Folklore and American Literary Theory*. Amherst: University of Massachusetts Press, 1972.

Bucke, Richard Maurice. *Walt Whitman*. Philadelphia: David McKay, 1883.

Buell, Lawrence. *Literary Transcendentalism: Style and Vision in the American Renaissance*. Ithaca: Cornell University Press, 1973.

———. "Transcendentalist Catalogue Rhetoric: Vision versus Form." *American Literature* 40 (1968): 325–39.

Burroughs, John. *Notes on Walt Whitman as Poet and Person*. 2d ed. New York: American News Company, 1871.

Cameron, Kenneth W. "Emerson's Recommendation of Whitman: The Remainder of the Evidence." *Emerson Society Quarterly*, no. 3 (1956): 14–20.

————. "Rough Draft of Whitman's 'By Emerson's Grave.'" *Emerson Society Quarterly*, no. 13 (1958): 32–34.

Campbell, Killis. "The Evolution of Whitman as an Artist." *American Literature* 6 (1934): 254–63.

Carpenter, Edward. *Days with Walt Whitman*. London: George Allen, 1906.

Conway, Moncure Daniel. *Autobiography: Memories and Experiences*. 2 vols. Boston: Houghton, Mifflin and Co., 1904.

Couser, G. Thomas. "An Emerson-Whitman Parallel: 'The American Scholar' and 'A Song for Occupations.'" *Walt Whitman Review* 22 (1976): 115–18.

Crawley, Thomas Edward. *The Structure of "Leaves of Grass."* Austin: University of Texas Press, 1970.

De La Vega, Angeles Palacia. *Sobre La Influencia de Emerson en Walt Whitman: Fe en el Destino Manifesto de los Estados Unidos de America*. Madrid: Edicions Leira, 1968.

Dressman, Michael. "Another Whitman Debt to Emerson." *Notes and Queries* 26 (1979): 305–6.

Dykes, Mattie M. "'A Nondescript Monster' with 'Terrible Eyes.'" *Missouri Teachers' College Studies* 4 (1940): 3–32.

Emerson, Edward. *Emerson in Concord*. Boston: Houghton, Mifflin and Co., 1889.

"Emerson and Whitman: Documents on their Relations (1855–88)." In *The Shock of Recognition*, ed. Edmund Wilson. New York: Doubleday, Doran & Co., 1943.

Foerster, Norman. "Whitman and the Cult of Confusion." *North American Review* 213 (1921): 799–812.

Furness, Clifton J. "Walt Whitman Looks at Boston." *New England Quarterly* 1 (1928): 353–70.

Gohdes, Clarence. "Whitman and Emerson." *Sewanee Review* 37 (1929): 79–93.

Grover, Edwin O. "The First Words of Warm Approval." *Walt Whitman Review* 5 (1959): 30–33.

Howard, Leon. "For a Critique of Whitman's Transcendentalism." *Modern Language Notes* 47 (1932): 79–85.

Johnson, Jane. "Whitman's Changing Attitude Towards Emerson." *PMLA* 73 (1958): 452.

Kaplan, Justin. "'Half Song-Thrush, Half Alligator.'" *American Heritage* 31 (1980): 62–67.

Kennedy, William Sloane. "Identities of Thought and Phrases in Emerson and Whitman." *The Conservator* 8 (1897): 88–91.

A Leaf of Grass from Shady Hill, with a Review of Walt Whitman's "Leaves of Grass." Introduction by Kenneth B. Murdock. Cambridge: Harvard University Press, 1928.

Lefcowitz, Allan B., and Lefcowitz, Barbara F. "James Bryce's First Visit to America: The New England Sections of His 1870 Journal and Related Correspondence." *New England Quarterly* 50 (1977): 325.

Loving, Jerome. "Emerson's 'Constant Way of Looking at Whitman's
    Genius.'" *American Literature* 51 (1979): 399–403.
_____. "'A Well-Intended Halfness': Emerson's View of *Leaves of Grass*."
    Studies in American Humor 3 (1976): 61–68.
Matthiessen, F. O. *American Renaissance: Art and Expression in the Age of
    Emerson and Whitman*. New York: Oxford University Press, 1941.
Moore, John B. "The Master of Whitman." *Studies in Philology* 23 (1926):
    77–89.
Moss, William M. "'So Many Promising Youths': Emerson's Disappoint-
    ing Discoveries of New England Poet-Seers." *New England Quarterly*
    49 (1976): 46–64.
O'Connor, William Douglas. "Emerson and Whitman." New York
    Tribune, 18 June 1882. Reprinted in *Walt Whitman's Champion: William
    Douglas O'Connor*, ed. Jerome Loving. College Station: Texas A&M
    University Press, 1978.
Poirier, Suzanne. "'A Song of the Rolling Earth' as Transcendental and
    Poetic Theory." *Walt Whitman Review* 22 (1976): 67–74.
Pressley, Ruth Peyton. "The Indebtedness of Whitman to Emerson."
    Ph.D. dissertation, University of Texas, 1930.
Price, Kenneth M. "Whitman on Other Writers: Controlled 'Gracious-
    ness' in *Specimen Days*." *ESQ: A Journal of the American Renaissance* 26
    (1980): 79–87.
Rosenfeld, Alvin L. "Emerson and Whitman: Their Personal and Literary
    Relationship." Ph.D. dissertation, Brown University, 1967.
Ross, Donald. "Emerson's Stylistic Influence on Whitman." *American
    Transcendental Quarterly*, no. 25 (1975): 41–51.
Rubin, Joseph Jay. *The Historic Whitman*. University Park: Pennsylvania
    State University Press, 1973.
Rusk, Ralph L. *Life of Ralph Waldo Emerson*. New York: Columbia Univer-
    sity Press, 1949.
Shephard, Esther. *Walt Whitman's Pose*. New York: Harcourt, Brace and
    Co., 1938.
Stovall, Floyd. *The Foreground of "Leaves of Grass."* Charlottesville: Univer-
    sity Press of Virginia, 1974.
Sutcliffe, Emerson Grant. "Whitman, Emerson and the New Poetry." *New
    Republic* 19 (1919): 114–16.
Thomas, Bee Cotton. "An Analysis of the Influence of Ralph Waldo
    Emerson on Walt Whitman." M.A. Thesis, University of Southern
    California, 1932.
Tilton, Eleanor M., ed. *"Leaves of Grass*: Four Letters to Emerson." *Harvard
    Library Bulletin* 27 (1979): 336–41.
Trowbridge, John Townsend. "Reminiscences of Walt Whitman." *Atlantic
    Monthly* 89 (1902): 163–75.
Waggoner, Hyatt H. *American Poets from the Puritans to the Present*. Boston:
    Houghton Mifflin Co., 1968.

White, William. "Walt Whitman on New England Writers: An Uncollected Fragment." *New England Quarterly* 27 (1954): 395–96.

———. "Whitman on American Poets: An Uncollected Piece." *English Language Notes* 1 (1963): 42–43.

Willson, Lawrence. "The 'Body Electric' Meets the Genteel Tradition." *New Mexico Quarterly* 26 (1956–57): 369–86.

Index

Emerson, Whitman, and the American Muse is not an "influence study" but a rigorous examination of the intersection of two poets whose work shaped what F. O. Matthiessen called the American Renaissance. In the first book on the relationship of Ralph Waldo Emerson and Walt Whitman, Jerome Loving has skillfully gathered together the relevant documents, sifted through the mass of criticism, and emerged with a study that thoroughly and imaginatively explores a connection that has concerned critics for more than a century.

Loving's focus is not on Emerson's influence on Whitman but (at the outset) on their common apprenticeship, one in which each writer independently made the discovery of Character. What Whitman found in Emerson was himself, the same discovery Emerson made in his own apprenticeship as a writer. This study observes, then, a neat symmetrical pattern in the relationship. Beginning with their intersection in 1842, the year in which Whitman heard Emerson lecture on "The Poet," the study proceeds with an examination of the "foregrounds" of each writer and then brings the two back together in the 1850s when the Concord poet greeted the Brooklyn bard "at the beginning of a great career." In his discussion of the literary "scandal" that resulted from Whitman's unauthorized publication of Emerson's famous letter, Loving not only illuminates that episode but goes on to cast much-needed light on Emerson's so-called silence about *Leaves of Grass* after 1855.